I0118431

IF CONFIRMED

An Insider's View of the National Security Confirmation Process

Arnold L. Punaro

BOOKS BY ARNOLD L. PUNARO

If Confirmed: An Insider's View of the National Security Confirmation Process (2024)

The Ever-Shrinking Fighting Force (2021)

On War and Politics: The Battlefield Inside Washington's Beltway (2016)

IF CONFIRMED

AN INSIDER'S VIEW OF THE NATIONAL SECURITY CONFIRMATION PROCESS

COPYRIGHT © 2024 BY ARNOLD L. PUNARO

All rights reserved. No part of this publication may be reproduced or transmitted in any form or by any means, electronic or mechanical, including photocopying, recording, or any information storage and retrieval system now known or to be invented, without permission from the author.

ISBN 978-1-962729-05-5 (PAPERBACK)

PUBLISHED IN THE UNITED STATES OF AMERICA BY FORTIS, AN ADDUCENT NONFICTION IMPRINT IN COLLABORATION WITH PUNARO PRESS.

FORTIS

ADDUCENT, INC.
JACKSONVILLE, FLORIDA
ADDUCENTCREATIVE.COM

THE PUNARO GROUP
MCLEAN, VIRGINIA
PUNAROGROUP.COM

DEDICATION

To paraphrase Theodore Roosevelt, this book is dedicated to the men and women, civilian and uniformed, who served or aspire to serve "in the arena" of public service, committed to doing the best job possible for our citizens and our form of government. One of our most important missions is to ensure our brave troops are the best trained, best equipped, and best led in a dangerous and unstable world. These are no timid souls.

"To be prepared for war is one of the most effectual means of preserving peace."

—President George Washington, First Annual Address to Congress, January 8, 1790

CONTENTS

PRAISE FOR

IF CONFIRMED: AN INSIDER'S VIEW OF THE NATIONAL SECURITY CONFIRMATION PROCESS

"The selection and preparation of nominees for top positions at DOD is a mixture of science and art. It is also a mysterious process, even for Beltway insiders—until now. Arnold Punaro always tackles topics in military affairs that are under-examined. In this case, he covers subjects that literally no one in the world knows more about: the processes of nominating, confirming, and appointing top brass at the Pentagon. These are important topics, considering that every American has an intrinsic interest in leadership selection outcomes at the nation's largest, most complicated, and by many measures, most important agency."

DR. MATTHEW AUER, Dean and Arch Professor of Public and International Affairs, School of Public and International Affairs, University of Georgia.

"With *If Confirmed*, General Punaro masterfully distills the wisdom and insights accumulated from a career intimately involved in the confirmation of thousands of civilian and military leaders. I have seen General Punaro's candor save-the-day repeatedly over the years. Whether for nominees, policy enthusiasts, or public servants, this book is an essential primer on the history and inner workings of a critical component of American governance."

THE HONORABLE BARBARA BARRETT, Former Secretary of the Air Force; Former Ambassador to Finland.

"There is literally no one alive better able to comment on the nomination and confirmation process in both the Executive and Legislative Branches for military and civilian nominees who must pass through the Senate Armed Services Committee and the

i

Senate floor. I also served as the staff director of the Armed Services Committee, and I relied on Arnold's expertise and advice to help me navigate the complicated and, at times, very difficult process of guiding or stopping nominees from confirmation. He is simply the master. None better, in my opinion. Arnold has a command of the history, back door deals, trials, and process rules that no one else can claim. This is a must-read book for those wishing to be confirmed and those trying to help them achieve that goal."

JOHN BONSELL, Former Staff Director of the Senate Armed Services Committee.

"The Senate's confirmation power is found in a brief clause of the Constitution's Article One. In today's Washington, the process now requires a complex legal and political navigation for even the most qualified candidates nominated to serve. No guide is more experienced or knowledgeable than Arnold Punaro, and *If Confirmed* is must reading for citizens and candidates wanting to understand what exactly is 'advise and consent.'"

THE HONORABLE RUDY DE LEON, Senior Fellow of National Security & International Policy, Center for American Progress; Former Deputy Secretary of Defense; Former Under Secretary of Defense for Personnel and Readiness; Former Under Secretary of the Air Force; Former Staff Director of the House Armed Services Committee.

"There is no one who has a better understanding of the Senate confirmation process than Arnold Punaro. He has assisted countless senior officials in navigating the process. I was fortunate to be one of the individuals he coached, mentored, and prepared for Senate confirmation hearings. I found his counsel to be "pure gold." Those interested in the process will find this book informative. For those willing to serve in a confirmed position and preparing for a hearing, this book demystifies the process and provides invaluable insight. It reflects Arnold's decades of experience, his deep understanding of the process and the Senate, and his gift for clarity."

GENERAL JOE DUNFORD, USMC (Ret); Former Chairman of the Joint Chiefs of Staff; Former Commandant of the Marine Corps.

"Leave it to Washington's most trusted expert to identify a significant gap in knowledge and so masterfully provide vital insight for those seeking to lead federal agencies at the commander-in-chief's request. There is no better or more respected practitioner with such unparalleled views deep from the policy foxholes of Washington D.C. on the intricacies of the Senate confirmation process than the intrepid Arnold Punaro. A trusted colleague to all, Arnold's shared wisdom built on a 40-year proficiency of intimately shepherding novices through the good, bad, and the ugly of the confirmation process is the key that will unlock the doors to many futures in the next generation."

MACKENZIE EAGLEN, Senior Fellow, American Enterprise Institute.

"Arnold Punaro's nearly 50 years of experience and expertise in this arena is unmatched. Navigating the Senate confirmation process can be daunting without the right support. Thanks to Arnold and his team, I was well prepared for my own hearings to become secretary of the Army and secretary of defense. More importantly, Arnold has always worked in a bipartisan fashion with senior military and civilian nominees alike to do what's best for our country. I can think of no better person to write this much-needed book."

THE HONORABLE DR. MARK ESPER, Former Secretary of Defense; Former Secretary of the Army.

"The confirmation process has become torturous. Arnold Punaro has participated in this from every possible direction. *If Confirmed* is valuable, either for surviving the current process or as a guide to improve it going forward."

THE HONORABLE JOHN J. HAMRE, Ph.D., President, CEO and Langone Chair in American Leadership of Center for Strategic and International Studies; Former Deputy Secretary of Defense; Former Under Secretary of Defense Comptroller.

"If you are interested in understanding, guiding others in navigating, or are participating yourself as a nominee in the oft-bewildering, sometimes maddening, but absolutely critical Senate confirmation process for defense officials, there is absolutely no individual with more experience, knowledge, insights, or field craft regarding every part of the process than Arnold Punaro. You want him in your foxhole and this fine book puts him there with you. Arnold helped me in my own nomination process and then in successfully winning confirmation of countless nominees to Department of Defense positions thereafter, including no shortage of politically fraught and procedurally challenging instances. He is a master."

THE HONORABLE STEPHEN HEDGER, Former Assistant Secretary of Defense for Legislative Affairs; Former Special Assistant to the President for Senate Affairs.

"I can't think of anyone better than Washington insider Arnold Punaro to outline the do's, the don't's as well as the good, bad and ugly of the confirmation process. From his time in the Senate to his time in the military to his time as an advisor helping thousands of nominees, Punaro knows the process from the inside out. *If Confirmed* offers a must-read history and playbook for anyone wishing to serve at the highest levels of government."

THE HONORABLE DEBBIE LEE JAMES, Former Secretary of the Air Force; Former Assistant Secretary of Defense for Reserve Affairs; Former President of Technical and Engineering Sector, SAIC.

"*If Confirmed* is an unprecedented, one-of-a-kind guide to navigate the Senate confirmation process, written by a genuine master of that process. I have been through three Senate confirmations, and there is no better coach than General Arnold Punaro.

Arnold knows the issues, the process, the personalities who run the process, and the minefields to avoid. When necessary, Arnold is not afraid to cut a presidential nominee down to size in preparation for cross-examination by a United States senator. I have been 'murdered' by Arnold more than once and lived to talk about the experience. Above all, Arnold is the consummate Washington insider, who, year after year, knows everything and everybody in the close-knit national security community."

THE HONORABLE JEH JOHNSON, Former Secretary of Homeland Security; Former Department of Defense General Counsel; Former General Counsel of the Department of the Air Force.

"I have known and served with the author since 1979 and know of no one who has so willingly and consistently given freely of his time and effort to making our national security organizations better. His first two books are "must read and retain" efforts, and this one is no different. In fact, because it touches on the thousands of candidates for public office who require Senate confirmation, this book is, at once, an expert education of one of the most important rites of passage to government positions, and it also reveals the intensely personal pressures and results of the confirmation process itself. There have been those who turned down the opportunity for a trial run by the author and his committee of experts. Most have lived to regret that decision. The overwhelming majority of those who subjected themselves to this advanced course of confirmation preparation, sometimes more than once, were successful in being confirmed. Put this book on your bookshelf for future use, either for yourself or perhaps for someone you know who has been nominated to an office that requires U.S. Senate confirmation."

GENERAL JAMES L. JONES, USMC (Ret); Former U.S. National Security Advisor; 32nd Commandant of the Marine Corps; Former Commander, U.S. European Command and Supreme Allied Commander Europe.

"Arnold Punaro's experience in the layered world of Senate confirmations is singular, spanning multiple administrations. A trusted advisor to generations of Department of Defense leaders, he has helped countless officials navigate the unpredictable politics and sometimes difficult process of getting through the U.S. Senate. This is the book that Arnold had to write, as there is no equal to the experience, perspective, and insight that he brings to this issue."

LOUIS LAUTER, Former Acting Assistant Secretary of Defense for Legislative Affairs.

"In *If Confirmed,* Arnold Punaro gives an informed insider's account of the history of the Senate confirmation process for nominees in the national security world, as well as providing a guide for current nominees and suggestions on how to make the system work more effectively. We need our most dedicated and talented people to serve in these important Senate-confirmed positions, and if our confirmation system continues to become more sclerotic and less productive, it will harm our ability to attract and retain the right people for these demanding jobs. *If Confirmed* is a comprehensive look at a topic that is as important as it is complex."

THE HONORABLE GENERAL JAMES N. MATTIS, USMC (Ret); Former Secretary of Defense; Former Commander of U.S. Central Command.

"Every nominee, and potential nominee, needs to read and heed Arnold Punaro's sage advice. His deep and diverse career of service at the very highest levels of the Senate and the Pentagon brings him unparalleled insight and an unmatched understanding of the often uncertain and politically charged confirmation journey. Arnold's prudent counsel has singularly ensured countless nominees successfully navigated their Senate confirmation with ease—ensuring needed continuity of key national security posts across administrations and party lines."

LAURA MCALEER, Former Deputy Assistant Secretary of Defense for Senate Affairs; Former National Security Advisor at the U.S. Senate; Associate Vice President, Federal & Washington Relations at the University of Notre Dame.

"Arnold Punaro is unparalleled in his knowledge of the Senate confirmation process and his ability to prepare a political or uniformed nominee to testify in front of the Senate Armed Services Committee."

THE HONORABLE RYAN D. MCCARTHY, Former Secretary of the Army; Former Under Secretary of the Army.

"*If Confirmed* provides a rare glimpse behind the curtain into a process with far-reaching national security implications. Any prospective nominee would be well-served by examining Arnold Punaro's lessons learned and strategies for navigating Senate confirmations. Demystifying pathways into government service, especially with respect to the Senate confirmation process, will help ensure that our nation has qualified candidates prepared to serve at the highest levels."

JAMIE JONES MILLER, CEO and Dean, Northeastern University Arlington Campus; former Principal Deputy Assistant Secretary of Defense for Legislative Affairs.

"A few times in your life, you find the expert in an area where only a very few exist. Arnold Punaro spent a greater part of his career helping others, including myself, get confirmed by the United States Senate for all matters regarding our national security. Beforehand, he was the lead in determining who would "be anointed" by the Senate Armed Services Committee for literally every Senate-confirmed position in the Department of Defense. Arnold is a culmination of experience and knowledge in this daunting process. His work to bring in the very best to serve our country continues today. Anyone going through it, either as a nominee or one who works to get highly qualified people into these critical government positions, will serve themselves well to read this book."

THE HONORABLE JIM MORHARD, Former Deputy NASA Administrator; Former Deputy Sergeant at Arms of the United States Senate; Former Staff Director, Senate Appropriations Committee.

"I am one of the many who benefited from Arnold Punaro's preparation for a confirmation hearing. In my case, to be secretary of Veterans Affairs. His long history with and deep knowledge of the process was evident. This book, *If Confirmed*, is a wonderful contribution to those who are called upon to serve our country. It is valuable in context, expectation setting, and for framing one's thoughts in responding to the many stakeholders in the nomination and confirmation process. Arnold Punaro is singularly qualified to bring all aspects of the process together, which he does in this readable and eminently useful book. It is a "must read" for any embarking on the journey of service in the Executive Branch."

THE HONORABLE JAMES B. PEAKE, M.D. Lieutenant General, USA (Ret.); Senior Vice President, CGI Federal; former Secretary of Veterans Affairs.

"The ultimate guide on the confirmation process from the ultimate guide through it! Arnold Punaro brings unmatched experience, expertise, and insights to this subject. I benefited from his wisdom and guidance in preparing for four Senate confirmations (as well as several high-stakes hearings), and this book will be invaluable to any nominee for high office or any individual helping a nominee navigate the confirmation process."

THE HONORABLE GENERAL DAVID PETRAEUS, U.S. Army (Ret.); former Commander of the Surge in Iraq, U.S. Central Command, and Coalition Forces in Afghanistan; Former Director of the CIA; Co-author (with Andrew Roberts) of *Conflict: The Evolution of Warfare from 1945 to Ukraine.*

"Arnold Punaro has amassed a lifetime of wisdom in the process of Senate confirmation. With well over a half-century of service to our nation, he shares that wisdom in *If Confirmed*. This book is indispensable for anyone set to embark on that process or interested in this critical function of the American government."

THE HONORABLE PATRICK SHANAHAN, Former Deputy Secretary of Defense.

"The Senate confirmation process has become more contentious over time, and yet, we need capable leaders who can enter public service and take on the challenging roles facing our nation. There is no more qualified servant to the nation than Arnold Punaro in preparing leaders for this grueling process. Punaro has the experience, expertise, and reputation for developing nominees to engage this process with legitimacy and a focus on the benefits they will contribute to the country. Punaro's book will become **THE** source for preparing and fulfilling the responsibilities of this important and increasingly difficult process."

DR. DAVID M. VAN SLYKE, Dean and Louis A. Bantle Chair in Business-Government Policy, The Maxwell School of Citizenship and Public Affairs, Syracuse University.

"General Punaro has shepherded my confirmations from assistant secretary to the cabinet. In my first tour at the Pentagon, I put the nomination of Robert Gates in his safe hands. No one knows the history and traditions of the Senate nor has better relationships on both sides of the aisle than Arnold Punaro. He is a patriot and a Washington institution. The trust he has from conservatives and liberals harkens back to a better, more civil time in the nation's capital. Wish there were more like him."

THE HONORABLE ROBERT WILKIE, Former Secretary of Veterans Affairs; Former Under Secretary of Defense for Personnel and Readiness; Former Assistant Secretary of Defense for Legislative Affairs.

"I have had the pleasure of knowing Arnold since the early 1970s and sat with him on the 'murder board' process. In addition to a unique commitment to wanting to make the DOD and government work better, what sets Arnold apart in my mind are his remarkable instincts to understand relevant issues and shape them to reach better outcomes. When he brings these talents to help the extremely capable people nominated for senior positions in the government improve their prospects for confirmation in the contentious atmosphere, such nominations are too often considered, and the country benefits."

THE HONORABLE KIM WINCUP, Former Assistant Secretary of the Army for Manpower and Reserve Affairs; Former Assistant Secretary of the Air Force for Acquisition; Former Staff Director of the House Armed Services Committee.

FOREWORD

In his exciting and inspiring novel, *Advise and Consent*, Allen Drury shined a bright spotlight on the awesome responsibility of the Senate under the advice and consent powers set forth in Article II of the United States Constitution.

From unrestrained ambition to corruption, the fictional characters in this novel revealed both human flaws and selfish motives, but they also offered inspiring examples of senators who placed honor above ambition and who cherished the Senate's role in our constitutional system. In my early 20s, I was deeply moved by this powerful novel and its portrayal of the Senate as an institution—the good, the bad, and the ugly. In Drury's book, the good prevailed, and he made it clear what the Senate can be at its best.

As a member of the Senate, and from 1987-1995, as chairman of the Senate Armed Services Committee (SASC), charged with oversight of the Pentagon, my appreciation of the Senate's unique role in the confirmation process deepened. There were few functions that I approached as seriously as I did the confirmation of nominees, both civilian and military, to lead the Department of Defense. I viewed our constitutional duty of advice and consent not only as a check on the president's power of appointment but as a vital responsibility to ensure the readiness and capability of our military and civilian control of the armed forces.

During the years of my Committee leadership, Arnold Punaro was by my side at the Committee as staff director. Like Allen Drury, Arnold understands and cherishes the Senate's advice and consent role.

In this valuable and insightful book, Arnold clearly outlines how and why the Senate's important role has moved recently from "badly bent" to "broken" and is in need of urgent and major repair. Arnold wisely analyzes the problem and offers workable solutions.

When a single senator can prevent Senate action that the SASC has recommended on hundreds of senior military nominations for reasons that have nothing to do with the intended job or the job performance of the nominee, it is time for the Senate leadership of both parties to declare this is an abuse of power and end it. The abuse we are witnessing today is an effort to misuse the confirmation process to achieve objectives that should be addressed through the normal legislative process.

These delays are clearly unfair to the nominees. This abuse of the Senate Rules also significantly weakens the important influence of committees and committee leadership. It undermines the credibility of the Senate majority and minority leaders, whose job is to ensure that the Senate carries out one of its most important constitutional duties.

The reforms that Arnold proposes in *If Confirmed* are both crucial and achievable—first, addressing the many inefficiencies and duplications in the requirements of the Legislative and Executive Branches related to nominees that slow down the process; second, bringing an end to the practice used by a few senators who abuse their power to delay nominations—even after the nominees have been carefully screened and recommended for confirmation by the appropriate Senate committees.

Arnold Punaro is a man of discerning intellect, political savvy, and inexhaustible energy, tempered by personal humility and abiding care and concern for the men and women who wear the uniform of our country and their families. In *If Confirmed*, he issues a heartfelt and urgent plea for action by the Senate leadership, including the committee chairs and ranking members. I encourage both the Senate and the Executive Branch—and those who cherish the Senate as an institution–to give these proposals by an experienced professional, careful consideration and to begin the essential process of correcting the dysfunctions that damage the Senate's advice and consent role under the Constitution.

Taking these steps will help restore trust in the Senate as an institution and enhance the effectiveness of our federal government.

—SAM NUNN, FORMER SENATOR (GEORGIA, 1972-1997), FORMER CHAIRMAN, SENATE ARMED SERVICES COMMITTEE (1987-1995)

INTRODUCTION

"The importance of appointments is registered most clearly in their impact on public policy. The driving force in the appointment process, its fundamental dynamic, is the widely held assumption that who you get in government directly affects what you get out of government." —G. Calvin Mackenzie, *The Politics of Presidential Appointments*, 1981

NEWSFLASH | Washington D.C. The Senate Armed Services Committee (SASC) is holding up the nomination of a senior Air Force officer. The SASC is seeking more information about his qualifications for promotion to the grade of brigadier general.

In today's Senate confirmation process, such news would not be surprising or unusual. Holds on nominations are almost commonplace. But this was back in 1957, and the Senate Armed Services Committee (SASC) was holding up the nomination of the famous actor James M. Stewart based on questions about his qualifications. The hold on Jimmy Stewart 67 years ago is only one example that underscores the gravity with which the SASC has approached its constitutional power of advice and consent since the modern Committee was formed at the end of World War II.

In 1942, Stewart became the first major American movie star to enlist to fight in World War II. His lifelong love of flying quickly led to his commission as a pilot in the Army Air Corps. He earned the Distinguished Flying Cross for actions while serving as deputy commander of the 2nd Bombardment Wing, the French Croix de Guerre with palm, and the Air Medal with three oak leaf clusters. By the war's end in 1945, he had been promoted to colonel. In 1946, James Stewart starred as George Bailey in his first postwar film, *It's a Wonderful Life*. He earned an Oscar nomination for Best Actor in the iconic role, one of many accolades in his life. In

4

1956, Stewart was nominated by President Eisenhower for promotion to brigadier general in the reserve component of the United States Air Force, the nation's newest Military Service. As a distinguished movie star and decorated World War II combat veteran, many saw his promotion as a no-brainer. Everyone believed the Senate would merely check the box and advance his nomination.

Article I, Section Eight of the Constitution establishes Congress's role in defense and national security matters. In the Senate, the SASC exercises this power directly through its oversight of the Department of Defense (DOD) and the enactment of annual legislation authorizing DOD funding and programs. From Article II, Section Two of the Constitution, the SASC draws its duty to provide its advice and consent concerning the principal civilian and military officers nominated by the president for service in DOD. In its early decades, neither public sentiment nor the nation's political tides altered the Committee's mission-focused approach to nominations. The confirmation process has provided the Committee a powerful tool to determine which senior leaders should be approved to serve in critical institutional positions and which should lead American military operations globally. Its role in confirmations also affords the Committee a unique avenue to examine and oversee DOD. Unsurprisingly, the SASC has applied itself with utmost seriousness to its role in the confirmation process over many decades.

Stewart experienced this firsthand. On May 2, 1957, during the hearing for his and other reserve officers' promotions, Senator Margaret Chase Smith (R-ME) noted discrepancies between Stewart and his peers in total reserve points earned. Public support for Stewart's nomination had been bolstered by a *Washington Daily News* article identifying him as a regularly-training reservist, who in 1952 had even trained as a B-52 pilot with the Psychological Warfare Division of the Air Force at Strategic Air Command in

Omaha, Nebraska.[1] However, based on her office's research, Smith asserted Stewart could not have flown the B-52 at Strategic Air Command that year because the plane had not come into regular service until 1955. And Stewart had not completed his annual qualifications to fly. Then-Air Force Deputy Chief of Staff for Personnel, Lt. Gen. Emmett O'Donnell, a witness at the hearing, conceded: "He could not be the command pilot [for a B-52]... he is not fully qualified on any military aircraft."[2]

Stewart's nomination stalled and did not move forward for two years. Senator Smith's extensive research and attention to detail turned what was considered a routine promotion hearing into a thorough examination of why the Air Force believed Stewart was qualified for advancement, other than the promotion boosting the Service's recruitment numbers with the draw of a famous actor.[3] Ultimately, Stewart was confirmed and continued to serve in the Air Force reserve until he reached the mandatory retirement age of 60 on May 31, 1968—27 years in total.

This event wasn't out of the ordinary. Almost a decade later, Air Force Colonel Samuel P. Goddard was nominated for promotion to brigadier general. A popular former governor of Arizona then running for election once more, Goddard's promotion was held up "on grounds he had not met all qualifications" by Senator Smith, no less.[4] Committee Chair, Sen. Richard B. Russell (D-GA), wrote a personal letter to Sen. Carl Hayden (D-AZ) regarding the nomination:

> Like Stewart, Colonel Goddard had an excellent war record, and I think that the members of the Committee on both sides of the aisle regretted that he had not made the few additional points which would have entitled his promotion to approval.[5]

Historically, the confirmation of nominations processed through the SASC has come down to a single factor: a nominee's qualifications for the position to which he or she is nominated. Political favoritism and popular opinion rarely influenced the Committee's focus on the diligent execution of its constitutional duty. The senators serving as members of the SASC recognize the leaders confirmed by the Senate directly impact U.S. national security and foreign policy, with ramifications reaching beyond politics to the lives of service members, both in and out of combat, and the defense of our freedoms.

Unfortunately, that norm is currently being put to the test. As this book goes to press, we have just witnessed what happens when the Senate confirmation process gets hijacked, misused, and derailed. In February 2023, Senator Tommy Tuberville (R-AL) placed a hold on hundreds of general and flag officer promotions, not because of a concern for any nominees' qualifications, but because he disagreed with a Biden Administration policy. Senator Tuberville's use of military promotions as pawns in a pitched political battle was a significant disruption of the Senate's long-standing nonpartisan, non-political military promotion process and of civil-military relations more broadly.

You will see me discuss the use of holds throughout this book. But it's important to note none had ever risen to the level in the combination of scale, breadth, and length that we witnessed with Sen. Tuberville's actions. And my hope is that none will again. The saddest part was that, in the end, it was all for naught.

It's important that the American people have confidence that the SASC ensures that only those who are highly qualified to take charge of our national security are confirmed. Therefore, properly vetting nominees is complex and steeped in procedural precedent and historical convention. Confirmed officials—DOD civilian and military personnel—establish and implement U.S. defense policy and may be called upon to make decisions of considerable import under extremely challenging circumstances. From crafting the National Defense Strategy to commanding our nation's warfighters to budget and personnel decisions... these individuals exercise immense power and influence when they take the oath of office. For example, the confirmed civilian leaders of the Military Departments (the Army, Navy, and Air Force) are charged with organizing, training, and equipping the armed forces to support the warfighting combatant commanders. For these reasons, the SASC has never lost focus on the importance of a sound process underpinning its review of DOD nominations or the vigorous oversight of the actions and decisions taken by those officials once confirmed and appointed.

I spent 24 years in the U.S. Senate, from 1973 to 1997. I worked in various roles for Senator Sam Nunn (D-GA), including as his staff director of the SASC for eight years when he was chairman and the staff director for the minority for five years when he was ranking member. I have served as an official and unofficial confirmation advisor for the Executive Branch since 1997, handling national security and myriad other nominations. From 1983 to 1996 alone, as staff director, I was involved in approximately 50,000 military nominations and as many as 50 civilian nominations every year.

From my earlier days as a Senate staffer starting in 1973, I was made keenly aware of the Senate's role in confirming presidential appointments. When Governor Jimmy Carter was elected president in 1976, many Georgians were nominated for key positions. Senator Nunn and I, as a member of his personal staff, were heavily involved. That's when I had my first hands-on experience with the nomination process.

Senator Nunn was also on the Government Affairs Committee, so we dealt with what became the controversial nomination of

Bert Lance to be head of the Office of Management and Budget (OMB) in 1977. Another troubled nomination that same year was that of Paul Warnke to be head of the Arms Control and Disarmament Agency and the negotiator of the Strategic Arms Limitation Talks. Although I was always glad that SASC did not handle judicial nominations, Senator Nunn was involved in the 1991 nomination of Judge Clarence Thomas, a Georgian, to the Supreme Court. This required significant staff support. As a member of Senator Nunn's staff, I was in the middle of these nominations. We took away many lessons about the best ways to handle nominations and pitfalls to avoid that were applicable to the SASC process.

Arnold Punaro taking notes at a meeting with Secretary of Defense Leon Panetta on major defense policy issues. Punaro helped prepare Sec. Panetta to be secretary of defense while he was still the director of the CIA.

All these nominations and the Senate's process of considering them were far from routine. The White House played a direct role in each of them. I learned early on the difference between a routine nomination and one of high visibility and a top priority for the president.

Regarding the almost 1,200 government-wide civilian positions that today require Senate confirmation, each nominee considers his or her nomination the most important.[6] Yet it is undeniable that the individual positions in the DOD and the Department of Energy (DOE) nuclear weapons complex requiring confirmation by the SASC are some of the most consequential in government.

DOD spends over $400 billion annually on goods, services, supplies, and equipment. It is the world's largest energy consumer, using roughly 12 million gallons of fuel daily. It maintains one of the world's most extensive property books, operating over a half million facilities on nearly 5,000 sites on 25 million acres of land. It has an enormous capital stock of over 13,000 aircraft, 300 naval ships, and 250,000 wheeled vehicles. An estimated 10 million people fit under the DOD umbrella, including over two million active and reserve personnel (plus their family members), 751,000 civilian employees, and 2.3 million retirees. In short, DOD remains the largest and most complex organization in our government and the world. The now 65 Presidentially-Appointed, Senate-Confirmed (PAS) positions range from the secretary of defense to the assistant secretaries of each Military Service, the DOD inspector general, general counsel, and other key positions. (See Appendix A for a list of all PAS positions under SASC jurisdiction.) The DOE nominees under SASC jurisdiction include the leadership of the National Nuclear Security Administration and another four positions responsible for the nation's nuclear weapons programs and stockpile. Strong leadership is essential, and these political appointees must be highly qualified for positions of immense responsibility and impact.

Throughout this book, I'll outline that there are hundreds of personnel involved in the nomination process, which includes Executive Branch vetting, the Senate's role in confirmation, and the president's appointment authority. It is one of the most time-consuming aspects of government across all three branches, including judicial nominations, which have become highly contentious.

The SASC follows a comprehensive and organized process for all nominations. The Committee's staff director must ensure the process is followed and make individual staff recommendations when a nomination is non-routine or high-profile. Nominations can prove unpredictable. One that appears routine can quickly become controversial, and one that promises to be highly controversial can become utterly routine.

Although I was involved in every aspect of the confirmation process as SASC staff director from 1983 to 1997, I have also been a pro bono confirmation advisor to the DOD since 1997. The White House has frequently asked me to advise on cabinet nominations outside the DOD, including at the Department of Veterans Affairs (VA) and the Department of Homeland Security (DHS). From staff director to confirmation advisor, I have been directly involved in the confirmation process for 12 secretaries of defense, 12 Joint Chiefs of Staff chairmen, over 40 service chiefs, and at least 2,000 civilian officials. In this capacity, I have advised DOD's leadership on handling specific nominations and met with individual nominees (both military and civilian) to prepare them for their confirmation hearings. In troubled nominations, my involvement was often much more extensive. I often called on other former SASC staff directors—experts in all aspects of the hearing process—to help me prepare a nominee to answer any question a senator might ask them. My team's preparatory sessions were called "murder boards." I was asked to serve officially on the confirmation teams for several key nominees, including several secretary of defense nominations, and was designated as a Special Government Employee. These included Secretaries Ash Carter, Patrick Shanahan, and Mark Esper.

Secretary of Defense Ash Carter recognized my efforts in assisting with DOD nominations and confirmations in January 2017 with the Department of Defense Medal for Distinguished Public Service, the highest civilian award given to someone outside the Department.

Secretary of Defense Ash Carter presents Arnold Punaro with the Department of Defense Medal for Distinguished Public Service (January 2017). Presented for exceptionally distinguished service of significance to the Department of Defense, the Medal is the highest award the secretary of defense can present to a private citizen. The award referenced the hundreds of civilian presidential appointees and military general and flag officers Punaro guided through the Senate confirmation process, including 12 secretaries of defense and 12 chairmen of the Joint Chiefs of Staff. For the full text of the award citation, see Appendix B.

I have also helped a handful of nominees in both Democratic and Republican administrations outside of DOD prepare for their confirmations. Some examples include Jeh Johnson for secretary of Homeland Security; Robert Wilkie and Jim Peake for secretary of the Department of Veterans Affairs; Jim Morhard, deputy administrator of NASA; and two ambassador examples are Mark Lippert, ambassador to South Korea and Georgette Mosbacher, ambassador to Poland. Thanks to the rigorous process we developed over the years for DOD nominees, all these nominees benefited from our team's comprehensive prep.

Beginning with initial vetting in the Executive Branch, this book will explore the various "detonation" points that nominees might experience. The book also covers the Federal Bureau of Investigation (FBI) full-field investigation, extensive written and verbal questionnaires, review of tax filings, and financial and organizational conflicts of interest. In most cases, all are required before the president approves and submits the nomination to the U.S. Senate. Depending on how each White House prepares materials for the president's decision, this process can take months or up to a year for those below the cabinet level.

It is essential to point out that people considering public service face the nagging question of whether they want to deal with the hassles that come with government work, beginning with the confirmation process. Those who answer the call to public service follow a noble tradition from the late 18th century, when Thomas Jefferson and Alexander Hamilton helped guide policy as cabinet secretaries during the presidency of George Washington. Paul C. Light put public service in this historical context:

> American government was designed to be led by citizens who would step out of private life for a term of office, then return to their communities enriched by service and ready to recruit the next generation of citizen servants. The Founding Fathers believed in a democracy led by individuals who would not become so enamored of power and

addicted to perquisites that they would use government as an instrument of self-aggrandizement.[7]

This book is a reference guide to the SASC confirmation process for civilian and military nominees. It details the good, the bad, and the ugly, the actual process, and how it has changed over time (in many ways, not for the better). And it offers suggestions for streamlining its operation. This book will delineate what I have termed the "dos and don'ts" of the confirmation process and the many lessons learned over 50 years of working in this arena. I hope this book makes a nominee's path easier should he or she choose to answer the call to service. Most importantly, I hope this helps the highly qualified individuals our government needs choose willingly to go through the process with a better understanding of how to be successful.

The DOD is a complex organization with our government's most critical mission: deterring and defeating those trying to take away our democratic freedoms. The people who serve in key confirmed civilian and military positions must lead in achieving this goal. Working with Congress, they determine how best to ensure that the defense of our freedoms is successful. The confirmation process in the Senate is the crucial step in putting this leadership in place. It ensures that each nominee follows through on the goals he or she establishes and promises in testimony before the Committee when they answer each senator's question with: "If confirmed...."

SECTION 1: The Process From 30,000 Feet

1

THE CONSTITUTIONAL PROCESS

This chapter provides a high-level overview of the confirmation process, including the president's and Congress's powers. The process is firmly anchored in the Constitution in both branches of government. It applies to civilian nominees for presidential appointment to key positions in the Executive Branch and to military officers. The president's appointment powers and the Senate's advice and consent role are addressed in Article II, Section Two of the U.S. Constitution:

> He [the President] shall nominate, and by and with the Advice and Consent of the Senate, shall appoint Ambassadors, other public Ministers and Consuls, Judges of the Supreme Court, and all other Officers of the United States whose Appointments are not herein otherwise provided for, and which shall be established by Law: but the Congress may by Law vest the Appointment of such inferior Officers, as they think proper, in the president alone, in the Courts of Law, or in the Heads of Departments.

The president first nominates an individual for a specific position, after which the Senate assumes control in determining whether to approve, disapprove, or act on the president's nominee. If the Senate's advice and consent regarding a nominee is favorable and the nominee is confirmed, the power returns to the president to appoint the nominee to the position for which confirmed.

The president retains the right to withdraw any nomination (civilian or military) before a full Senate vote to confirm or not occurs. Although infrequent, the president withdraws a handful of nominations in each administration. Sometimes a nomination is withdrawn to permit the correction of a technical error in the paperwork. For example, in July 2021, President Biden withdrew the nomination of Andrew Hunter, whose paperwork reflected he had been nominated to serve as an assistant secretary of the Army. In fact, Biden had intended him to serve as an assistant secretary of the Air Force. The White House corrected the paperwork, and Hunter was renominated for the Air Force position within days.

In other cases, however, the withdrawal of the nomination is based on a concern about the nominee. Undoubtedly, the very public aspect of the process subjects a nominee to intense personal scrutiny. It is not uncommon for the spotlight cast by the White House's announcement of a nomination or its posting on Congress.gov (the publicly accessible website of the Senate and the House) to generate reports from media, aggrieved members of the public or "watchdog" organizations alleging the nominee has engaged in misjudgments or dishonest acts that render him or her unsuitable for the position for which nominated. Sometimes, an inquiry undertaken by individual senators or the SASC professional staff as part of the confirmation process yields potentially adverse information about a nominee.

In most cases, the White House was aware of and considered this so-called adverse information before proceeding with the nomination. Even if new negative information arises, it is often resolved in favor of the nominee. But sometimes the adverse information—regardless of when or how it became known—is of such magnitude or so fraught politically it soon becomes plain the nominee cannot or will not be confirmed by the Senate. In such cases, the White House may withdraw the nomination to minimize the distraction and embarrassment.

In April 2021, early in his administration, President Biden nominated Ms. Brenda Sue Fulton to be the assistant secretary of defense for Manpower and Reserve Affairs. Fulton, a West Point graduate who, after leaving the service, would be appointed to and lead the West Point Board of Visitors, was a well-respected advocate for LGBTQ causes. She had been instrumental in persuading then-Secretary of Defense Ash Carter to change DOD policy in 2016 to permit transgender persons to serve openly in the military and to receive necessary medical care and services in military treatment facilities; her confirmation was taken as a given. Yet at her hearing before the SASC in October 2021, a slew of prominent Republican senators, Tom Cotton of Arkansas, Rick Scott of Florida, Josh Hawley of Missouri, Dan Sullivan of Alaska, and Marsha Blackburn of Tennessee, drilled Fulton on a cache of social media posts, formerly called tweets, in which she had labeled all Republicans as "racists" and criticized the Supreme Court for having "twisted [the tenets of religious freedom] to mean conservative Christians can dictate their beliefs to the rest of us." Fulton was never voted out of Committee. Following Senate Rules, her nomination was returned to the president on January 3, 2022, at the end of the first session of the 117th Congress.

Many were surprised when the president renominated Fulton for the same position a day later when the second session of the 117th Congress started. Her nomination was received in the Senate, referred to the SASC, and sat without action for almost nine months. Finally, on September 29, 2022, President Biden withdrew Fulton's nomination and concurrently nominated Mr. Ron Keohane in her place. Fulton, meanwhile, had already been appointed to a non-career senior executive position in the Department of Veterans Affairs. This role did not require Senate confirmation. Fulton's experience, as well as those of other recent Biden Administration nominees such as Colin Kahl, who was narrowly confirmed by the Senate to be the under secretary of defense for policy without having garnered a single Republican vote, and Neera Tanden, Biden's initial pick to lead the OMB, whose nomination was withdrawn, also offer a caution to would-be nominees who use or have used social media as a venue for personal expression.

An example of the SASC not voting on a nomination occurred during the Clinton Administration when Morton Halperin was nominated as assistant secretary of defense for democracy and peacekeeping. Then-Secretary of Defense Les Aspin was a vigorous advocate because of Halperin's extensive background and experience in arms control. Aspin had previously consulted with then-Chairman Sam Nunn (D-GA) and me as staff director. We thought the nomination could be problematic and unlikely to be approved. There were allegations Halperin leaked classified information and had worked on the Pentagon Papers. (He ended up on the Nixon enemies list.) But we felt that should he be nominated, we would ensure he got a fair hearing and would be treated with respect during the process.

Halperin's nomination created a firestorm on the Republican side of the Committee, even with some conservative Democrats. I knew from the outset he would never get out of Committee, as the votes were not there, and I asked those in opposition to tone it down. This didn't happen. Halperin ended up having a hearing, and even though he acquitted himself well, the SASC never acted on his nomination. He was subsequently appointed to a non-confirmed position on the National Security Council. None of the allegations were ever substantiated. Former Secretary of State Henry Kissinger ultimately wrote Mr. Halperin a letter of apology for some of the misinformation promulgated about him during the Nixon Administration. Mr. Halperin went on to serve with distinction in the Obama Administration and other key positions. He was confirmed by the Senate to several commission positions in that timeframe.

In other cases, a nominee will act on his or her own accord to withdraw from further consideration. Such withdrawals are almost always honored by the White House and interpreted as the "end of the matter." But the president's submission of a formal notice of the nomination's withdrawal to the Senate is still required. On July 14, 2021, Mike Brown, a prominent businessman who had been nominated on April 2, 2021, as under secretary of defense for acquisition and sustainment, asked to withdraw his nomination because of an ongoing DOD inspector general (IG) review of personnel practices at the Defense Innovation Unit, which Brown headed. The president withdrew the nomination on July 20, 2021. Although Brown had been cleared of those allegations prior to his nomination, once he was nominated, the allegations resurfaced. The IG finally cleared him again, but their review took over a year and wasn't completed until September 9, 2022.

The president also retains full authority not to appoint an individual to a position, even if the Senate has confirmed that individual. But this rarely occurs. All this to say... all three steps of the process: nomination by the president, confirmation by the Senate, and appointment by the president, in that order, must take place before that nominee can hold the position and lawfully exercise the authorities associated with it. It is important to note Senate confirmations are specific to a particular nominee and a particular job or position (for civilian nominees) or for promotion to a specific military grade or duty position (for military officers). If the president nominates a confirmed civilian appointee for a new job or a military officer for further promotion (even if the original confirmation occurred recently), a new Senate confirmation process is required.

THE THREE PHASES OF THE CONSTITUTIONAL PROCESS AS AP-PLIED TO CIVILIAN NOMINEES

The process of advice and consent, or confirmation, has three main phases, each of which requires time and dutiful preparation:

1. Nomination,
2. Confirmation, and
3. Appointment.

Although the three-phase constitutional process is the same for nominees for civilian positions and military officers, each phase can be very different, depending on the type of nominee. This chapter focuses on the process as it applies to civilian nominees. The procedure applicable to military nominees will be addressed in Section Four.

1. Nomination. The nomination of an individual to a Presidentially-Appointed, Senate-Confirmed (PAS) position is the president's sole province. The term "PAS" applies only to civilian positions. Before the president makes a formal nomination for one of the 1,200 federal PAS positions, the White House recruits and screens candidates. The Office of Presidential Personnel (PPO) plays the lead role in preparing a list of potential candidates for each vacancy and, depending on the president's preferences, recommends one or more finalists for the president's consideration. Candidates for PAS positions may be recruited via a White House website established for that purpose (as during the Administration of President George W. Bush) or recommended by members of Congress or other officials serving in the administration. Often the president will draw on prospective candidates suggested by persons with close personal ties or bonds of trust or to whom the president perceives an owed obligation, whether for campaign support, donations, or other reasons. Presidents often recall persons who served in political appointments in past administrations of the president's party.

Once a candidate is tentatively selected, they are asked to submit to a full-field FBI background investigation. (We will review these requirements in detail in a later chapter.) In most cases, the background investigation occurs before the president formally decides on the nomination. Therefore, the candidate and the FBI should be as discreet as possible during this process. Depending on the prospective nominee's circumstances, the full-field investigation can take six to eight weeks or longer. Once the investigation and all of the nominee's paperwork are complete and reviewed by the White House Counsel's Office, the nomination is forwarded to the president. If the president decides to move forward with the nomination, then it is submitted to the Senate for its advice and consent.

Misunderstandings about the exact status of nominations are not uncommon. There can be many preliminary signals about a nomination before its actual formal submission to the Senate or the committee of jurisdiction. There can be "speculation" about who the president might nominate for a senior position. Sometimes this is the administration's way of flushing out congressional, media, and public sentiment about a prospective nominee. It becomes a "dipstick" test to see whether a prospective nominee is confirmable to a particular PAS position. An informal "intent to nominate" may be circulated to the media, or a more formal official announcement of the president's "intent to nominate." Recent administrations signified this by posting a statement and biographical information about the intended nominee on the publicly accessible White House website. None of these count as the "nomination." Only the actual nomination—signed and submitted by the president and received by the Senate—sets the wheels of the Senate confirmation process in motion. The lapse between an announcement of an intent to nominate and the actual nomination can range from a few days to several weeks or months. This has been the case in every administration. Rumor and speculation notwithstanding, the Senate, the SASC, and most other Senate committees cannot and will not act on a nomination until it is formally received in the Senate and referred to the Committee.

Arnold Punaro discusses the organization of the Office of the Secretary of Defense and the new National Defense Strategy with Secretary of Defense Jim Mattis. Mattis served in the position from 2017-2019. The note below is from Jim Mattis to Punaro after he helped him with his confirmation.

Dear Arnold, I know I would not be using this stationary but for your extraordinary support in getting me through confirmation. Thank you for all you did—the coaching, the papers and the murder boards. Nothing takes the place of experience and I'm grateful for your willingness to share yours. Semper Fi, Jim.

THE SECRETARY OF DEFENSE
WASHINGTON

24 JAN 2017

Dear Arnold,

I know I would not be using this stationary but for your extraordinary support in getting me through confirmation. Thank you for all you did — the coaching, the papers and the murder boards. Nothing takes the place of experience and I'm grateful for your willingness to share yours.

Semper Fi,

Jim

2. Confirmation. The Senate confirmation process starts only when the nomination is received and referred to the SASC. How the Senate and the SASC treat it varies, depending on the importance of the position involved, existing political circumstances, and policy implications. Unsurprisingly, past Committee chairmen and ranking members have leveraged White House or DOD commitment to a particular nominee or need for an expeditious confirmation to prompt other desired and relevant actions by the administration or the Department.

But inevitably, the process begins with yet another round of paperwork for the nominee to complete. Once all paperwork is completed, it is provided to all senators on the SASC, along with the majority and minority staff directors and other designated staff members of the Committee. Nominees can then meet with senators on the Committee one-on-one in meetings known as "courtesy calls."

From there, the Committee chairman (with the consultation of the ranking member) will set a hearing date. The nominee will be sent a set of Advance Policy Questions (APQs), which must be completed before the hearing.

On the day of the hearing, the chairman begins by asking a series of standard questions to ensure the nominee has not taken any actions to presume the outcome of the confirmation process and to affirm the Committee's oversight role of the Department. Senators then proceed to ask questions about the nominee's background, qualifications, and the administration's policies and programs.

A quick aside about the "presumption of confirmation." The principle that nominees who have not yet been confirmed by the Senate must avoid actions and statements that "presume confirmation" or **appear to do so** originated with the SASC. Avoiding the "presumption of confirmation" is now inculcated in DOD culture and processes. Periodically, usually at the beginning of a new administration, the DOD general counsel will issue a memorandum to all nominees and prospective nominees entitled "Guidelines on Activities Prior to Confirmation." This memorandum, the most recent issued in April 2021 by then-Acting General Counsel Beth George, reinforces that until a nominee is confirmed by the Senate and appointed by the president, they must act in a manner consistent with his or her pre-confirmation role, which is limited to preparing to assume new duties and responsibilities as a PAS. It lists several specific activities to which a nominee must steer clear—activities that the SASC has previously indicated will be interpreted as "presuming confirmation."

The "presumption of confirmation" is no more apparent than with Graham Allison, nominated in the Clinton Administration in March 1993 as the assistant secretary of defense for policy and planning. I was the staff director of the SASC at the time. While

Allison was highly qualified for the role he had been nominated for, he behaved as if oblivious to the policies against "presumption." Allison ensconced himself in the Pentagon almost immediately after being nominated and began making policy recommendations and personnel decisions affecting the Policy and Planning Office. The SASC soon determined Allison was using authorities and availing himself of privileges that would come to him only once confirmed by the Senate and appointed by the president as assistant secretary.

He was put in the "penalty box" and required to meet personally (and uncomfortably) with several SASC senators. They reinforced in no uncertain terms that Allison's nomination would not proceed unless he made it clear he understood and would conform to the "rules of the road." Eventually, after a lengthy delay and significant personal embarrassment, Allison, much chastened, was confirmed.

Avoiding the "presumption of confirmation" is also why prudent nominees, when answering senators' questions about "how they might address or change this or that DOD policy or program," frequently preface their answers with the phrase: "If confirmed...." Senators and Committee Staff expect nominees to use this phrase. It's a mark of professionalism and an indicator the nominee understands and respects the primacy of the Senate's constitutional role in the confirmation process.

Another example to illustrate this principle occurred in 2023, when General Eric Smith, USMC, was nominated to succeed General David Berger as commandant of the Marine Corps. General Berger's term expired on July 11, 2023, before General Smith could be confirmed by the Senate due to a hold by Senator Tommy Tuberville (R-AL). As the assistant commandant, Title 10 gave Smith the authority to serve as the Marine Corps' senior official. But Smith was precluded from taking any action that would "presume the outcome" of the confirmation process, such as issuing the traditional "Commandant's Guidance." The same prohibition on "presumption" applied in 2023 to the incoming service chiefs.

The SASC remains extremely watchful for "presumption missteps" and responds swiftly and firmly when they occur.

After the nominee answers any post-hearing Questions for the Record (QFRs), the SASC must vote on whether to report a nominee out of Committee. If the SASC reports the nominee favorably, the nomination is placed on the Senate Executive Calendar. The Senate majority leader controls when and which nominees are voted on by the full Senate. Nominees can be confirmed by either a unanimous consent agreement or a roll call vote, where a simple majority is needed to pass. In some cases, the majority leader will need cloture to overcome a hold on a nominee—also a simple majority vote.

3. Appointment. After the Senate has confirmed a nominee, the president must sign the warrant of appointment to complete the process. This usually takes a few days, though it can take longer if the president is traveling. Only after the official appointment can the nominee take the oath of office and begin serving in their new position.

All three phases must be completed for the appointment to be constitutionally valid. While both the Executive and Legislative Branches undertake to process most presidential nominations as soon as possible, it is, for most nominees, a plodding and paper-driven experience. Although the appointment process to a PAS position has become far lengthier over the years, none of the three phases outlined above can be bypassed or curtailed. There are no shortcuts. Nominees who wish to serve as a PAS have no option but to move through the three phases, taking each step as directed.

(Section Two of this book will go into more details of each phase and outline the timeframes.)

THE PLUM BOOK

The president appoints many civilians to political positions in the federal government during any administration. The Senate's focus is on presidential appointments requiring Senate confirmation. The official list of all federal government positions subject to a presidential or political appointment—PAS officers, officers who can be appointed by action of the president alone, political senior executives, and so-called "Schedule C" political appointees who are identified and screened by the White House and appointed to their positions by officials in the department or agency to which they are assigned for duty—is outlined in the "Plum Book."

First created in the Eisenhower Administration, a new edition of the Plum Book is released by the Senate Committee on Homeland Security and Government Affairs and the House Committee on Oversight and Reform after each presidential election. The Plum Book is an invaluable reference for the White House PPO and individuals interested in presidential or other political appointments. It is quite possible, however, that the 2020 Plum Book will be the last released in hard copy. The Plum Act of 2022, enacted as part of the National Defense Authorization Act (NDAA) for Fiscal Year (FY) 2023, requires that not later than December 23, 2023, the director of the Office of Personnel Management (OPM) create and maintain a publicly accessible website presenting the information currently published in the Plum Book. There is an understanding that the site's data will be updated and validated annually. Effective January 1, 2026, the hard copy Plum Book will no longer be published.

SUMMARY OF POSITIONS SUBJECT TO NONCOMPETITIVE APPOINTMENT

PAS	=	Positions Subject to Presidential Appointment with Senate Confirmation
PA	=	Positions Subject to Presidential Appointment without Senate Confirmation
GEN	=	Positions Designated as Senior Executive Service "General"
NA	=	Senior Executive Service General Positions Filled by Noncareer Appointment
TA	=	Senior Executive Service Positions Filled by Limited Emergency or Limited Term Appointment
SC	=	Positions Filled by Schedule C Excepted Appointment
XS	=	Positions Subject to Statutory Excepted Appointment

PAS	PA	GEN	NA	TA	SC	XS	Total
1,118	354	2,510	724	83	1,566	723	7,078

A table from the 2020 Plum Book depicts the different types of presidential appointments, including those that require Senate confirmation, together with the total numbers of such appointees in the federal government.

VACANCIES, ACTING OFFICERS, AND PERFORMING THE DUTIES OF

It's rare that all 65 PAS positions in DOD are encumbered by Senate-confirmed persons. Yet it's widely accepted that continuity of senior leadership is essential to DOD's critical national security mission and good government overall. A topline understanding of the Vacancies Act is useful to anyone interested in government and politics. In enacting the Federal Vacancies Reform Act (FVRA) of 1998, as amended, Congress established a procedure by which the duties associated with a vacant PAS position could be temporarily performed by an Acting official. The temporary nature of "Acting" status under the law was intended to incentivize the president to nominate for confirmation by the Senate persons he had selected to fill PAS positions in his administration. One essential purpose of the law—particularly relevant to the focus of this book—is to preclude a president from depriving the Senate of its constitutional role in providing advice and consent on nominations for key government positions by stocking his administration with a series of Acting officials, none of whom have been subject to the crucible of the confirmation process, and who may thus perceive themselves less accountable to congressional oversight.

When a civilian position that requires Senate confirmation and appointment by the president becomes vacant for any reason, the FVRA kicks in. The law applies to PAS positions that have not yet been filled by a person confirmed by the Senate and appointed by the president (a relatively common occurrence at the beginning of a new administration) and positions filled by a presidentially appointed, Senate-confirmed official who has since died, resigned, or otherwise cannot fulfill the duties of the post (e.g., incapacitating illness).

It's important to understand which positions the FVRA applies to and those it does not. The FVRA applies only to vacancies in PAS positions. It does not apply to any other types of civilian jobs in the DOD or other federal departments and agencies, and it does not apply to the military.

The FVRA limits who can serve as an Acting in a PAS position and for how long. A person who is properly Acting in a PAS position can perform any duty or function required of that position, even if the Acting is not him or herself a PAS. But once the FVRA's time limit on service as Acting has expired, no one may serve as Acting, and the "statutory duties" of the vacant office must be performed by the secretary of defense in his role as the head of DOD.

Under the FVRA, only three categories of people can serve as Acting in a vacant PAS position:

CATEGORY 1: The person serving as the "first assistant" to the PAS whose position is vacant. The first assistant in DOD usually carries the title of principal deputy or deputy. Sometimes the top "deputy" is also a PAS. But they can also be a non-career (political) member of the Senior Executive Service (SES), a career SES, or the military. The first assistant *fleets up automatically* to Acting as soon as a vacancy occurs unless the president (and only the president) intervenes and designates someone in Categories

Two or Three to serve as Acting. Unless expressly authorized in law, a military officer serving as a deputy to a PAS is prohibited from serving as an Acting PAS. For example, the law governing the PAS position of assistant secretary of the Navy for research, development, and acquisition establishes the position of a principal military deputy. It expressly provides that this military deputy may serve for up to one year as Acting assistant secretary in the absence of the PAS.

CATEGORY 2: The president (and only the president) can designate another PAS from anywhere in the federal government to serve as Acting. When Secretary of Defense Mark Esper was fired by President Trump, the president bypassed his DOD-approved succession plan that would have placed Deputy Secretary of Defense David Norquist in the Acting role. He used his authority under the FVRA to appoint Christopher Miller, previously confirmed by the Senate as director of the National Counterterrorism Center, a PAS position, to be the Acting secretary of defense.

CATEGORY 3: The president (and only the president) can designate another senior agency employee to serve as Acting, provided that this senior employee is from *the same executive agency* in which the vacancy occurs (for our purposes, from any component of DOD); has served in DOD for at least 90 days during the 365 days *preceding* the date on which the vacancy occurred; and during those 90 days, served in a position for which the *rate of pay was at least GS-15, Step 1.*

The FVRA limits the time that an Acting can serve. The Vacancies Act does not provide a set number of days for an Acting to serve. Instead, the period involves a series of interrelated provisions tied to the president's submission of a nomination for the vacant position. In the most common situation, an Acting officer can serve for only 210 days, measured *from the date the vacancy first occurs* (not from the date an Acting begins to serve). But as soon as the president submits a nomination to the Senate to fill the vacant position, the 210-day clock *stops*. The Acting official can continue to serve without limitation until the nominee is confirmed, or the nomination is rejected, returned by the Senate, or withdrawn by the president. Because the Senate confirmation process is so lengthy, it is not uncommon for an Acting official in DOD to serve for as long as 12 to 18 months before the nominee for the vacancy is confirmed.

However, if the president's first nomination is rejected, returned, or withdrawn, the 210-day Acting clock starts anew as of that date. This cycle can repeat itself with a second presidential nominee. But the second nomination's rejection, return, or withdrawal starts a third and final 210-day period during which an Acting may serve. This situation is atypical and has not occurred in DOD for at least 10 years.

The FVRA provides extra time for a new president to submit nominations for PAS positions across a new administration. Specifically, an Acting official can serve 300 days in any vacant PAS position beginning the day a new president takes the oath of office (regardless of when the vacancy occurred), or that becomes vacant during the new president's first 60 days in office. This special authority does not apply to a president elected to a second term.

The FVRA, as interpreted by the courts, also imposes restrictions on a person being both the nominee and serving as Acting for the same vacant PAS position. Generally, if the president nominates a person permanently for the vacant position, that person may not serve as an Acting officer. The president must name another qualified person as Acting instead of the nominated person.

Secretary of Defense Mark Esper and Arnold Punaro stop for a photo in January 2020 before delving into discussions on key challenges facing the Department. When Esper was Acting secretary of defense, the FVRA required him to return to his role as secretary of the Army during his nomination and confirmation process for secdef. Punaro was part of his confirmation prep team.

There is an exception to this limitation, however. A person nominated may serve as Acting during the pendency of his or her nomination to that same position if he or she is the first assistant and has served in that role for at least 90 days during the year preceding the vacancy or the first assistant is also a PAS position to which the person was previously confirmed by the Senate. This restriction is why Mark Esper had to step down on July 15, 2019, as Acting secretary of defense when he was nominated for the position.

Mark T. Esper

Nov 7

Arnold,

I know I've shared this with you a few times, but I wanted to put pen to paper and formally say Thanks! once again for all of your support, guidance, and insights. From working with the Chairman, to advising OSD, to our hearing prep sessions, your involvement really made a difference. So thanks again for your help.... and friendship.... and I hope to stay in close contact with you in the months ahead.

Sincerely,
Mark

Arnold, I know I've shared this with you a few times, but I wanted to put pen to paper and formally say Thanks! once again for all of your support, guidance, and insights. From working with the Chairman, to advising OSD, to our hearing prep sessions, your involvement really made a difference. So thanks again for your help... and friendship... and I hope to stay in close contact with you in the months ahead. Sincerely, Mark

President Trump had tapped Esper to serve as Acting secretary of defense after the resignation of Patrick Shanahan, pulling Esper from his confirmed position as secretary of the Army. Esper served as Acting from June 24 to July 15, 2019, when Trump formally nominated him to be secretary of defense. But because Esper had not served previously as the deputy secretary of defense—the first assistant to the secretary—he did not meet the law's criteria.

Esper returned to his confirmed role as secretary of the Army while his nomination was processed by the SASC. Trump installed Navy Secretary Richard Spencer as Acting secretary of defense from July 15 to July 23. There was an arrangement from the SASC to expedite Esper's nomination, which they did. He was sworn in as secretary of defense on July 23, 2019.

Once the FVRA time limit on service as Acting (usually, but not always at the 210-day mark after the vacancy occurs) has expired, *no one* may serve as Acting in the vacant position, and the statutory duties, if any, must be performed by the secretary of defense in his role as the head of DOD.

A statutory duty is a duty or function reserved by law or regulation to a specific PAS and only to that PAS. For a duty to be considered statutory, the law or regulation imposing it must read: "The PAS *and only the PAS* may approve...." Statutory duties are rare; most PAS positions have none.

If a person serves in an Acting role in contravention of the Vacancies Act, his or her actions and decisions are viewed as without force and effect under law. Critically, the Vacancies Act also prohibits an agency from subsequently curing a violation by reissuing an otherwise invalid decision through the proper official or process. The FVRA can be enforced both through political processes and private litigation.

The Government Accountability Office (GAO) monitors the service of Acting officers across the federal government. It is bound to report violations of the Vacancies Act to Congress.

Should GAO make such a report, it could prompt Congress to use its oversight mechanisms to pressure the Executive Branch to comply with the Act. In addition, in some cases, private litigants may sue in federal court to invalidate noncompliant agency actions.

Mindful of the need to ensure the continuity of leadership in the Department, DOD developed the administrative construct of Performing the Duties Of (PTDO) to address situations in which no one qualifies to serve as Acting or the FVRA time limit on Acting service has expired. Again, we emphasize that PTDO status *is not* part of the FVRA.

The secretary of defense or secretary of the Military Department concerned *can designate any employee* to Perform the Duties Of a vacant PAS position under that secretary's supervision. Further, there is *no time limit* an employee can serve PTDO. But PTDO designees may not perform the statutory duties—if any—of the vacant PAS position. PTDO designees may not perform duties that laws or regulations reserve to an official who is Presidentially-Appointed and Senate-confirmed—unless the employee designated to Perform the Duties Of is a PAS in his or her own right.

The SASC maintains awareness of who serves in an Acting or PTDO role in vacant DOD PAS positions. Although each case of Acting or PTDO must be analyzed based on its own specific facts and circumstances, at the beginning of the Biden Administration, SASC advised DOD it would consider a nominee who is Performing the Duties Of the same position for which nominated as "presuming confirmation" unless that nominee met the criteria in the FVRA.[8] Although the Pentagon uses PTDO status judiciously, some recent examples have been considered egregious and deliberate attempts to circumvent the Senate confirmation process.

In the Spring of 2020, retired Army Brigadier General Anthony Tata was appointed as a senior adviser to Secretary of Defense Mark Esper. President Trump nominated Tata to be under secretary of defense for policy in June of that year. The nomination provoked an almost immediate outcry. CNN reported that Tata had once called President Obama "a terrorist leader" and derided Islam as "the most oppressive violent religion I know of."[9] Tata was also reported to have retired from the military in 2009 after an Army inquiry found he conducted at least two adulterous affairs while serving.

There was also a sense that President Trump was interested in positioning Tata to replace Esper, with whom Trump had publicly voiced his dissatisfaction. Significant opposition to Tata's nomination began to build among Democrats and Republicans on the SASC; 15 minutes before Tata's confirmation hearing was slated to start on the morning of July 30, 2020, SASC Chairman Jim Inhofe announced a delay in the proceedings. There were "many Democrats and Republicans who didn't know enough about Anthony Tata to consider him for a very significant position."

Yet less than a week later, the Pentagon announced Tata had withdrawn from the confirmation process and would be appointed to Perform the Duties Of the deputy under secretary of defense for policy. Tata would report to Dr. James Anderson, who was presently serving as the Acting under secretary of defense for policy, the position to which Tata had been nominated. Anderson was confirmed by the Senate to the deputy under secretary's position in June 2020.

But because the position of under secretary had been vacant since John Rood's resignation at President Trump's request in February 2020, Anderson had served as Acting under secretary immediately after his confirmation to the deputy first assistant's position. It left the deputy under secretary's position unmanned and open for Tata.

Less than four months later, Tata would be catapulted into PTDO the under secretary when Anderson resigned a day after President Trump sacked Esper. In effect, Anthony Tata now performed the identical job he had originally been nominated for—a nomination that had failed because he could not garner the support of the SASC. The move was widely condemned in the Senate as a maneuver to sidestep the Senate's constitutional advice and consent role. Tata would continue to serve PTDO for the remaining three months of the Trump Administration.

It is no idle speculation to say that, under other circumstances, the SASC would have taken severe measures vis-à-vis the Pentagon and administration for flouting the confirmation process.

RECESS APPOINTMENTS

Under the Constitution, the president and the Senate share the power to appoint high-level policymaking positions in federal departments and agencies. The president nominates individuals for these positions, and the Senate must confirm them before they can be appointed. The Constitution also provides an exception to this process. When the Senate is in recess, the president may make a temporary appointment, called a recess appointment, to any such position without Senate approval.

During the country's early years, both houses of Congress had short sessions and long recesses. Until the early 20th century, Senate sessions were less than half the year. Presidents used their recess appointment power to maintain the continuity of administrative government by temporarily filling offices when the Senate was not in session and nominees could not be considered or confirmed.

But presidents have also sometimes used the recess appointment power for political reasons, temporarily installing an appointee who probably would not be confirmed by the Senate. Although recess appointments are only temporary, they strain relationships between the executive and Congress. The Senate does not favor appointments made without their advice and consent. Presidents rarely preferred these appointments because of the limited time a recess appointee could serve.

In 2007, the Senate began using *pro forma* sessions to create a situation in which the Senate never formally moved into a recess status. These usually comprised the Senate reconvening every three days during a scheduled absence for less than five minutes of the day, and no official business is conducted. But that the Senate is technically not in recess denies the president the ability to make an appointment during this period.

In 2012, President Barack Obama, frustrated by the Senate's refusal to confirm many of his nominees, challenged the Senate's use of *pro forma* sessions and made a series of recess appointments to the National Labor Relations Board (NLRB). Obama asserted the appointments were valid exercises of the president's constitutional authority and that the *pro forma* sessions were intended only to stymie executive power.

Two years later, however, the Supreme Court settled the debate between the Executive and Legislative Branches, ruling unanimously in *NLRB v. Noel Canning* that the appointments in question were, in fact, unconstitutional. The Senate's regular use of *pro forma* sessions continues today, and recess appointments have found little to no use since then.

POLITICAL APPOINTEE GROWTH OVER TIME

	1960	2012*	2020**
Secretary	10	15	15
Deputy Secretary	6	16	28
Under Secretary	15	44	91
Assistant Secretary	87	154	535 ***
Deputy Assistant Secretary	78	293	1,070
Total	196	522	1,739

Political Appointee Growth Over Time

* Reflects enactment of S.679, Presidential Appointment Efficiency and Streamlining Act on July 31, 2012.

** Source for 2020 figures: Light, Paul C. "Federal Bloat is at a 60-Year High." Brookings, October 5, 2020. https://www.brookings.edu/blog/fixgov/2020/10/05/federal-bloat-is-at-a-sixty-year-high/

*** The Executive Level IV Assistant Secretary rank includes a variety of titles that include Directors, General Counsels, Chief Financial Officers, Chief Information Technology Officers, Chief Human Capital Officers, and other Executive Level IV titles. Under 2008 legislation, Senate-confirmed Inspectors General were elevated from Executive Level IV to Executive Level III, making them equivalent in this analysis to an Under Secretary

GROWTH IN TOP-LEVEL POSITIONS

Over the years, the federal government's management and overhead layers have steadily increased. The chart above depicts the growth in the number of political appointee positions over the last 60 years.

While we may not get a perfect apples-to-apples comparison for each of the above positions as titles and levels change throughout the years, the trend is clear: growth in numbers across the board. And with that comes an increased number of PAS officials in government, each requiring precious Senate time to confirm:

POLITICAL APPOINTEES
(as of 2020 Plum Book)

194	881	91	93	60	65	1,118	7,078
Ambassadors	Judges	Under Secretary	U.S. Attorneys	State	Defense-Civilians	Total Requiring Senate Confirmation (PAS)	Political Appointees Grand Total

Today, when including just the DOD civilian nominees, the full Senate must vote on the secretary of defense, the deputy secretary, six under secretaries of defense and their six deputy under secretaries, as well as seven other senior officials designated as principal staff assistants (PSA).[10] One level down, we add a host of assistant secretaries of defense—each of whom already reports to a PAS official.

As DOD has grown in size over the years, the number of PAS positions has increased. Positions that were once at or near the top of the hierarchy are now layered under more senior PAS officials. For example, over the years, the number of ASDs has waxed and waned between single and double digits. In his last years as chairman of the Armed Services Committee, Senator John McCain led an effort to curtail growth in ASDs, but to little avail. In fact, between 2020 and 2023, Congress created four new assistant secretaries of defense—all subject to Senate confirmation—for an all-time high of 19.

In addition, the Senate-confirmed secretary of each Military Department is supported by an under secretary, Senate-confirmed, and no fewer than four assistant secretaries and a general counsel.[11] All told, the Military Department assistant secretaries and general counsel number 17 PAS positions.

I'll stop our tally here because it seems that the cohort of DOD's assistant secretaries and Military Department assistant secretaries/general counsels is the right level to say: enough is enough. This single level of DOD and Military Department leadership numbers 36 PAS positions—well more than half of the DOD total of 65.

2

THE SENATE ARMED SERVICES COMMITTEE (SASC)

This chapter will focus on the SASC's historical role in the confirmation process and the factors that make its process different from those in the rest of the Senate.

President Harry S. Truman established the SASC on August 2, 1946, when he signed the Legislative Reorganization Act of 1946. Before then, the three Senate committees on Military Affairs, the Militia, and Naval Affairs, created in 1816, oversaw the military. In 1858, the Committee on the Militia merged with the Committee on Military Affairs. In 1872, the Committee dropped "Militia" from its name.[12] The Legislative Reorganization Act combined the Committee on Naval Affairs and the Committee on Military Affairs. For the first time in the history of the U.S. Senate, a single committee was responsible for all elements of the common defense: the SASC.

The new Committee comprised 13 senators and was granted broad jurisdictional authority over "proposed legislation, messages, petitions, memorials, and other matters relating to... the common defense generally," and, more specifically, to the War Department and the Military Establishment and the Navy Department and the Naval Establishment. In addition, the Committee was directly responsible for all policies, programs, and personnel of the armed forces.[13]

The Committee's impact over the years has proven nothing short of extraordinary. Consider its leading role in establishing the All-Volunteer Force in 1973, the military officer personnel policy in the Defense Officer Personnel Management Act of 1980, clarifying military command and institutional relationships and responsibilities and the governance authorities in the Goldwater-Nichols Act (GNA) of 1986, implementing the Packard Commission's defense procurement system recommendations, and creating the U.S. Special Operations Command, among other accomplishments. The Committee also played an integral role in any Senate consideration of arms control legislation and treaties.[14]

Even since its earliest days, the SASC has never been shy about flexing its muscle through the confirmation process. For example, in the 81st Congress, President Harry Truman nominated his close friend, Mon C. Wallgren, to be chairman of the National Security Resources Board. Wallgren unexpectedly faced backlash from Sen. Harry P. Cain (R- WA), a member of the SASC, who spoke for over six hours on the Senate floor and wrote a 261-page book claiming Wallgren was unfit for the position.[15] Even though the president's party controlled the Senate, the SASC voted seven to six to table Wallgren's nomination, and the Truman Administration withdrew his name shortly after that.

Sen. Richard B. Russell, Jr. (D-GA), who served as chairman of the SASC from 1955 to 1969, left a lasting mark on the Committee and its approach to the confirmation process. He solidified the traditions of a strong chairman, bipartisanship, and the Committee as a forceful voice for a strong national defense in the Senate. Though he had strict respect for the Executive Branch and its responsibility to enact policy, Russell recognized the Committee's ability to use the confirmation process to implement policy preferences. Russell strongly believed that while the actual selection of nominees and policy development belonged primarily to the Executive Branch, the SASC could provide oversight, accountability, and guidance through the confirmation process. In Russell's SASC, questioning nominees became an opportunity for members of the Committee to send a powerful (and often persuasive) message to nominees on the issues they should be focused on, if confirmed.

A primary example was Clifford Furnas, nominated in 1955 to be assistant secretary of defense for research and development. In questioning Furnas during his confirmation hearing, Russell and other senators repeatedly probed Furnas's views about the consolidation of science and technology programs within the DOD. In response, Furnas took an "I'll see what I can do" stance. Furnas was confirmed but understood that the Committee would call him to testify in the future and expected answers to their earlier questions.[16] In this manner, the SASC knew it could flex its power over the Executive Branch by placing expectations on and holding nominees accountable. This is a tradition the SASC continues today.

The SASC has consistently been vigilant about conflicts of interest as well. With the nomination of Louis A. Johnson to be secretary of defense in 1949, the Committee took months to inquire into perceived conflicts of interest before reporting favorably on his nomination. When Charles E. Wilson, then president of General Motors (GM), was nominated to be secretary of defense by President Eisenhower, the Committee required him to sever all ties with GM before favorably reporting his nomination. The same would be asked of Robert McNamara, then at Ford Motor Company, upon his nomination less than a decade later. Similarly, the 1968 nomination of David Packard, co-founder of Hewlett-Packard (HP), encountered objections because of his stockholdings and considerable investments in DOD suppliers. Packard turned over his HP stock to a Bank of America-managed trust. During his tenure, he was prohibited from keeping dividends or collecting from stock appreciation. He also resigned as HP chairman and CEO and from the boards of other corporations doing business with the Defense Department and divested those holdings. He was confirmed on January 23, 1969.[17]

The SASC's earnest approach to confirmations continued after the Russell era. During Sen. Sam Nunn's first term in the Senate, he voted in favor of President Carter's pick for head of the Arms Control and Disarmament Agency (ACDA), Paul Warnke, but against Warnke's nomination as Lead Negotiator of the Strategic Arms Limitation Talks (SALT II).[18] Nunn, a first-term senator from the same party and home state as the president, was unafraid to voice his reservations about that nomination, which is a testament to how seriously he and the Committee approached their role in the confirmation process. In addition to surfacing concerns about Warnke's views on disarmament, Nunn sought to leverage the confirmation process to demonstrate to the president that the Senate could and would block a future treaty that failed to maintain U.S. nuclear superiority over the Soviets. Although the Senate ultimately confirmed Warnke to both positions, confirmation for the negotiator's role passed by a slim voting margin of 58-40, far short of the two-thirds required to ratify any future treaty he might negotiate. Nunn had achieved his goal; he and a group of moderate Democrats continued to oppose the SALT II Treaty initially negotiated by Warnke. The Soviet invasion of Afghanistan sealed its fate, and the proposed treaty was never approved.

In mid-1988, before the November presidential election, Chairman Nunn and Ranking Member John Warner sent a letter to the candidates of both parties: the incumbent Vice President George H.W. Bush for the Republicans and Massachusetts Governor Michael Dukakis for the Democrats.

Both Nunn and Warner agreed that as to some prior DOD nominees, particularly those nominated for positions as secretaries of the Military Departments, leadership skill and experience in national security matters appeared to have taken a back seat to the nominee's coziness with the political establishment of the party in power. Both perceived that, in some cases, the most critical positions in the most critical cabinet agency had been filled on the basis of campaign contributions rather than qualifications. And both were deeply convinced that public respect for the U.S. military— or the dearth of same—was a direct consequence of the merit of the Department's civilian leadership. Both recalled favorably the example of James Schlesinger, who had served as secretary of defense under former Presidents Nixon and Ford, bringing to the position an unparalleled depth of experience in defense matters, having previously served in the Bureau of the Budget, the Atomic Energy Commission, and the CIA. On many an occasion, Schlesinger had swayed the views and decisions of the Joint Chiefs by the sheer intellectual power of his arguments. Both Nunn and Warner were of the firm view that the incoming president needed to nominate DOD leaders, including the secretaries of the Military Departments, with the leadership and technical chops for the demanding jobs on which they would enter, if confirmed. They must be "ready on day one" to exercise appropriate civilian control of the military while earning and maintaining the respect of military leaders, service members, and the American public.

The senators' bipartisan letter urged both candidates to consider the skills, experience, character, and integrity of those they considered for nomination, particularly to positions of leadership in the Department of Defense. The letter observed that whichever party's candidate emerged victorious in the upcoming election, the identification of respected, highly qualified, and responsible persons to lead the Department of Defense should be a top priority for the president-elect, applying a rubric in which qualifications were preeminent over politics. Both senators emphasized that in guiding the Senate Armed Services Committee's vetting of a nominee's suitability for a DOD position and informing the advice and consent function of the whole of the Senate, they would carefully appraise the candidate's skill, experience, character, and integrity. This letter ranks among one of the most important that Senators Nunn and Warner would author together over the many years of their partnership—it was the first formal articulation of Sen. Nunn's approach to national security nominations, and it remained the approach he would apply to nominations throughout his Senate career.

When he became SASC chairman in 1987, Senator Nunn also used the confirmation process to hold the DOD accountable for issues beyond nominations. Often, an office in the Pentagon would inquire about the status of a nominee pending before the SASC. If the SASC was waiting for DOD to provide information or documents (as was almost always the case), even if not related to the nomination at issue, Nunn would respond with: "And where is this item we're waiting on from your office?" Senator Nunn and I (as his staff director) standardized and formalized certain aspects of the confirmation process still used today, such as APQs, standard forms, and the questions the current SASC chairman poses at the start of every confirmation hearing.

WHAT MAKES SASC CONFIRMATIONS DIFFERENT FROM THE REST OF THE SENATE

There are several key differences between the SASC's approach to confirmations and the processes in other committees in the Senate. Including military promotions, the SASC handles over 50,000 nominations each year.[19] By comparison, the Senate Foreign Relations Committee considers roughly 2,000 nominations (the vast majority are foreign service promotions), and the Senate Judiciary Committee considers over 870 federal judgeships.[20] Despite the significant workload, the SASC devotes considerable time and attention to the confirmation process and to individual nominees, without exception. This is a testament to the hard work and dedication of both senators and Committee professional staff and exemplifies SASC members' unflagging commitment to fulfilling their constitutional duty without fail.

The members of the SASC in the 101st Congress, 1990, in the formal hearing room in Russell 212. Seated left to right: Sens. Jeff Bingaman, Ted Kennedy, Carl Levin, Jim Exon, Chairman Sam Nunn, Ranking Member John Warner, Strom Thurmond, Bill Cohen, and John McCain. Standing left to right: Sens. Robert Byrd, Dick Shelby, Tim Wirth, Al Gore, John Glenn, Alan Dixon, Arnold Punaro, Pat Tucker, Sens. Malcolm Wallop, Slade Gordon, Trent Lott, and Dan Coats.

One crucial difference between the SASC and other committees is its traditional bipartisan approach that underscores the adage: "Politics should stop at the water's edge on national security matters." This approach extends to most issues before the Committee and holds true for nominations. The general sense for civilian nominations is, regardless of party—absent substantive concerns over qualifications, ethics, or past conduct—the sitting president deserves to have his or her chosen team in place, the precedent established by Chairman Russell. However, this does not prevent vigorous questioning from the Committee.

The SASC assesses each nominee's ability to work with senators from both sides of the aisle, notwithstanding the party of the administration or the party in the Senate majority. In most cases, hearings are far less contentious than those for civilian nominees before other committees. This has changed with more nominees facing questions highlighting potential differences between the administration's policy and approach and the views of an individual senator.

In recent years, the SASC has never called "opponents" of the nominee to testify publicly, as in some other committees. That said, in at least one high-profile case during the 116th Congress, Chairman Jim Inhofe (R-OK) and Ranking Member Jack Reed (D-RI) agreed to a series of confidential "executive sessions" in which a female officer testified she had been sexually assaulted by a senior military officer whose nomination for appointment to another position of "trust and responsibility" was pending before the Committee.

The SASC took these allegations seriously and set up a process for both the victim of the alleged assault and the officer accused to provide information. After hearing both sides of the story and reviewing all available evidence, including several independent investigations, the nominee was approved in a solidly bipartisan vote.

Past SASC chairmen also have used the Executive Session format—with only senators and select senior Committee staff in attendance—to address sensitive and serious issues that, if true, would call into question the suitability of a nominee. But as a matter of policy and practice, the SASC has never been inclined to handle these sensitive issues before the public and press. Most civilian and military nominees are voted out of the Committee *en bloc* on a bipartisan voice vote.

Senator Nunn, SASC chair; Arnold Punaro, staff director; Pat Tucker, minority staff director; and Senator Warner, SASC ranking member have a serious discussion about a pending vote on a major civilian nomination.

Although it is rare for the Committee vote to divide along partisan lines, the case of Dr. Colin Kahl presents a notable exception. Dr. Kahl was nominated as President Joe Biden's under secretary of defense for policy on January 20, 2021. Kahl was a former DOD official and National Security Advisor to Biden during his tenure as vice president. He supported several Obama-era policies Republicans disliked, such as the Iran nuclear deal. Further, after leaving his position within the administration, Kahl made numerous volatile posts criticizing the Trump Administration and other Republicans. In the Trump Administration, several nominees failed because of their vitriolic social media presence. The SASC and Senate Republicans applied this same standard to Biden nominee Kahl. Even though Kahl used his March 4 confirmation hearing to apologize for the "disrespectful language" he used in the posts and pledged a nonpartisan approach to his Pentagon job, SASC Republicans uniformly asserted he was far too partisan.

On March 24, the SASC failed to advance Kahl's nomination due to an evenly split vote along party lines. (The Senate was split 50/50, so both parties had equal representation on the Committee.) This required a Senate motion to discharge the nomination from the Committee, which occurred on April 21, with Vice President Kamala Harris casting a tie-breaking vote to advance the nomination to the Senate floor. Kahl was confirmed on April 27 on a party line roll call vote of 49-45. Several Republicans were unavoidably absent from the vote, which afforded Democrats a 4-vote majority, a wider margin of victory than expected.

Kahl is the first DOD nominee in history not to receive a single vote from the minority in Committee. He also received no minority votes on the Senate floor. Although he was eventually confirmed, the specter of partisanship continued to hang over him. As then-Ranking Member Inhofe stated, "The under secretary of defense for policy position has always, until now, received bipartisan support during the confirmation process. That Dr. Kahl did not garner a Republican vote is really saying something."[21]

An administration risks its relationship with the SASC and challenges the bipartisan tradition of the Committee when it advances a clearly partisan nominee. The precedent established by a Democratic president and Democratic chair (when I was staff director) was that nominees without significant bipartisan support were not taken to a vote in Committee. Instead, the administration was informed, and the nomination was ultimately withdrawn. DOD civilian political leaders need to work across the aisle, and any nominee that can't get some bipartisan support should not be confirmed.

I recommended an initiative instituted in 1987, supported by Chairman Nunn and Ranking Member John Warner (R-VA), that underscores another aspect of the SASC's unique confirmation approach. Each civilian nominee and some military nominees for 3-

and 4-star positions must complete APQs before their hearing. There were several reasons to institute the APQs. A primary reason was to have on record the views of all civilian and senior military nominees in favor of the GNA, passed in 1986 over the objections of all the senior civilian and military leadership in the Pentagon. The APQs always included 4-5 questions at the beginning to ascertain the nominee's positions on the GNA reforms. The GNA questions were included in APQs all eight years of Nunn's chairmanship and for decades after by subsequent chairmen until, ultimately, they were no longer needed, as the GNA was fully supported and implemented.

Another reason the APQs were important was to have the nominees answer questions that might not warrant verbal questions from a senator during the hearing. This allowed senators, who were allocated only five or six minutes per round for questions, to focus on the most critical issues. The APQs often number into the hundreds for senior nominees, ranging from their qualifications to their plans to tackle specific issues related to their prospective positions. Other committees do not always require nominees to submit answers to a long list of policy questions, but SASC does.

APQs highlight issues the Committee cares about, giving the nominee a sense of the SASC's interests and policy preferences. Senators pay close attention to the nominee's answers. They read through the dozens of pages to prepare for the questions to pose at the confirmation hearing. If an answer does not sit right—either on policy or because it seems written by Pentagon "yes-men" (the bureaucrats or career staff)—they never hesitate to raise the matter with the nominee, either individually during a pre-hearing "courtesy call," or at the hearing itself. DOD nominees must walk the fine line between providing thoughtful answers to their APQs—getting prior approval for their responses from the Executive Branch and often the White House—and avoiding a purely "party line" answer (which could antagonize senators not of the party) on tough issues.

The APQs typically require review and approval at the Office of the Secretary of Defense (OSD) level and go through the pre-clearance process at the Office of Management and Budget (OMB) and the White House Counsel's Office. Over time, nominees have learned that SASC has a long memory. The Committee does not hesitate to use the nominee's APQ responses as an oversight mechanism, reminding the nominee of commitments and plans documented in those pre-confirmation responses and inquiring why the nominee's specific promises have not yet been fulfilled or objectives attained as intended.

Most confirmation hearings in the Senate begin with the Committee chairman swearing in the nominee to affirm his or her testimony is accurate to the best of their knowledge. In the SASC, however, nominees are rarely sworn in, demonstrating trust and respect for the national security nominee. In these cases, the chairman will begin with a series of yes/no questions intended primarily to assert the Committee's constitutional oversight role vis-à-vis the Executive Branch and to document the nominee's commitment to helping the Committee execute its oversight function. These questions are generally the following or some variation:

1. Have you adhered to applicable laws and regulations governing conflicts of interest?
2. Have you assumed any duties or taken any actions that appear to presume the outcome of the confirmation process?
3. Exercising our legislative and oversight responsibilities makes it important that this Committee, its subcommittees, and other appropriate committees of Congress receive testimony, briefings, reports, records, and other information from the Executive Branch on a timely basis. Do you agree, if confirmed, to appear and testify before this Committee when requested?

4. Do you agree to promptly provide records, documents, and electronic communications when requested by this Committee, subcommittees, or other appropriate committees and to consult with the request regarding the basis for any good faith delay or denial in providing such records?
5. Will you ensure your staff complies with this Committee's deadlines for producing reports, records, and other information, including timely responses to hearing Questions for the Record?
6. Will you cooperate and provide witnesses and briefers in response to a congressional request?
7. Will those witnesses and briefers be protected from reprisal for their testimony or briefings?

The expected answer to these questions is an unqualified "yes" or "no," as appropriate. These same questions are included in the nominee's SASC Questionnaire and APQ package. Still, their public restatement at the beginning of the confirmation hearing highlights a unique facet of SASC's approach. It underscores the importance with which the SASC views its oversight role.

Military nominees for 3- and 4-star positions are asked an additional question: "Do you agree, when asked before this Committee, to give your personal views, even if your views differ from those of the administration?" This question is not posed to civilian nominees because civilian administration officials are always presumed to reflect and represent the views of the president (and administration) who has nominated and appointed them. When requested by civilian leaders in our government, including Committees of the Senate and House of Representatives, our military leaders are expected to give their personal opinions, even on professional matters. This expectation persists regardless of politics, a hallmark of our civil/military relations system.

When Sen. John McCain (R-AZ) was chairman of the SASC, he insisted that civilian political nominees also give their personal views when he or another member of the Committee asked. If a DOD civilian nominee refused, McCain announced he would not proceed with further consideration of the nominee. The Trump White House relented and gave nominees special permission to give their personal views when asked.

One of the better examples of this was the contrast between two nominees in the Obama and Trump administrations over U.S. policy toward Syria. During McCain's tenure as chairman, President Obama nominated Elissa Slotkin as assistant secretary of defense for international security affairs. McCain asked her a question on Syria, and she could not provide her personal views because of a prohibition by the Obama Administration, so McCain refused to process her nomination. She was never confirmed despite her overwhelming qualifications for the position.

When David Trachtenberg was nominated to be deputy under secretary of defense for policy in the Trump Administration, McCain held up his nomination over the same issue of his personal opinions on Syria policy. This time, the White House gave Trachtenberg leeway to share his views. His nomination proceeded, and he was confirmed.

About halfway through the Trump Administration, the White House began requiring nominees to qualify their answers to the standard questions used for decades. For example, in 2019, when Dr. Mark Esper was nominated to be secretary of defense, his APQ responses were changed during administration review to:

> I respect Congress's authority to seek information from the Department. If confirmed, I agree to accommodate all congressional requests for information by supplying the requested information to the fullest extent, consistent with

the constitutional and statutory obligations of the Executive Branch.[22]

Sen. John McCain, then-chairman of the Senate Armed Services Committee, and Arnold Punaro discuss Committee business, including nominations, back in 2015.

In contrast, when Dr. Esper responded to the APQs for his nomination to become secretary of the Army (earlier in the administration), he answered all the standard questions with a simple "Yes." And those simple responses were transmitted to the SASC without change.[23] I have known and worked with Dr. Esper closely. The more convoluted responses in 2019 were not changes he insisted on.

Another answer commonly proffered during the Trump Administration became: "If confirmed, I agree to accommodate in a timely manner all congressional requests for information by supplying the requested information to the fullest extent, consistent with applicable statutes and the U.S. Constitution."[24] This "quibbling" did not go over well in the SASC. Within a few months, the Committee updated each standard question in the SASC

Questionnaire and each nominee's APQs to read: "Do you agree, without qualification... please answer with a simple Yes or No."[25] Some nominees were informed that until such a time as their "administration-required" responses were changed to a simple "Yes" or "No," they would not be scheduled for a hearing.

Another important distinguishing feature of the SASC is its strong working relationship with the DOD and the Executive Branch, somewhat unique among Senate committees and the departments they oversee. The powerful working relationship is a two-way street, grounded in tradition and mutual respect. Several practices help to maintain this relationship. The Department's custom of timely notification to the SASC about events and policy decisions has proven essential to the relationship. For example, senators, especially the chairman and ranking member of the SASC, dislike learning about breaking Pentagon news from the media or via social media posts. The SASC also appreciates the Department's advance consultation and coordination on major nominations or significant policy changes, as well as the Department's policy of providing witness testimony before the SASC when asked. Other examples of this positive working relationship include the Department's respect for the Senate's role in the confirmation process and upholding time-honored agreements, such as that governing above-threshold reprogramming.[26]

The Trump Administration saw several of these norms violated, which strained the relationship between the SASC and the DOD, even though Republicans then controlled the Senate. One such example was the designation of Anthony Tata as "Performing the Duties Of" the under secretary of defense for policy, the exact position for which the Committee had previously declined to confirm him, as discussed in Chapter One.

Breaking such norms breeds suspicion and distrust between the Committee and the Department. It can cause rejected nominations and new, often cumbersome, and unwelcome legislation to codify these norms into law. Rebuilding the relationship can take significant time and effort from both branches of government. Still, it's well worth the effort and upkeep. When an administration respects the SASC's constitutional role, norms, and traditions, the Committee inevitably reciprocates with an appropriately deliberative, inclusive, and bipartisan confirmation process. The Committee understands good and bad behavior and responds accordingly.

3

THE ROLE AND IMPORTANCE OF THE SHERPA

The beginning of a new presidential administration is a challenging time. Political appointees of the outgoing administration usually resign effective January 20, timed with the incoming president's inauguration, leaving the new president's transition team with over 7,000 political jobs to fill. At least 1,200 require nomination by the president with the advice and consent of the Senate.[27] At DOD, the new administration typically asks select members of the prior administration's team to remain until the initial leaders are nominated, confirmed, and appointed. (Typically, one person at OSD and one each in the Military Departments are asked to remain temporarily.)

Each civilian nomination is important to the new administration and the individual nominated. But there are certain nominees—particularly the most senior and for those positions deemed critical to the continuity of government and national security—accorded special, personalized handling. They are assigned a "Sherpa" to help them through the process.

Like their mountaineering namesake, a Sherpa guides top-level civilian nominees through the nomination, confirmation, and appointment processes. Although the use of a Sherpa is not exclusive to the period of a presidential transition, they're frequently used during the often-raw political process associated with a change in administration. In these cases, Sherpas are almost always drawn from outside the government. They are trusted agents of the administration, specially selected for their experience, savvy, and ability to bring order out of chaos at a critical inflection point.

Also important is whether a particular Sherpa is a good match for the nominee with whom he or she will be paired. The Sherpa must be capable of instilling in the nominee the will to buckle down and persevere through the often-arduous process of confirmation. They must also inspire the nominee's confidence in their advice and help.

Presidential candidates typically begin planning their transitions many months before the election.[28] The transition involves a team carrying out pre-election planning by the non-incumbent candidates. Activities include vetting candidates for positions in the new administration, briefing the incoming administration on the operations of the Executive Branch, and developing a comprehensive policy platform.[29]

Under the Intelligence Reform and Terrorism Prevention Act of 2004, major party candidates for president are encouraged to submit—before the general election—requests for security clearances for prospective transition team members who will require access to classified information to carry out their responsibilities.[30] The law requires that, to the extent practicable, the background investigations and eligibility determinations must be completed by the day after the election. The transition team has little over two months—early November to January 20 of the following year—to prepare the new president and administration to hit the ground running and ensure the continuity of government.

The law also urges the president-elect to submit candidate names for the high-level national security positions in the new administration to the FBI as soon as possible after the election. The FBI is required by law to undertake and complete, as expeditiously as possible, the background investigations necessary to provide security clearances to these candidates before the new president is inaugurated.

The Presidential Transition Act also expresses the Sense of the Senate that after the election, the president-elect should submit the nominations even before the inauguration, if possible, of candidates for high-level national security positions through the level of undersecretary of cabinet departments. For the nominations received by the inauguration, the law encourages the Senate committees to complete their consideration and report the nominees to the Senate floor, where the full Senate should vote to confirm or reject them within 30 days of their submission.

The Sherpa's work starts well before the initial confirmation hearing in the Senate. For high-level national security nominees, like the secretary of defense, it should occur even before the new president is sworn in. The secretary of defense is traditionally confirmed and sworn in on the same day as the inauguration, with the deputy secretary following shortly after.

A Sherpa must be deeply familiar with the confirmation process and have an in-depth understanding of the committee(s) with jurisdiction over their nominee, the senators on those committees, and their priorities (especially those of senators not of the same party as the new president), the committees' professional staff, and the senators' personal staffs.

The Sherpa is the person closest to the nominee and the battle rhythm of his or her nomination. They assemble a small team of key people to coordinate activities supporting the nominee. This hub establishes the conditions for a nomination's successful outcome through the spokes of multiple lines of effort operating concurrently.

Arnold Punaro with then-Secretary of Veterans Affairs Robert Wilkie at a Comfort for America's Uniformed Services (CAUSE) event. Punaro assisted Wilkie with his three Senate confirmations—as assistant secretary of defense (2006), under secretary of defense (2017), and secretary of Veterans Affairs (2018). Wilkie was the leader of the Sherpa team for incoming Secretary of Defense James Mattis in late 2016 and early 2017. Wilkie's note reads: "General, You are a Patriot and Gentleman of the highest order!"

THE SHERPA AS LEAD MEMBER OF THE CONFIRMATION TEAM

Assembling the following team members enables a seamless confirmation process:

1. TEAM LEAD—THE SHERPA. Must make timely decisions and speak with authority for the nominee and the administration.
2. LEGISLATIVE AFFAIRS AIDE. Must be familiar with the specific cabinet department of the nominee and have strong ties to the transition team and new White House leadership.
3. POLICY AIDE. Full-time subject matter expert who can address policy issues on the spot, review briefing papers, reach out to policy organizations for rapid response to questions, and correctly advise the nominee on the administration's position on any issue.
4. PUBLIC AFFAIRS AIDE. Full-time media-savvy expert who understands both conventional and social media and monitors the media flow to determine when a rapid response is required and to recommend what that response should be.
5. SCHEDULER. Controls the nominee's schedule and works Senate schedules. Helps decide the priority of a nominee's engagements in coordination with the Sherpa.
6. CONFIRMATION EXPERT. Outside expert with significant experience handling cabinet-level and other senior civilian confirmations, with strong ties to the leadership of the committee of jurisdiction. (Precedent and longstanding relationships are essential to Senate committees.)
7. WHITE HOUSE TRANSITION REPRESENTATIVE. Commits to attending the confirmation team's early morning and late evening coordinating meetings and possesses the expertise and clout to speak authoritatively for the White House.
8. ADMINISTRATIVE AIDE. Keeps track of tasks, generates and disseminates completed written materials, supports a wide range of administrative functions, and ensures that all Committee

requirements are tracked and completed on time and to standard.

9. ADVANCE POLICY QUESTION (APQ) RESPONSE LEAD. Must have expertise in the department in which the nominee will be appointed, the policy issues of greatest import to that department, and to the committee of jurisdiction. Develop and enforce a process for reviewing proposed APQ responses, which typically must be vetted and approved by the transition team and the White House at the beginning of an administration.

10. TALKING POINTS LEAD. Handles talking points for courtesy calls, unique to each senator, and prepares a one-page backgrounder on each senator, setting forth basic demographic information and lists of key legislation sponsored and policy issues and programs of particular interest.

11. PERSONAL PAPERWORK LEAD. Assists with all Executive and Legislative Branch forms and questionnaires. (An outside attorney who can ensure all the forms are properly prepared is recommended but can be expensive—an expense that will not be subsidized by the government.)

It is also helpful to identify a speechwriter and chief of staff to be a part of the confirmation team. Although it is not unusual for personnel in these positions to take on a role in the government, it would be inappropriate, and a presumption of confirmation, to hire them at this stage of proceedings. Many who fill these positions at the outset do so as volunteers.

For the most senior cabinet-level nominees, the team should set up a "war room" or "command center." This is where the team will work daily, coordinate priorities and assignments, and direct research. The key to effectiveness is for the Sherpa to be as inclusive as possible and keep the team members informed and fully engaged. Collective knowledge and wisdom are better; no single person can handle every issue or occurrence.

The Sherpa must identify and scope the top issues or the "hot topics" his or her nominee will face. They must ensure that any policy position the nominee will espouse on any issue is properly coordinated throughout the administration and/or transition. The Sherpa must ensure the formulation and coordination of the nominee's answers to potential APQs, responses to questions posed by senators during courtesy calls, and any statements the nominee might make in a media interview or chance engagement (which should be avoided if possible) before the confirmation hearing and the responses to questions the nominee is likely to receive from senators on both sides of the aisle during the hearing. To ensure the accuracy and consistency of policy positions across the administration, nominees' APQs must be cleared by the lawyers of their respective department or agency, the Office of Management and Budget, the National Security Council, and the White House. The Sherpa must exercise great care to avoid a situation in which their nominee expresses a policy view or position different from the president or president-elect. Nominees for the secretary of defense, secretary of state, CIA director, and the director of National Intelligence must be coordinated and in lockstep on key policy issues, such as the U.S. policy toward Taiwan. These nominees appear before different Senate committees for confirmation, and a new administration will not want different answers on major policy issues.

Sherpas (and their nominees) should understand what impression they want their nominee to convey to the American public and those they will lead in their department, if confirmed. For example, much can be learned from Robert Gates's multiple nominations through several presidential administrations. Gates was nominated by President Ronald Reagan to be CIA director in 1987. His nomination was withdrawn because some Democrats attacked his role in the Iran-Contra affair, and rumormongering spun out of control. However, in 1991, when nominated a second time to be

CIA director by President George H. W. Bush, Gates himself insisted on tackling the issue head-on and was confirmed. He had the help and powerful support of Sen. Sam Nunn, then-chair of the SASC, and Sen. David Boren (D-OK), then-chair of the Senate Select Committee on Intelligence.

Gates was then nominated to be secretary of defense by President George W. Bush in 2006, and I was involved in his confirmation preparation. We were worried about Iran-Contra being re-litigated. I asked Eleanor Hill, an Iran-Contra Senate committee staffer, federal prosecutor, and former DOD inspector general, to research the issues and ensure we had every Iran-Contra topic identified and suggested answers for the nominee ready for the toughest questions. No Iran-Contra issue arose during the hearing (although some came up during the office courtesy calls, and Gates was more than ready in these cases). His robust preparation made him far more confident going into the hearing this time. We decided that the best message Gates could deliver to the Senate and the country was: "I am not Don Rumsfeld. The quicker you confirm me, the quicker Rumsfeld leaves." There was a strong anti-Rumsfeld sentiment then, and this approach worked well. Gates was nominated on December 4, 2006, and confirmed by the Senate two days later by a vote of 95-2. There is no better approach than being over-prepared to handle complex issues and having a plan going into the confirmation process.

Nominees will face both fair and prejudicial questions during their hearings. The role of the Sherpa and his or her team is to uncover any issue in advance that the nominee might be called on to address. Senators are always ready to lob a controversial question at the nominee. The department in which the nominee will serve—if confirmed—is not always up to this kind of detective work. The nominee must be prepared to rebut the tough questions and any strategic narrative a senator may try to establish. The

Sherpa must prepare his or her nominee for the worst-case scenario so that not only will the nominee be confirmed, but he or she will make a good impression during the hearing and start from a position of strength.

Once the lead DOD team is in place, the role of confirmation support shifts from the Sherpa to the Office of the Assistant Secretary of Defense for Legislative Affairs and the legislative liaison teams in the Military Departments. A Deputy Assistant Secretary of Defense (DASD) for Senate Affairs typically leads the administration's confirmation process for all further defense nominees at OSD. The Senate Affairs DASD is almost always supported by a Senate Director, an active-duty military officer, usually an O-6 colonel or Navy captain, who handles the day-to-day paperwork and logistics of all three nomination process phases.[31]

I have worked with and trained Sherpas for many administrations. I even taught part of a course preparing these Sherpas. I developed a "Sherpa 101" briefing, reviewing the same tenets outlined in this chapter. To prepare them for the demanding jobs, I outlined the tough questions and narratives their nominees might face—both fair and unfair—and how best to prepare the nominee to counter them. For example, a hostile question might look like this for General James Mattis (who became Trump's secretary of defense): "General Mattis, you have indicated that you do not favor torture. President-elect Trump has said he favors torture. Should he—as president—order our troops, through you in the chain of command, to engage in torture, would you obey that order? Do you support civilian control of the military in all cases, or just when you agree with the president?" That question tried to establish the narrative that Mattis's nomination and Trump's lack of national security knowledge would erode civilian control of the military.

For President-elect Biden's team, an example I used in the Sherpa training was Neera Tanden, nominated as director of the OMB. A hostile question for her would be: "Do you stand by your posts calling the leader of the Senate "Moscow Mitch" and insulting Republican members of Congress? Is that the proper demeanor and character we want in our country's cabinet officials?" The underlying narrative being pushed by Tanden's opponents was that she was temperamentally unfit for the position.

The Sherpa team's goal is to have a counter-narrative ready. In Mattis's case, he was the right person to be in the chain of command because he's tough, smart, experienced in warfare, and won't be pushed around by the Pentagon. In Tanden's, she had the expertise and breadth of knowledge to lead OMB, regardless of her mild political commentary as a private citizen on social media. Mattis successfully combated the negative narratives surrounding his nomination and was confirmed 98-1. Tanden, unfortunately, did not. She faced the exact pushback I had predicted. Ultimately, she withdrew her nomination after her contentious confirmation hearing.

SECTION 2: The Need-to-Know Details for National Security Nominees

4

THE NOMINATION PROCESS

Chapters Four, Five, and Six explore what is expected of nominees for civilian positions requiring presidential appointment following Senate confirmation (PAS positions) and what civilian nominees for these positions can expect throughout each step of the nomination, confirmation, and appointment processes. A comprehensive checklist for nominees can be found in Appendix C. This chapter focuses on the nomination process.

NOMINATION

The first step is for an administration to identify and recruit candidates for the roughly 1,200 PAS positions across the federal government. What often varies across administrations is how nominations in a particular department or agency (e.g., DOD) are coordinated or socialized with the head of that agency (e.g., the secretary of defense). On its headquarters-level staff, each cabinet-level department or agency has a political official known as the White House Liaison Officer (WHLO), who serves as the agency's connection to the Presidential Personnel Office (PPO). In some administrations, the secretary of defense and the DOD WHLO have engaged closely with the PPO to identify and vet candidates for DOD PAS positions. It was thought that Secretary of Defense James Mattis correctly insisted he, in coordination with his chief of staff and WHLO, approve each prospective PAS nomination before President Trump finalized it.

In other administrations, the opposite approach prevailed. All authority was reserved to the PPO, and some secretaries of defense learned of a PAS nomination at almost the same time as the public—when the president announced it and transmitted the nomination to the Senate. At that point in the process, the secretary could not decline to accept a particular nominee or suggest someone else in his or her stead.

Most administrations strike a balance somewhere between these two extremes. Usually, the White House and the secretary of defense (or a high-level designee) interview and provide input on finalists for a nomination to a PAS position in the Defense Department before the director of PPO recommends the top choice to the president. Some presidents have wanted more than one option, so they would ask the secretary of defense to evaluate all candidates and show their preference for the president's consideration.

Once a candidate is tentatively selected, the White House Personnel Security Office applies criteria established by the administration to conduct an initial suitability review of the prospective nominee. In the Obama Administration, this involved a review of the individual's resume, social media presence, and an interview to assess whether the nominee could and would be able to carry out the president's directives and policies. Of course, a candidate's prior campaign donations or support to the campaign, such as volunteering in a local campaign office or participating in door-to-door or telephonic neighborhood canvassing for the candidate, benefit a prospective nominee. In most cases, they are not a hard and firm prerequisite. If found suitable, the candidate is invited to submit the battery of forms required by the FBI to start a full-field background investigation. Because of the significant time and resources associated with conducting that background check, most administrations undertake this extensive vetting only after the president makes a final, albeit cautious, choice of a nominee. If a hiccup disqualifies the candidate, the process must begin again with a new name.

Heather Wilson, secretary of the Air Force, pictured with Arnold Punaro after he assisted with her confirmation process before the U.S. Senate. She was confirmed in 2017.

PAPERWORK

At a minimum, each prospective nominee must submit the following paperwork:

- Biographical Information Sheet.
- Appointee Release and Consent for Background Investigation.
- SF 86 Security Questionnaire: A 130-page questionnaire used to collect preliminary data on an individual whose government employment requires access to classified information. The FBI uses this form as the jumping-off point for their background investigation. All potential nominees for PAS positions must complete the form, even if the position does not require access to classified information. This form requires detailed and

highly personal information, often dating back to an applicant's teen years. The electronic questionnaire for investigations processing (e-QIP) must be used to submit the information. The SF 86 incorporates many additional but necessary forms, including:

o SF 86 Supplement and SF 86 Certification;
o Authorization for Release of Information required for the background investigation;
o Authorization for Release of Medical Information Pursuant to the Health Insurance Portability and Accountability Act (HIPAA); and
o Disclosure and Authorization to Obtain Consumer (Credit) Report and Fair Credit Reporting Disclosure and Authorization.

• Office of Government Ethics (OGE) Form 278e (Executive Branch Personnel Public Financial Disclosure Report) as opposed to the OGE Form 450 (Confidential Financial Disclosure).

o For many civilian candidates, this will be their first exposure to the complexity of federal government ethics standards and requirements. Completing the OGE 278e requires the prospective nominee to disclose detailed information about his or her financial assets, debts, positions held in other organizations, and the assets, debts, and organizational affiliations of the nominee's spouse and minor children.
o OGE and the DAEO of the department or agency with which the nominee will serve—for our purposes, the DOD or Military Department Standards of Conduct Offices (SOCO)—are available to guide the prospective nominee in completing the 278e. A completed 278e is reviewed by OGE and SOCO experts. They determine what steps the nominee may need to take to avoid conflicts of interest and conform

with Executive Branch ethics laws and rules as they apply to the specific PAS position for which the individual is being considered. In addition, the Senate committee with jurisdiction over the nomination has often established specific requirements for nominee ethics compliance. More detailed information about SASC ethics requirements for civilian nominees is provided in Chapter Five.

- IRS Form 4506
  - Allows the Internal Revenue Service to release copies of the prospective nominee's tax returns to a third party, namely the FBI and the White House. Nominees must release copies of the tax returns filed for the three most recent years. The SASC also requires civilian nominees to submit their federal tax returns for the three most recent tax years but permits them to submit their returns directly to the Committee rather than requiring IRS involvement.
- Personal Data Statement.
- Fingerprint Card.

The background investigation can begin once the FBI reviews the full complement of the nominee's paperwork and determines that all required information has been provided.

BACKGROUND INVESTIGATION

The first step is often a detailed personal interview of the nominee by the FBI agent charged with the investigation. Because the FBI assigns a top priority to the background investigations of prospective presidential nominees, this interview will probably take place within 10 to 20 days after the candidate submits completed paperwork. The FBI agent in charge will use the interview to clarify any ambiguities in the nominee's SF 86 and to identify additional references (not already listed) who know the nominee well.

After the interview, the FBI will disseminate requests for interviews with the nominee's family, colleagues, and references across its global network of agents. A candidate should not be surprised when friends and family members report being questioned by a different FBI agent than the agent who interviewed the candidate. These interviews, which follow a standard format, will usually be conducted in person by an agent in the same geographic area as the interviewee. The FBI will review the candidate's publicly accessible social media, which can open another optic into candidates' lives and expand the pool of individuals the FBI may seek to interview.

It's not unusual for the FBI to reengage with the prospective nominee throughout the background investigation. This usually occurs when the FBI seeks additional references and their contact information to clarify or explain information that may come to light as the investigation proceeds or for other purposes. However, candidates should not be alarmed if they *do not* hear from the FBI. I have never known the FBI to contact the subject of a background investigation simply to provide an update or for purely social reasons. As frustrating as "no contact" may be, it shows the investigation is proceeding apace.

With few exceptions, the background investigation occurs before the president decides on a candidate's nomination. The prospective nominee's discretion and that of the FBI are essential to ensure a thorough investigation is conducted without generating undue publicity. In most cases, the FBI and the prospective nominee are prohibited from disclosing the true purpose of the background investigation.

To avoid leaks and the premature release of information that may constrain the president's decisions about a prospective nominee, the nominee's references and other witnesses interviewed by the FBI are often told only that the individual under investigation is "updating his or her security clearance." The inconvenience of such a tight-lipped policy notwithstanding, its benefits are readily discernable when contrasted with several embarrassments suffered by the White House of President George W. Bush. Early in the administration, the White House would publicly announce a nomination before the completion of a nominee's background investigation, only to withdraw the nomination when significant derogatory information surfaced that cast doubt on the nominee's suitability and rendered confirmation unlikely.

A full-field background investigation is laborious and time-consuming and is not rushed. Even though the FBI prioritizes White House requests, a full-field can take six to eight weeks to complete under ordinary circumstances. Anything unusual, such as a prospective nominee with extensive overseas travel or foreign contacts, will take far longer. This may be like a security clearance investigation for potential nominees currently or only recently employed by the federal government. Still, it will almost always be more expansive. It will probably include periods not reviewed in prior government employment, especially if the individual is considered for nomination to a more senior position or one of particular sensitivity.

The FBI provides the White House Security Office and nominations counsel in the Office of the White House Counsel with periodic updates as the background investigation proceeds, especially if information of concern is developed. Such updates are handled with great concern for the privacy of the prospective nominee, and information is released only to those who have an official "need to know." On completion, the final investigation result is provided to the White House Security Office and the Office of White House Counsel. The FBI officer who delivers this information may be required to verbally brief the designated nominations counsel on anything significantly derogatory.

It doesn't matter whether the content of the background investigation is harmful or benign. Ownership and adjudication of the investigation and the decision to proceed with a nomination lie solely with the president and the White House. However, the SASC requires that the FBI full-field investigation be made available for the personal review of the Committee chair and ranking member before any SASC vote on a nomination. The Committee's leaders will apprise other SASC senators of anything that may generate concerns about the nominee's suitability. This allows other members of the SASC to consider the information in casting their vote on the Committee's disposition of the nomination. Such information is rare, and its dissemination is tightly controlled.

A prospective nominee must be completely transparent with the White House and the FBI. It is a rare person who lives a perfect life without past missteps. Past mistakes, as embarrassing as they may be in the present day, do not disqualify a nominee for a presidential appointment. *Lying* about past mistakes or being less than candid with the White House or the FBI inevitably sets off alarms that will quickly take a nominee out of the running for a PAS position. Similarly, a lack of integrity or candor can quickly sink even the most technically qualified nominees.

Vic Stello's nomination to be an assistant secretary of energy for defense programs showcases the importance of nominee integrity and how integrity issues—whether actual or perceived—can adversely affect the trajectory of a nomination. On July 24, 1989, President George H.W. Bush nominated Stello as assistant secretary of energy for defense programs.

Stello's nomination was referred to the SASC, where, at first blush, he was received as the type of "hands-on manager" needed to oversee the cleanup and operation of the nation's nuclear weapons complex (17 production facilities and laboratories in 12 states). Many had been shut down because of safety problems created by an infrastructure crumbling under years of neglect and mismanagement. Stello, an expert in nuclear operations safety, had spent almost a quarter of a century with the Nuclear Regulatory Commission (NRC). He became executive secretary, only one level below the commissioners themselves. I met with Stello during the regular staff director review and was impressed with his directness and cumulative experience.

Almost immediately, however, complaints about Stello filtered in. The Committee soon learned that Stello had been the subject of a lengthy grand jury investigation in 1984 and 1985. Although the Justice Department ultimately decided not to prosecute Stello, the investigation was to determine whether he had committed a crime by failing to enforce regulations at Three Mile Island, the site of the most significant accident in U.S. commercial nuclear power plant history, and at the Zimmer nuclear plant in Moscow, Ohio, which had to be abandoned. The grand jury also investigated whether Stello blocked his staff from submitting allegations of Atomic Energy Act violations to the Justice Department for potential prosecution. Stello's conduct at the NRC had also been the subject of three congressional investigations.

Two days before Stello's scheduled hearing before the SASC, Senator Howard Metzenbaum (D-OH) urged President Bush to withdraw Stello's nomination. Metzenbaum and four other Democratic senators signed a letter asking Bush to select someone else. "Based on [Stello's] record of circumventing health and safety regulations and obstructing investigations while at the NRC, we strongly believe that Mr. Stello is not the proper candidate for this responsibility and that the Senate should reject his confirmation." The five senators asserted that even if confirmed, the controversy surrounding his nomination would significantly impair his ability to execute the functions required of his job.[32] As Chairman, Sen.

Nunn, along with Sen. Warner (as ranking member), decided Stello deserved his "day in court" at a hearing.

On November 15 and 16, 1989, the SASC held two full days of hearings on Stello's nomination. Stello told the Committee that his actions at the NRC had been geared toward ensuring public health and safety, sometimes at the expense of finding fault. While remaining open to confirming Stello, Chairman Nunn voiced his annoyance that the Justice Department still had not turned over documents on Stello's grand jury investigation.

The Committee's request had been pending for four months. Senator Tim Wirth (D-CO) said that he could never vote for Stello because he had no confidence that he would put safety on par with production. And Senator Edward Kennedy (D-MA) said he would vote against Stello because of the way he had handled the licensing of the Seabrook nuclear plant in New Hampshire.

In addition to hearing from Stello, the Committee called seven other witnesses. One of whom, sitting Secretary of Energy James Watkins, stated unequivocally that Stello's confirmation to head the nation's troubled nuclear weapons program was his top priority. Watkins noted that four other candidates had refused the job because the pay, $80,700 per year, was too low.[33] Committee members also heard from Julian Greenspun, the former deputy chief of litigation at the Justice Department, who stated, "Stello lied to me" during the Justice Department's investigation of the Three Mile Island incident. Greenspun told the Committee: "Based on my extensive experience with the NRC, I can unequivocally state that I know of no other regulatory or investigatory agency where senior agency officials have taken as many bizarre and deliberate actions intended to hamper the investigation and prosecution of individuals and companies in the industry the agency regulates."

Rep. Sam Gejdenson (D-CT), whose House Interior oversight committee in 1987 condemned Stello's performance on several safety issues, told the Committee: "Stello was consistently on the wrong side of every issue, all the time. He stifled independent inquiry, and he was such a believer that he didn't have the temperament necessary to be a watchdog of the industry."[34]

On January 25, 1990, the SASC was set to meet and act on Stello's nomination but balked upon learning he was the focus of yet another investigation, this time by the NRC inspector general. The latest allegations were that Stello had authorized a $6,000 cash payment to an informant pursuing a "vendetta" against Roger Fortuna, an NRC investigator assigned to examine wrongdoing at nuclear plants. It was alleged that Stello was "out to get" Fortuna because he was too hard on the commercial nuclear industry. The Committee decided to hold on further consideration of Stello's nomination until it reviewed the outcomes of this latest investigation.

On April 20, 1990, after months of inaction on his nomination, Stello withdrew his name from consideration, saying that the president needed to find someone who could win confirmation to the sensitive job "at the earliest opportunity.... It has become clear to me I cannot be that person."[35] The president formally withdrew Stello's nomination four days later. Stello remained at the Department of Energy in a civil service job that did not require Senate confirmation. Toward the end of his career, he had an annual safety award named in his honor.[36]

To put a finer point on the imperative for complete transparency, I tell the cautionary tale of the nomination of Don Remy. On April 20, 2009, President Obama nominated Don Remy as the general counsel of the Department of the Army. Remy was highly qualified and a logical choice for the position. During his service as an Army officer, he was assigned for four years as assistant to the Army general counsel as part of that office's Honors Program. Remy left the service, clerked for a federal judge, then returned to government as a deputy assistant attorney general in the Department of Justice.

From 2000 to 2006, Remy was the senior vice president, chief compliance officer, and general counsel for Fannie Mae. Fannie Mae is the informal name for the Federal National Mortgage Association, one of two government-sponsored enterprises that provide lenders with the cash needed to fund home loans with affordable mortgage rates. Unfortunately for Remy, his tenure at Fannie Mae overlapped with the company's $11 billion accounting scandal that rocked a mortgage industry already in crisis.

After an extensive three-year investigation, the Office of Federal Housing Enterprise Oversight issued a blistering report alleging that senior executives at Fannie Mae had manipulated accounting to collect millions of dollars in undeserved bonuses and to deceive investors—the Securities and Exchange Commission fined Fannie Mae $400 million. Thirty executives and employees at the company, including many who had left and the current president and CEO, were reviewed for possible disciplinary action or termination.

It is important to clarify that there was no hint Remy had engaged in harmful acts during his time at Fannie Mae. Still, during his confirmation hearing before the SASC on April 28, 2009, he was questioned pointedly by Senators John McCain (R-AZ) and Mel Martinez (R-FL). Remy's timing could not have been worse. At the time of his nomination and hearing, the housing bubble had burst, and the global economy was in recession. President Obama had recently signed the $787 billion American Recovery and Reinvestment Act into law, but economic recovery was still months away.

Unsurprisingly, Sen. Martinez questioned Remy about why the biographical sketch submitted by the White House had not clearly called out Remy's service with Fannie Mae. The resume submitted by the White House stated Remy had "served as an attorney and businessperson for a major U.S. company" and the specific positions he had held and his duties and responsibilities. But the name of the company and the dates of Remy's employment were conspicuously absent. Working from the same biographical sketch, Senator Mary Landrieu (D-LA), who had introduced Remy at the hearing, and Senator Mark Warner (D-VA), who had written Remy a letter of recommendation, also mentioned only that he had served as an attorney for a major U.S. company.

During my team's prep session for Remy, Kim Wincup, former House Armed Services Committee (HASC) staff director and former assistant secretary in both the Army and Air Force, noted the bio Remy submitted to the SASC did not list Fannie Mae. Wincup worried this would be a red star cluster for the SASC. To his great credit, Remy said he agreed and would change it. The White House, however, disagreed with this approach, so the bio was not changed; what followed was just what Kim Wincup predicted.

Senator Martinez's exchange with Mr. Remy follows:

Senator MARTINEZ. "Mr. Remy, I want to ask a question of you, and I think it is, frankly, one of candor. I want to suggest to you that I think it is important to have good communication with the Committee and to be clear. I have looked at your resume, and I find it astonishing that you do not list your employer for a number of years. I can't even see the number of years because also your resume does not state when you began and when you ended your employment with what you describe as "a major U.S. company." Now I know by description and also what Senator McCain said that it appears to have been Fannie Mae, but you don't disclose that or the years that you were at Fannie Mae. Am I correct that it is Fannie Mae?"

Mr. REMY. "Yes, Senator. Yes, Senator."

Senator MARTINEZ. "When did you go to work there, and how long did you work there?"

Mr. REMY. "Senator, I worked at Fannie Mae from the years of 2000 through 2006."

Senator MARTINEZ. "To my knowledge, there is nothing wrong with having done that, and I think it should be on your resume clearly stated for all to see. Although there has been some controversy with the company, I know a lot of honorable people who have worked there, and I just don't think it is appropriate not to disclose it clearly."

Remy took responsibility for the incomplete biography submitted to the Committee. But he emphasized that many versions of his biography were in circulation and that he had disclosed his employment with Fannie Mae on his SASC Questionnaire and the Financial Disclosure forms filed with the Committee. Remy noted, "[s]ome shameful things may have happened [at Fannie Mae], but I have nothing to hide from my responsibilities."

After the hearing, at Chairman Levin's request, Remy submitted a detailed statement of his duties at Fannie Mae and an updated version of his biography that clearly called out his employment with the troubled organization. Remy also responded to an exhaustive set of Questions for the Record from Sen. Martinez, focused on Remy's employment with Fannie Mae and how, in his role as chief compliance officer, he had failed to detect the widespread fraudulent conduct in which other Fannie Mae executives had engaged.

But the damage was done. Less than a month later, on June 17, 2009, the president withdrew Remy's nomination. Remy went on to a successful career in the private sector and, in April 2021, was nominated by President Biden as the deputy secretary of Veterans Affairs. Having learned from experience, Remy ensured that his biography and nomination paperwork appropriately referenced Fannie Mae and addressed his work at Fannie Mae frequently during his confirmation hearing on May 19, 2021.

Issues associated with Fannie Mae never even came up, and Remy was favorably voted out of Committee on May 26, 2021. But once reported to the Senate floor, Remy's nomination was one of four to Veterans Affairs (VA) leadership posts blocked temporarily by Senator Marsha Blackburn (R-TN) and others.

Sen. Blackburn's concerns were unrelated to Remy or other nominees. Rather, she had pledged to hold the nominations over a lingering complaint about the VA's lack of response to the Senate on the cost of legislation that would grant more generous benefits to victims of military toxic exposure cases. The VA took steps to resolve Senator Blackburn's concerns in early July. On July 15, Remy was confirmed in the Senate by 91-8.

Once the prospective nominee's completed background investigation, ethics paperwork, and other essential documents are reviewed by the Office of White House Counsel and other appropriate agencies, the nomination is forwarded to the president for his decision and signature. The nomination then must be delivered to the Senate, presuming the Senate is in session and available to receive nominations. (The Senate cannot formally receive a nomination during a recess or pro forma session.)

The hard copy of the president's signed nomination is received and processed by the Office of the Executive Clerk and placed on the Executive Calendar (a separate document from the Senate's Calendar of Business, which lists pending bills and resolutions).

The executive clerk assigns each nominee a Presidential Nomination Number (PN). The first nomination received in any new Congress is designated as PN1. Each nomination is assigned the next available PN in sequence by the executive clerk through the end of the Congress.

Each nomination, with its PN, is added to the publicly accessible Senate website, listed as "pending." Usually, within 24 to 48 hours of receipt, the nomination is referred to the committee of jurisdiction determined by Senate Rules and precedents of many years.

James E. McPherson was nominated in 2018 to be the Army general counsel. Unlike Remy's situation in 2009, McPherson not only sailed through that process but was also nominated two years later for promotion to be the 34th under secretary of the Army and achieved the same positive results. I was privileged to assist him through the confirmation process both times, and he penned the following note that reads:

*Dear General Punaro: Thank you for your support during my confirmation process to be the 34th under secretary of the Army. Your group's collective expertise, judgment, and wise counsel was instrumental to my hearing preparation, and I am truly appreciative of your assistance. Please express my sincere gratitude to your team. Thank you for your time, friendship, and dedicated service to our nation. Sincerely, Jim. *Couldn't have done it without your help and support. Jim*

THE UNDER SECRETARY OF THE ARMY
WASHINGTON, D.C. 20310-0102

APR 0 3 2020

Major General Arnold Punaro
United States Marine Corps (Retired)
1313 Dolley Madison Boulevard, Suite 404
McLean, Virginia 22101

Dear General Punaro: / *GENERAL,*

Thank you for your support during my confirmation process to be the 34th Under Secretary of the Army. Your Group's collective expertise, judgment, and wise counsel was instrumental to my hearing preparation, and I am truly appreciative of your assistance. Please express my sincere gratitude to your team.

Thank you for your time, friendship, and dedicated service to our Nation.

Sincerely,

Jim

James E. McPherson

COULDN'T HAVE DONE IT WITHOUT YOU HELP AND SUPPORT -

Jim

5

THE CONFIRMATION PROCESS

This chapter explores what nominees can expect during the confirmation process after their names have been officially submitted to the Senate for advice and consent. The Senate's role begins only after the president formally submits a nomination and is referred to the committee of jurisdiction—in this case, the SASC.

Before the SASC moves on the nomination, the nominee must complete and submit the following documents and information to the Committee. Submissions are usually made through DOD and the White House:

- The nominee's OGE Form 278e and a letter from the nominee to the SASC chairman regarding conflicts of interest and other matters. The nominee is provided a template letter from which to begin work and is expected to change it to reflect his or her unique personal circumstances. Nominees are also expected to use the letter to elaborate on sensitive matters revealed in their financial disclosure forms or responses to the SASC Questionnaire for Civilian Nominees (discussed below).
- In addition, OGE submits a letter documenting its review of the nominee's OGE Form 278e and addressing any financial or organizational conflicts of interest it may have identified. The Designated Agency Ethics Official (DAEO) of the department or agency the nominee will serve also submits a letter assessing the nominee's compliance with law, Executive Branch and DOD ethics regulations, and SASC divestiture policies. In DOD, this is usually the Standards of Conduct Office or the ethics official of a Military Department most familiar with the

duty requirements of the position for which the individual has been nominated. The letter also explains the actual or perceived conflicts of interest identified. It spells out steps the nominee must take—including the divestiture of certain assets or resignation from certain outside positions—to eliminate or mitigate the conflict or correct any violation. The letter concludes with a certification that, subject to the nominee's compliance with these required steps, the nominee does not have a conflict of interest or the appearance of one concerning the position for which nominated.

SASC's pre-hearing role in vetting civilian nominees includes a rigorous scrub for compliance with Executive Branch ethics rules and the Committee's ethics policy. For years, the SASC policy on civilian nominee financial conflicts of interest was among the most restrictive of any Senate committee. At its core, the policy required civilian nominees to divest *all* stock holdings of any value in any company with defense contracts of $25,000 or more in the preceding fiscal year. (Practically, each nominee's holdings had to be scanned against the over 30,000 large and small businesses.)

Effective February 22, 2021, the SASC revised its policies about the divestitures required of civilian nominees for PAS positions. Under the new policy, DOD PAS nominees must divest holdings in companies appearing in the "Top 10" slots of the General Services Administration (GSA) published Top 100 Contractors listing over the last five fiscal years.[37] This new requirement is consistent with Title 10 of the U.S. Code, Section 988. It puts civilian PAS appointees on a level playing field with general/flag officers and members of the Senior Executive Service serving in key acquisition positions.[38] Although the GSA's "Top 10" list rarely changes, the 5-year timeframe was chosen to promote transparency and longer-term predictability in identifying prohibited holdings.

In addition, DOD PAS nominees may now avail themselves of the *de minimis* exception in OGE conflict of interest regulations. This means that a civilian nominee's stock holdings of less than $15,000 in any individual company—even companies in the "Top 10" of the GSA 5-year list—are considered by OGE and the SASC to be *de minimis*. They need not be divested.[39] Civilian nominees are required to divest only direct stock holdings. Divestiture of Excepted Investment Funds (EIFs) or Mutual Funds is not required (unless OGE, DOD SOCO, or the Military Department DAEO determines them to be a "sector fund," the ownership of which could present an actual or perceived conflict of interest, considering the specific duties of the position for which the individual is nominated).[40]

These limitations on specific holdings, the types of holdings, and the amounts of same apply throughout the individual's service in the specific position to which confirmed. If confirmed, it will be the nominee's responsibility to ensure that such investments do not grow to exceed the $15,000 threshold during his or her service in a PAS position. Should an investment accrue value above the *de minimis* level, the appointee can divest the holding in full or partially in an amount sufficient to return the value of the shares held to or below the threshold. Although the $15,000 Executive Branch threshold has been static for decades, SASC policy will automatically adjust to any new *de minimis* standard should OGE increase the threshold going forward.

The 2021 change in SASC policy also eliminated the longstanding requirement that civilian nominees who, under past private sector employment, had a defined benefit retirement plan with a company that did business with DOD obtain a "surety." The surety was essentially an insurance policy to guarantee such benefit payments should the company become insolvent.[41] After the situation involving Secretary of the Army

Thomas White's pension payments by the insurance company when Enron went insolvent, getting such a "surety" proved almost impossible. OGE and DOD ethics officials had long opined that such a surety was unnecessary given that ethics laws require a DOD PAS to recuse himself or herself if called upon to make a decision that could affect a past employer and, by implication, the solvency of the defined benefit plan the PAS may receive from that employer.[42] The confirmation of Gordon England to be deputy secretary of defense was stalled for months when the SASC insisted he obtain an insurance policy for his General Dynamics pension. Due to what occurred with Enron, the cost was prohibitive, and finally, the SASC processed his nomination.

There is always the possibility that as part of the nomination clearance process, OGE, the DAEO, or in extremely rare cases, the SASC, may advise a nominee that, if confirmed, he or she must sell or otherwise divest of an asset to avoid a conflict of interest or the appearance of one. Most times, selling the asset will cause an unplanned and unwelcome capital gain, given that the requirement to sell likely was not part of the nominee's long-term investment strategy. The sale must occur within a minimal period after the nominee is confirmed (usually 90 days), regardless of the market conditions. In such cases, the nominee may be eligible for an OGE Certificate of Divestiture. This approach was updated by Chairman Nunn working with the Finance Committee to lessen somewhat the burden of the SASC's total divestiture policy.

The Certificate of Divestiture permits a nominee to defer tax on the capital gain because of the requirement to sell the asset to comply with government conflict of interest rules associated with nomination, confirmation, and appointment to a PAS position.[43] Minimizing the burden associated with public service should help attract and keep highly qualified personnel in the Executive Branch while maintaining public confidence in government officials' integrity and decision-making processes.

These financial divestiture requirements can prove too much of a burden on some nominees. On December 19, 2016, then-President-elect Donald Trump announced his intent to nominate Vincent Viola for the secretary of the Army position. Viola, a retired Army major, and West Point graduate, had played a key role in launching the Combating Terrorism Center at West Point shortly after the 9/11 attacks. After leaving the service, Viola had launched several successful businesses. In 2008, Viola founded Virtu Financial, a digital trading firm he took public in 2015. Viola was also the owner of the Florida Panthers, a National Hockey League franchise, and the co-owner of the 2017 Kentucky Derby winner, Always Dreaming. At the time of his nomination, Viola was worth $1.8 billion, according to Forbes, putting him among the 400 wealthiest Americans. Trump's choice of Viola was reported to be concerning to General James Mattis, whom Trump had nominated as his secretary of defense. Reportedly, Mattis had not been informed of the choice before the announcement and expressed concern about Virtu's digital trading practices, which were then under investigation by regulators. Senate Minority Leader Chuck Schumer (D-NY) praised his fellow New Yorker, saying: "I've known Vinnie Viola for over a decade, and his dedication to the Army is second to none," before adding that "of course, the president's nominees would be carefully vetted by the Senate."

Less than two months later, on February 3, 2017, Viola withdrew from consideration for the position. He cited his inability to comply with strict Defense Department ethics regulations regarding personal businesses. Viola had been searching for ways to divest from his business ventures, including transferring ownership of the Florida Panthers to his family members and transferring responsibility for operations to another businessman who served as vice chairman of the team organization. But it was reported that none of these proposals met the OGE and DOD criteria. Viola said he was "deeply honored" to be nominated for the post but concluded that he could not successfully navigate the confirmation process.

Viola was not the only Trump Military Department nominee with financial divestiture issues. Trump's first pick to be secretary of the Navy, Philip Bilden, withdrew from consideration because he could not meet the OGE requirements for the position without "materially adverse divestment" of his family's financial interests.[44] The nomination then went to Richard V. Spencer, who was confirmed as secretary of the Navy on August 1, 2017. Spencer was fired in November 2019.

Trump's second choice for Army secretary, Dr. Mark Green, also suffered severe headwinds because of some public statements and withdrew his nomination. (Now, he is a member of Congress who chairs the House Committee on Homeland Security.) Had Trump's first-choice nominees faced fewer hurdles throughout the confirmation process, the administration may have had more successful and timely appointments to these critical positions.

Certificates of Divestiture are not automatic. DOD SOCO or the Military Department DAEO will assist a civilian nominee in applying for a Certificate of Divestiture from OGE. The application must contain the nominee's unequivocal commitment to divest the property, even if OGE declines to issue a Certificate. The director of OGE may issue a Certificate of Divestiture on determining that divestiture of the specific asset is necessary to comply with federal laws or rules or if a congressional committee requires divestiture as a condition of Senate confirmation. The nominee must apply for a Certificate of

Divestiture within 90 days of becoming aware of the requirement to divest the property. A nominee must apply for a Certificate of Divestiture *before* selling the asset. OGE cannot and
will not issue a Certificate of Divestiture for a sold property.
Nominees are cautioned not to sell an asset until the DAEO
provides the OGE-approved Certificate of Divestiture or notifies the nominee that OGE has denied the request. Notice that
a Certificate of Divestiture has been granted is made available
to the public in the same manner as a nominee's OGE 278e.

The nominee will be required to sell the property within
three months of his or her Senate confirmation.[45] Exceptions
to the three-month deadline can be granted only in cases of
unusual hardship. Within 60 days of the sale, the nominee
must reinvest the proceeds in "permitted property." Permitted
property is limited to U.S. government obligations (i.e., Treas-
uries), diversified mutual funds, and diversified exchange-
traded funds.[46] The deferred capital gains tax will come due
only once the permitted property is sold.[47]

Four recent presidents have issued ethics executive orders,
each containing an "ethics pledge" that civilian appointees
must sign upon taking office. Those orders were issued by
Presidents Clinton (1993), Obama (2009), Trump (2017), and
Biden (2021); each touted the pledge as part of his drive to ensure that the administration was the most "ethical on record."
Except for President Clinton's order, all placed restrictions on
political appointees as they entered government service. All orders, including Clinton's, restricted appointees' post-government conduct.[48] President Biden's ethics pledge requires civilian appointees to commit to "conduct consistent with" the
pledge and to "decision-making on the merits and only in the
public interest, without regard to private gain or personal benefit." The pledge bans appointees from accepting gifts from
lobbyists, extends revolving door prohibitions from one to two

years, places restrictions on the activities of Executive Branch personnel formerly registered as lobbyists or foreign agents, places post-government employment restrictions on officials leaving government, and prohibits "golden parachute" payments from private sector firms as a reward for entering government service. Presidents Clinton and Trump rescinded their ethics pledges shortly before leaving office, freeing their appointees from compliance. President Obama left his pledge in place. Although the SASC and Senate understand civilian nominees must sign and comply with an administration's ethics pledge as a prerequisite to nomination, the pledge plays no other role in the confirmation process.

- The completed SASC Questionnaire for Civilian Nominees. Part A of the Questionnaire elicits the nominee's biographical information and commitments in furtherance of congressional and Committee oversight. Part B of the SASC Questionnaire requests additional personal information and information about employment relationships, potential conflicts of interest, legal matters and prior discipline or sanction, foreign affiliations, and financial data. SASC professional staff review the responses to ensure all questions are answered and to identify any responses showing something controversial or an item of interest to any senator.

- All documents must be signed by the nominee not more than 60 days before the date the nomination is received in the Senate.

- Concurrently, the nominee must submit complete copies of his or her last three federal tax returns.

- Civilian nominees must also submit a list of published writings (print and online), including titles, publishers, and dates written by the nominee or for which the nominee served as co-author or editor.

- The nominee must also submit two copies of formal speeches in the previous five years addressing matters relevant to the position to which he or she has been nominated.

The all-important confirmation hearing will not be scheduled until all the nominee's submissions are complete and the SASC professional staff has reviewed them.

The Committee takes its job vetting nominees incredibly seriously, and one example can demonstrate why. In 1981, President Reagan nominated Melvyn Paisley as assistant secretary of the Navy for research, engineering, and systems. Despite some ethical concerns in his record, he was confirmed on a bipartisan basis for the position. He served in his position until 1987.

Paisley was sued by the Justice Department for violating federal conflict of interest laws when he received a $183,000 severance package from his employer, Boeing, after accepting his DOD position in 1981.[49] Though the decision was later overturned by the courts in favor of Paisley, the issue demonstrates how fraught conflict of interest problems can be in DOD.

In 1991, Paisley also became wrapped in a major scandal in which he pled guilty to accepting bribes from and leaking classified information to defense firms.[50] This was a major scandal for the Pentagon and the Navy—but also for the SASC, which had confirmed him without issue for a position of power he seriously abused.

One special type of nomination bears mention at this point. Although most nominations for judicial positions are referred to the Senate Judiciary Committee, the SASC has jurisdiction over the nominations of judges of the United States Court of Appeals for the Armed Forces (CAAF). CAAF exercises worldwide appellate jurisdiction over members of the armed forces on active duty and other persons subject to the Uniform Code of Military Justice. The Court comprises five civilian judges appointed for 15-year terms by the president, with the advice and consent of the Senate. The Court's cases address a broad range of legal issues, and decisions by the Court are subject to direct review by the Supreme Court of the United States.[51] CAAF has adopted the Code of Conduct for United States Judges, which cautions a nominee for judicial office against public comments on issues that might come before him or her on the bench, if confirmed.[52] The SASC has adjusted its Questionnaire and APQs for CAAF nominees to reflect these limitations.

During the confirmation hearing, senators who ask a CAAF nominee to explain their views on a particular aspect of military law or how the nominee might decide a case under a specified set of facts should expect a response that judicial ethics preclude the nominee from providing the detailed response desired. This should be followed by assurances that the nominee will apply the law as enacted by Congress and as interpreted through the application of standing precedent. Finally, financial disclosure reports for most judges and judicial nominees—including nominees for appointment to CAAF—are filed on Form AO-10 with the Administrative Office of the U.S. Courts rather than the Office of Government Ethics. The Administrative Office reviews each nominee's report to ensure compliance with applicable laws and regulations. The CAAF nominee's Form AO-10 and a letter documenting review by the Administrative Office are provided to the SASC to support the nomination.[53]

All the information submitted by the president, the nominee, OGE, and DOD or the Military Department is made available to the senators comprising the SASC and the Committee staff director, the minority staff director, and designated members of the Committee's professional staff. The Committee reviews the information submitted and requests additional information as needed. Committee professional staff assigned by the chairman and the ranking member review the federal income tax returns of the nominee. They may enlist the expertise of the Joint Committee on Taxation for particularly challenging returns. Any senator and Committee professional staff member may raise questions associated with the nominee and his or her nomination package.

Questions that cannot be answered "in-house" are redirected to the Department or the nominee for response or clarification. Again, the SASC cannot and will not clear a nomination until it has received, thoroughly reviewed, and is satisfied with the content of all required documents. Although nomination packages contain highly sensitive and very personal information, I believe these files, to the current day, have never been breached or improperly disclosed by SASC senators or Committee professional staff. Nominees can rest assured great pains are taken to ensure the security and confidentiality of these documents to the greatest degree practicable in the context of the nomination process.

After all required documents are completed, received, and reviewed by the Committee, the Committee staff directors and/or majority and minority general counsels may request a nominee interview. Questions that have arisen throughout the Committee's nomination review may be addressed. Nominees should know that the SASC professional staff routinely checks a nominee's public social media presence. And staff often receives unsolicited input from outside groups regarding a nominee's suitability. The staff may use the nominee interview to explore in greater detail what they have learned about the nominee from these sources. The SASC also expects a senior nominee to meet with any member of the Committee who may request it. These meetings are known as "courtesy calls."

A hearing date is selected by the Committee chairman in consultation with the ranking member. Soon after the date is determined, Committee counsel provides Advance Policy Questions (APQs) to the nominee. In most cases, nominees have only 3-5 days to provide their completed APQ responses to the Committee. A nominee's APQ responses are almost always reviewed and sometimes adjusted by the general counsel of the department or agency where the nominee will work if confirmed. The Office of White House Counsel also often reviews APQ responses, ensuring that the nominee's answers comport with administration policies. Under SASC rules, public notice of the hearing's date, place, and subject must be issued at least one week before the hearing. Although the deadline for public notice may be waived, this is rarely done. Other deadlines also loom. The nominee's APQ responses and the text of any written statement the nominee plans to deliver at the hearing must be provided to the Committee no later than 48 hours before the hearing (not including holidays and weekends).

Before the hearing, Part A of the nominee's SASC Questionnaire, the nominee's OGE Form 278e and letter to the chairman of the Committee, the letters from OGE and the DAEO, and the nominee's responses to APQs are available in the Committee office for public inspection. After the hearing, this information will be entered into the hearing record, which is also available to the public. The nominee's responses to Part B of the SASC Questionnaire, financial data, and other confidential information are not public. They will be kept in the Committee's executive files. Nominee tax returns are available only to senators and Committee professional staff designated by the chairman. They are not open to public inspection and are returned to the nominee once the Committee completes its work on the nomination.

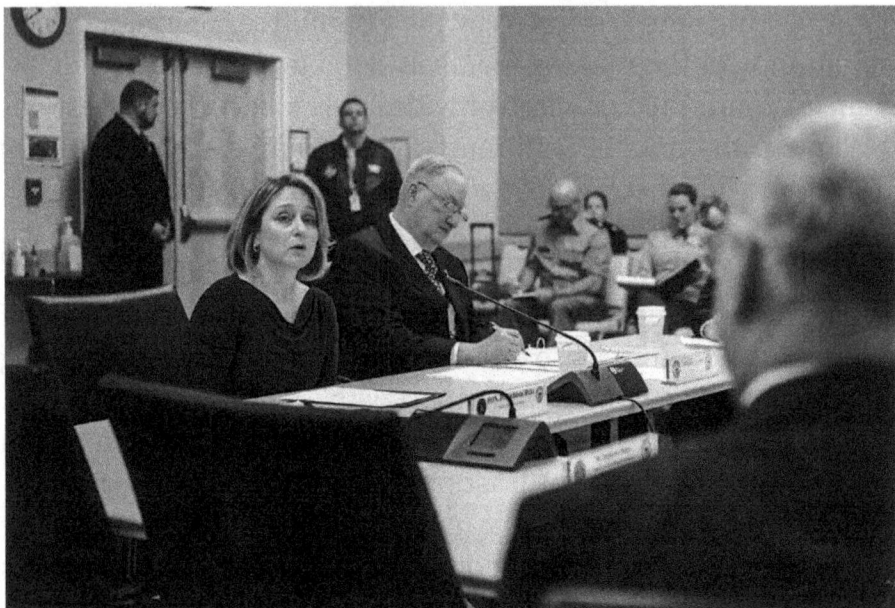

Arnold Punaro hosts Deputy Secretary of Defense Kathleen Hicks in his role as chairman of the Secretary of Defense Reserve Forces Policy Board.

A Committee hearing is conducted and chaired by the chairman or his or her designee. All confirmation hearings are open to the public, although matters relating to conflicts of interest or other confidential matters may be heard in a closed Executive Session that usually occurs immediately before or after the public hearing. Classified information may also be discussed in closed hearings or briefings in properly cleared spaces in the Capitol reserved for this purpose. In the context of civilian nominations, closed executive sessions or classified briefings are extremely rare, having occurred only once or twice in the last decade.

Unlike other committees, the SASC does not require nominees to testify under oath. I cannot recall a single instance where a nominee was sworn in during my tenure as staff director. The chairman asks each nominee to respond, "on the record," to a standard set of questions that ensure the nominee has not taken action or made any decisions that reflect a "presumption of confirmation." In addition, once confirmed, these questions secure each nominee's commitment to providing information to assist the Committee in its Department oversight.

After the hearing, each SASC member can submit written Questions for the Record (QFRs), which a nominee must respond to in writing. A nominee's satisfactory responses to the QFRs must be received and reviewed before the Committee votes on his or her nomination. A word to the wise: many nominees respond to questions asked during the confirmation hearing and in QFRs by promising to "look into that matter if confirmed" or by committing to work with a senator "to address a particular issue if confirmed." Nominees need to follow up on these commitments. I always urge nominees I counsel to stick to their promises and, once confirmed, to reach out to senators and Committee staff with information of interest and collaboration offers. The benefits of such initiative and follow-through cannot be overstated.

Per SASC rules, seven calendar days must elapse after the Committee receives the nomination before the Committee votes on the nominee. This gives each SASC senator a meaningful opportunity to review each nomination and raise concerns. Although this rule can be waived, it rarely is. A White House Counsel's Office representative must brief the chairman and ranking member on the FBI background investigation of the civilian nominee before any Committee vote. Once these conditions are met, the chairman will schedule the Committee vote. Notice of the proposed date and time of the vote and the names of the nominees is provided to SASC senators, usually via an email to their military legislative assistant.

Recent SASC practice has precluded individual SASC members from "holding" a nominee in Committee. If any SASC member brings to the chairman or ranking member's attention a substantive concern about a nominee, the chairman and ranking member work through Committee professional staff to investigate the matter and resolve it. Once the concern has been resolved (and presuming the nominee has met all other Committee requirements), a Committee vote on the nominee will probably proceed. Before the vote, any senator may advise others of any ongoing substantive or political concern about a nominee. Any senator can vote "no" on any nominee, and any senator can place a hold on that nominee for any reason once the Committee reports the nomination to the Senate floor.

As required by Senate Rule XXVI, a Committee members' quorum must be present to report a nomination out of Committee. SASC has long believed—and Senate Parliamentarians agree—that rolling voting, in which senators "drop in" to a voting location, provide their vote to Committee professional staff, then immediately depart for other business, does not meet the Senate Rules. SASC insists that a quorum of senators be physically present for a vote. Even during the COVID-19 pandemic, rolling or "virtual" voting was not permitted by the Senate or the SASC.

In the 118th Congress, a quorum is achieved when 13 of 25 SASC members are physically present and voting. SASC practice is to assemble the requisite quorum of SASC members in a room off the Senate floor in conjunction with a series of scheduled roll call votes or to vote on nominations during a scheduled Committee hearing on another matter once enough members are in attendance. It is not uncommon for the chairman—having been advised by staff that a quorum is present—to halt an ongoing hearing mid-sentence, proceed with the nomination vote, and return to the hearing at hand, all within a few minutes and with minimal disruption.

Senate practice recognizes three possible motions for Committee action on nominations. These are: (1) voting the nomination out of Committee with a favorable recommendation (that the nomination be confirmed by the Senate); (2) voting the nomination out of Committee with an unfavorable recommendation (that the Senate decline to confirm the nomination); or (3) voting the nomination out of Committee without recommendation. Given that the nominations subject to vote have been reviewed and cleared per the SASC's established criteria and processes and have navigated a confirmation hearing and post-hearing QFRs, the Committee chairman invariably moves to vote the nominees out of Committee with a favorable recommendation.

Presuming the existence of a quorum, a simple majority of senators present and voting must vote in favor of the motion for it to succeed. A tie vote or a majority of votes against the motion leaves the nomination in Committee. Throughout my service as staff director and carrying through to the present day, I observed the thoroughness of the SASC process to screen out—before the vote— any civilian nominee who can't make it out of Committee or survive a vote by the full Senate, rather than being voted out of the Committee with an unfavorable or no recommendation. Such nominations are usually held in Committee without further action. They are returned to the White House upon withdrawal by the president or at the end of a session of Congress under the Standing Rules of the Senate.[54] If the president still wants that nominee to be considered, he must submit a new nomination to the Senate.

Most Committee votes on nominations are voice votes. Civilian and military nominations are often voted together. Still, any SASC member may request a roll call vote, in which each senator's name is called and his or her "Yea" or "Nay" vote on the nominations recorded. Most votes are *en bloc*, meaning the Committee votes on all cleared nominations. Any senator may request a separate "by name" vote on one or more individual nominations, but this is extremely rare.

If a majority of the SASC senators are present for the Committee vote and a majority vote in favor of the nominee's confirmation, the chairman immediately reports the nomination to the Senate. It is placed on the Executive Calendar, recommending the nominee be confirmed. In certain instances, the Committee may file a report on the nominee. Senate Rules require any nomination reported out of Committee to "lay over" on the Senate floor for one business day before the nominee can be confirmed. This allows all 100 senators, most of whom are not members of the SASC, to review the nominations and raise any concerns. At this stage, the Committee's work is done. From this point forward, the decision to call up a nomination for consideration by the full Senate resides with the Senate majority leader.

It is important to note that some nominations are eligible for an abridged process. So-called "privileged" nominations comprise a subset of PAS positions eligible for consideration under S. Res. 116, agreed to by the Senate on June 29, 2011. The creation of privileged nominations and the special procedures for their consideration were part of a larger effort to reform the Senate confirmation process during the 112th Congress (2011-2012). The intent was to reduce the Committee workload linked to nominations and allow uncontroversial nominees to avoid the lengthy delays often associated with the confirmation process and more quickly assume their essential duties in the Executive Branch.

Most of the 285 nominations designated as privileged are part-time positions on various boards and commissions. However, the roster of privileged nominations includes certain full-time PAS positions of interest to the DOD and the SASC. They include the chief financial officer (CFO) for the DOD (which is the under secretary of defense (comptroller)), the assistant secretaries for financial management in the Military Departments, and the assistant secretary for legislative affairs.

Unlike a typical nomination, a privileged nomination is not referred to a committee unless requested explicitly by a senator. Instead, upon receipt from the White House, the nomination is entered into the "Privileged Nominations" section of the Senate Executive Calendar. Committees are notified and required to request biographical, financial, and other information from each privileged nominee. Privileged nominees under SASC jurisdiction must complete and submit all the same paperwork as the "nonprivileged" civilian nominations discussed above. The SASC chairman informs the Senate clerk once the Committee receives and clears each nominee's information.

After that, 10 Senate session days must elapse before the nomination can be considered on the Senate floor.[55] This allows a nomination to become eligible for floor consideration even though the SASC did not hold a formal hearing or vote to report it. However, there are no expedited Senate floor procedures for privileged nominations. They are called up and considered under the same procedures as any other civilian nomination.

Any senator may request that a privileged nomination be referred to Committee, and any such request is automatically granted. It is standard procedure for the chairman of the SASC to request that the nomination for the under secretary of defense (comptroller)/CFO be referred to the Committee, given the significant budgetary, policymaking, and oversight responsibilities assigned to the position. Once an otherwise privileged nomination is referred to the SASC, it must be voted out of Committee before the full Senate can consider it. Most privileged nominations considered on the Senate floor were never referred to a committee.

As of the end of 2022, the Senate considered 634 privileged nominations, and only 58 of these were referred to a committee at the request of a senator.[56] Even though most privileged nominees are confirmed without a hearing, the SASC believes strongly in the committee's prerogative to require that any nominee—privileged or not—be referred to and appear before the Committee for a confirmation hearing.

Although some civilian PAS nominees may be exempt from the hearing process, others must undergo more than one Senate confirmation hearing. These are nominees whose positions span the jurisdictional boundaries of more than one Senate committee. Under a "sequential referral" process, a nomination may be referred to two or more committees for successive consideration, usually under some time limit set by a long-ago Senate Order to establish the terms of the Committees' shared control over the nomination. For example, the nomination of the assistant secretary of the Army for civil works is first referred to the SASC.

Once favorably reported out of SASC, the nominee is sequentially referred to the Committee on Environment and Public Works (EPW) for 20 Senate session days.[57] This committee exercises jurisdiction over the civil works programs of the U.S. Army Corps of Engineers, which reports to the assistant secretary of the Army for civil works, justifying EPW's longstanding role in this nomination. The nominee must submit to the separate procedures of the EPW Committee, including a confirmation hearing.

EPW must complete its process within the 20-session-day period, or the nomination will be automatically discharged from the Committee to the Senate floor. Similarly, the nomination of the director of the National Reconnaissance Office falls under the jurisdiction of the Senate Select Committee on Intelligence and the SASC, reflective of the fact that the director reports to the director of National Intelligence and the secretary of defense.[58]

Arnold Punaro and Secretary of the Army Ryan McCarthy exchange greetings before their meeting to discuss major Military Department issues and the role of the Service secretaries and service chiefs under Title 10. Punaro assisted McCarthy with his confirmations for under secretary and secretary of the Army.

All inspector general nominations are subject to a sequential referral from the committee of primary jurisdiction (the SASC in the case of the DOD IG) to the Senate Homeland Security and Governmental Affairs Committee for 20 calendar days.[59] Some inspector general nominees are sequentially referred to yet a third committee. On receipt from the White House, the nomination of the inspector general of the National Reconnaissance Office is first referred to the Senate Select Committee on Intelligence, then to the SASC, and then to Homeland Security and Governmental Affairs. All this occurs before his or her nomination can be considered on the Senate floor.[60]

Except for nominees to presidential cabinet-level positions— for purposes of this book: the secretary of defense, the deputy secretary of defense, and the secretaries of the Military Departments, who, because of their importance, are usually confirmed by a recorded vote on the Senate floor—most DOD nominees are confirmed by the unanimous consent process. Before the majority leader's motion for unanimous consent, all nominees considered for Senate vote are "hotlined." Hotlining is a system of telephonic and email messages transmitted to all senators' offices advising them of the nominations under consideration for confirmation by name. It allows each senator to object or withhold consent, placing a "hold" on one or more nominees.

A hold is a request by a senator to his or her party leader (either the majority or minority leader) to prevent or delay action on a nomination. A standing order of the Senate aims to ensure that senators publicly specify their objection to the nominee. Still, enforcement of this order has proven challenging.[61] Senators may place a hold on a nomination for many reasons. For example, a senator may want more time to review a nomination or consult with the nominee. Senators may also place holds because they disagree with the nominee's policy positions. Some place holds to gain concessions from the administration on matters unrelated to the nomination. Should a senator place a hold on a civilian nominee under SASC jurisdiction, the SASC professional staff is informed. The staff immediately reaches out to the office of the holding senator to find out the basis for the hold and endeavor to resolve it. But senators have the discretion to continue a hold for as long as they deem appropriate. Some holds continue for many months or may never be lifted at all.

If no senator objects to a nomination, it will be approved; routine nominations are grouped and brought up on the Senate floor *en bloc* and approved together by unanimous consent. I want to emphasize that if even one senator places a hold on a nomination, the unanimous consent process is scuttled. Holds on nominees used to be rare. They are commonplace now, which proves exceedingly frustrating for individual nominees and the administration.

The only remaining option is through the "full-up" invocation of cloture on the nomination, followed, after the requisite interval, by a vote on the individual nominee. Recently, because of intensifying political stalemates, Majority Leader Chuck Schumer has been required to employ the full-up process for almost every civilian nominee pending before the Senate.

Cloture is how the Senate limits debate on any measure or matter, including a nomination. A cloture motion filed on a nomination receives a vote after two days of Senate session. If a majority of senators voting favor cloture, then after a maximum of two hours of consideration (for all but high-ranking nominations that have up to 30 hours), the Senate will vote on the nomination. The final "advice and consent" on the nomination is subject to a simple majority vote.

The process for invoking cloture on a nomination is relatively straightforward but incredibly time-consuming and, thus, is disfavored. If Senate leaders reach a unanimous consent agreement to limit the debate or to set a specific time for a final vote, the expenditure of floor time can be minimized.

6

THE APPOINTMENT PROCESS

After the rigorous nomination and confirmation phases, the nominee finally enters the much more straightforward appointment phase. This is the last step before he or she assumes their new position.

After the Senate acts, the secretary of the Senate attests to a resolution of confirmation or disapproval and transmits it to the White House. The executive clerk updates the Senate website, and SASC staff notifies DOD. Although Senate action to confirm one of the president's civilian nominees is typically reported with great fanfare in the Washington media, several days often elapse before the message of Senate confirmation is received in the White House. The warrant of appointment is then prepared and signed by the president. At the appropriate time, the president will issue and deliver the warrant appointing the nominee to the confirmed position.

Delivery of the signed warrant to the newly confirmed PAS completes the third phase of the constitutional process. It is the prerequisite to the nominee taking the oath of office to assume the duties and responsibilities of the confirmed position. An appointee to a senior position in DOD can be "on duty," usually a week to 10 days following Senate confirmation. Sometimes the White House will delay signing and presenting the warrant to the successful nominee to accommodate the nominee's preference for a later start date. Nominees often need time to close out existing non-governmental work obligations or move geographically.

12 Feb

LISA E. GORDON HAGERTY

Dear Arnold,

I am not sure where to start after your over-the-top support! Your kindness and guidance mean so much to me and know it helped me make it through the hearing!

I also wanted to thank you for the book and look forward to reading it soon!

As I embark on this exciting journey, I am hopeful that our paths will cross again.

Finally, thank you again for your continued, dedicated service to our great Nation - we are better for it.

With best and warmest regards,

Lisa

Lisa Gordon-Hagerty, confirmed to be the head of the National Nuclear Security Administration on February 15, 2018, writes a thank you note to Arnold Punaro for his help in preparing for her SASC hearing. The note reads:

Dear Arnold, I am not sure where to start after your over-the-top support! Your kindness and guidance mean so much to me and know it helped me make it through the hearing! I also wanted to thank you for the book and look forward to reading it soon! As I embark on this exciting journey, I am hopeful that our paths will cross again. Finally, thank you again for your continued, dedicated service to our great nation. We are better for it. With best and warmest regards, Lisa

In the case of the secretary of defense, that person is usually confirmed in the afternoon of the new president's inauguration, appointed, and sworn in the same day. This is because the secretary of defense is in the operational chain of command from the newly inaugurated president to the military warfighting commanders.

On reporting to the department or agency for duty, the new appointee is sworn in by personnel specialists to permit him or her to begin work immediately. Often, a formal, more elaborate, and public swearing-in ceremony is scheduled for a later date. Multiple oaths of office present no issue, provided an appointee takes his or her first oath before beginning to work.

ADDITIONAL THOUGHTS ON RETIRED MILITARY OFFICERS SERVING IN CIVILIAN POSITIONS

To close out our discussion of civilian nominations, I want to focus on the most critical DOD civilian nomination, the secretary of defense, and our recent experience with the nomination, confirmation, and appointment of retired military general officers.

The principle of civilian control of the military has been central to American ethos and culture since we became an independent nation. Ultimate authority over the U.S. armed services lies in the hands of civilian leadership. There are two key civilian positions in the military chain of command: an elected president designated by the Constitution as commander-in-chief of the armed forces and the secretary of defense.[62]

The position of the secretary of defense was first established in 1947 when the lessons of World War II were still fresh. Congress saw a need to create greater unity of command over all the Military

Services while ensuring that the newly centralized "national defense establishment" and the individuals empowered to lead it would not threaten the principle of civilian control. From the very first, the law provided that the secretary of defense was "appointed from *civilian life* by the president, with the advice and consent of the Senate" and that "a person who has within 10 years been on active duty as a commissioned officer in a regular component of the armed services shall *not be eligible* for appointment as secretary of defense."[63] In an era where legendary generals and admirals who were credited with winning the "war to end all wars" were enormously popular with the American people, this "cooling-off period" was viewed as a vital mechanism to maintain civilian control of the armed forces.

U.S. involvement in the Korean War exposed significant deficits in the readiness of our armed forces, resulting in President Truman firing Secretary of Defense Louis A. Johnson. Realizing the need to appoint a person of "great national prestige" to head the DOD, President Truman believed that man was George C. Marshall. Marshall had retired from military service in 1947 with a 5-star rank. President Truman had previously asked him to serve as secretary of state, and Marshall had received a congressional waiver to do so. (He served from January 21, 1947, to January 20, 1949.) President Truman then asked him if he would serve as secretary of defense.[64]

Marshall agreed to serve as secretary of defense, provided his tenure would be limited to six months to a year. (He served from September 21, 1950, to September 12, 1951.) Truman immediately sent a legislative proposal to Congress. If enacted, the proposal would grant an exception to the 10-year cooling-off period to allow him to appoint Marshall as secretary of defense. After much debate—with some members of Congress arguing that the Korean crisis justified an exception and that Marshall was uniquely and

exceptionally qualified, while opponents asserted that the principle of civilian control over the military superseded all other considerations—the measure finally passed and was enacted in law.[65]
Public Law 81-788 suspended the 10-years-out-of-uniform requirement only for General Marshall's nomination. The law included a nonbinding section expressing:

> ...the intent of Congress that the authority granted by this
> Act is not to be construed as approval by the Congress of
> continuing appointment of military men to the Office of
> the Secretary of Defense in the future. It is hereby ex-
> pressed as the sense of the Congress that after General
> Marshall leaves the office... no additional appointments of
> military men to that office shall be approved.

After the legislation was enacted, President Truman submitted
Marshall's nomination to the Senate on September 18, 1950. Marshall's SASC confirmation hearing occurred the next day. The
Committee favorably reported the nomination to the Senate floor
within hours. On September 20, 1950, the Senate voted to confirm
Marshall's nomination by a vote of 52-11, with 28 senators not voting.

Future presidents appeared to take Congress at its word—it
would be many years before the matter would raise its head again.
In 2007, Representative Walter B. Jones (D-NY) introduced legislation to reduce the "cooling-off" period required before a former
military officer could be appointed defense secretary. Jones justified his proposal as "[reducing] an outdated prohibition and [en-
abling] the president to choose from a greater pool of qualified
candidates with relevant military expertise."[66] Ultimately, the provision was enacted in law, changing the time between relief from
active duty and appointment to secretary of defense to only seven
years.[67]

Then in 2017, President Trump nominated James Mattis, a retired United States Marine Corps general, to serve as secretary of defense. And in 2021, President Biden nominated Army 4-star Lloyd Austin, who had retired from active duty only five years earlier. Both nominees were within the seven-year window, and both—like Marshall—required an exception to the law to take office. Both nominations inspired public and congressional debate about how to best uphold the principle of civilian control of the military in a contemporary context, as well as the health of civil-military relations.

Both nominations followed a similar trajectory in Congress. President Trump's intent to nominate Mattis was widely known. On January 10, 2017, before Trump was inaugurated, the SASC held a hearing on civilian control of the armed forces.[68] No one questioned Mattis's competence or ability. But Senator Jack Reed (D-RI), then the Committee's ranking member, expressed concerns about the politicization of the military. Reed questioned whether granting Mattis an exception would set an undesirable precedent for future waivers. He noted that only one other waiver for secretary of defense (Marshall's) had been granted in over half a century, for good reason.

Experts Dr. Kathleen Hicks (who would become deputy secretary of defense under President Biden) and Dr. Elliot Cohen testified before the Committee. They expressed some of these same concerns. Cohen added, "There is a breadth of view and perspective in running the military and making war that is not likely to be found in someone who has spent 30 or 40 years in uniform." The witnesses wondered whether a recently retired officer serving as secretary of defense would favor one Military Service branch over another or prefer the advice of military personnel over that of the DOD civilians.

That same day, SASC Chairman John McCain introduced S. 84, a bill carefully crafted to permit President Trump to appoint Mattis (and only Mattis) as secretary of defense, notwithstanding the nominee's inability to meet the "seven-years-out-of-uniform" standard. Two days later, on January 12, the SASC held Mattis's confirmation hearing. That same afternoon, the Senate passed S. 84 by a vote of 81-17. Although Sen. Reed voted in favor of the measure, 17 Democratic senators, many of whom were members of the SASC and at least one of whom was a military veteran, voted against the bill.[69] Because such legislation requires the action of both chambers of Congress, the House also played a role in the confirmation process. It passed S. 84 the next day by a vote of 258-161. On January 20, 2017, President Trump was inaugurated and proceeded immediately to the Oval Office, where he formally nominated Mattis and signed S. 84 into law.[70] At 4:55 p.m. on Inauguration Day, the Senate confirmed Mattis as secretary of defense by 98-1, with only Senator Kirsten Gillibrand (D-NY) voting against him and then-Senator Jeff Sessions (R-AL) not voting.[71]

President-elect Joe Biden announced retired General Lloyd Austin as his nominee for secretary of defense on December 8, 2020. On January 12, 2021, the SASC—with incoming Chairman Jack Reed presiding—held a hearing with testimony by outside experts on civilian control of the armed forces. Many of the same points debated four years earlier were raised again, all against the backdrop of asking to what extent civilian control of the military might have been eroded during the Mattis years. Reed expressed the same concerns he had years earlier about the Mattis nomination. Many noted the Austin nomination brought an added dimension: the extent to which the nominee, if confirmed, might help address longstanding concerns some had raised about minority underrepresentation, particularly at senior levels of the Department of Defense.

On January 15, 2021, then-Chairman of the House Armed Services Committee, Adam Smith (D-WA), introduced H.R. 335. The waiver bill, almost a mirror of Mattis's S. 84, was carefully crafted to permit Biden to appoint Austin (and only Austin) as secretary of defense, notwithstanding his inability to meet the "seven-years-out-of-uniform" standard. SASC held a confirmation hearing for Austin on January 19, 2021. One of President Biden's first acts after inauguration was to forward Austin's nomination to the Senate. At 4:10 p.m. on January 21, 2021, the day after Biden's inauguration, H.R. 355 passed the House by a vote of 326-76. It was referred to the Senate, where it was called up and passed almost immediately by a vote of 69-27. In the House, Rep. Walter Jones voted in favor of the bill. In contrast, Rep. Mike Gallagher (R-WI) and 62 other Republicans opposed the bill. Interestingly, in the Senate, more Democrats than Republicans voted against the bill (14 Democrats; 13 Republicans). The "Nay" votes included those of veterans Tammy Duckworth (D-IL) and Tom Cotton (R-AR). A day later, on January 22, Austin was confirmed in the Senate by a vote of 93-2, with two Republicans, Sens. Josh Hawley (R-MO) and Mike Lee (R-UT), opposed and five Republicans not voting. Later that same day, President Biden signed the waiver bill into law and appointed Lloyd Austin as the first black secretary of defense in the nation's history.[72]

Perceiving a disturbing pattern in the Mattis and Austin nominations, Rep. Mike Gallagher proposed, and the NDAA for FY 2022 incorporated, a modification to the law about appointing the secretary of defense.[73] The law now bifurcates the required "cooling-off" period between a military officer's departure from active duty and appointment as secretary of defense. The appointment of a former or retired officer who last served in a grade below general or flag officer remains at seven years. But officers who last served in a general or flag officer grade must have a *10-year* break between service in uniform and appointment as secretary of defense. I take this as a clear signal Congress is intent on curtailing the trend in senior military officer nominations for the position of defense secretary. And future nominations of retired military officers will face significantly enhanced scrutiny from both houses of Congress.

The secretary of defense is not the only DOD official with an "out of uniform" requirement. A prerequisite "cooling-off period" following active military service applies to several other senior DOD officials, including the deputy secretary of defense,[74] the six under secretaries of defense,[75] the secretaries of the Military Departments,[76] and the assistant secretary of defense for special operations and low-intensity conflict (but not to any other assistant secretary of defense).[77] More recently, the NDAA for FY 2021 established the position of chief diversity officer in the Office of the Secretary of Defense[78] and a senior advisor for diversity and inclusion in the Military Departments and the Coast Guard.[79] The law expressly provided that a person may not be appointed to diversity-related positions within three years after relief from active duty as a commissioned officer.

Civilian control of the military is a fundamental principle for the United States to uphold, and this provision is an essential step in the right direction. Interestingly, General Marshall, who accepted the position as secretary of defense, did so only because of the Korean emergency and the need to restore prestige to the office. He did not believe that retired generals should serve in this position.[80] I strongly agree.

SECTION 3: Face-to-Face With Congress

7

PREPARING FOR A HEARING

This chapter discusses what nominees can expect leading up to and during their confirmation hearings. It includes strategies to set themselves up for success.

PRE-HEARING

A nominee should understand the legal description of the position for which he or she is nominated, pulled directly from Title 10 of the U.S. Code.[81] Understanding the requirements of the position differs vastly from a presumption of confirmation, which, as noted earlier, must be avoided at all costs. The nominee must also know the paperwork forwarded to the committee supporting their nomination. As discussed in Chapter Five, senators and Committee professional staff will have reviewed the paperwork, so the nominee must be prepared for questions about or references to the package.

I have always advised nominees to keep a low profile, avoid putting out public statements, and avoid taking media interviews before the hearing. (This is also DOD's position.) However, if negative stories are circulating about the nominee, this doesn't mean one stays quiet. If a nominee is taking flak, it's not sufficient to just put on his/her flak jacket and helmet. He or she may need to respond. And that decision should be coordinated carefully within the Executive Branch. Nominees should not allow any negative drag or a free-fire zone to develop in the lag time from announcing a nomination to the hearing. If it becomes apparent a campaign to attack the nominee is brewing, it should not go uncontested. If this occurs, there should be a serious discussion and decision on the timing and content of any rebuttal before the hearing, not an *ad hoc* approach.

The right person and approach are essential if a decision is made to counter attacks. In most instances, the nominee is not the best person to do this. Using a surrogate to build momentum and develop advocates for the nominee on the SASC itself will usually be necessary. The confirmation team must recruit both Senate and external supporters for this situation. For the hearing, a nominee will need advocates on the committee who can act as the "fire brigade." That way, the nominee does not have to take the brunt of the attacks and defend all positions. These advocates and surrogates need to be prepared in advance about the key issues expected to arise, the main attack lines, the key facts, and recommended counterattacks. This takes significant thought, advance preparation, and coordination.

In all cases, nominees should prepare sufficiently for the routine and tough questions they will get at the hearing. Nominees (along with their team) should create a list of "hot topics" that are likely to arise during the hearing. With former Secretaries of Defense James Mattis and Mark Esper, we compiled a list of 50 hot-topic issues that went through many iterations of fine-tuning. We refined these issues every day based on courtesy calls and external developments. Depending on the position and current events, issues can be added to the hot topic list as late as the morning of the hearing. Senators may question a nominee about events that occur up through when the chairman brings down the gavel to start the hearing.

A prime example was at a posture hearing for Acting Secretary of Defense Pat Shanahan in 2019. Sen. Jeanne Shaheen (D-NH), at the hearing, asked about a breaking news story in the *New York Times* that morning about DOD's pushback on PFOS/PFOA chemical contamination standards.[82] The question and the article caught Shanahan relatively unprepared to answer satisfactorily. As part of advance preparation, I recommend having the Sherpa and team develop a one-page fact sheet on each "hot issue" following this basic format:

<u>Possible Format for "Hot Topic" Issue Papers—**NAME OF TOPIC**</u>

Policy issue and critique: This presents how a Senator will challenge or push the nominee on an existing policy. Frame it as a tough, realistic critique (it can be drawn from lines of attack Senators on the committee have used at previous hearings). This should be summarized in two to three sentences. Maximum length here should be 100 words.

Key Facts of the Issue:
- In a bullet point format, we want to highlight the most important factual information, statistics, or background points the nominee can site for background of the subject. This information should come from <u>unclassified</u> sources, and should be available to someone outside of the Pentagon (as the nominee is).

- Examples include: size of the U.S. force; key figures about Asia's population and share of world trade; military sexual assault key statistics. (Example: "Sexual assault in the military is an enormous problem and needs to be addressed. For example, last year there were XX assaults.)

- Make sure that all facts provided in this section are DOUBLE CHECKED for accuracy. If in doubt about a "fact's" accuracy, do NOT include it.

The Current Administration Position
- Describe the DoD and Administration policy for this issue. You can quote often used POTUS, SecDef, and JCS language that are often referred to (not just rhetoric, but that speak to issues such as: Was the Sony cyber incident an attack?; Did Russia invade Ukraine?; POTUS language for the Afghan drawdown). This section is intended to frame for the nominee what the policy actually is. These are not just talking points.

- We want a total of 2-3 bullets, of about 2-3 sentences each. They should be formulated sentences- not talking points, put actual sentences.

Key Answer Points
- This is the most important section. These should be 3-5 bullets that the nominee will use to actually answer the question. These can be the "safe harbor" points the nominee can repeatedly return to.

- These bullets should be short, concise and be how the nominee would actually answer the question (as nominee, not as Secretary of Defense; not as an Administration official who has been making the policy for the past year). They need not be complete sentences.

- Remember that short and punchy is far more effective than a big, slow wind up.

MURDER BOARDS

I continue to emphatically advocate the uses of prep sessions or "murder boards." This format prepares nominees by staging a mock hearing, creating an environment and a series of staged events that are as close to reality as possible. This exposes the nominee to what is likely to occur in the hearing itself. It gives the nominee practice in navigating the many ups and downs that can occur in a few hours of testimony before a Senate committee.

Starting in 1997, when Sen. Nunn decided not to run for re-election for a fourth term, I left the Senate after 24 years to work in the private sector. At this time, I began to work pro bono on the Department of Defense Confirmation Prep Team, at the request of the Department leadership, with colleagues who were also very knowledgeable in these areas. We ran murder boards for most DOD military and civilian nominees. I, along with a handful of my colleagues, who had served as staff directors of the Senate and House Armed Services Committees, would act as the senators in the murder boards. We'd grill nominees on their qualifications, the main issues facing DOD and their positions, and questions that might arise at the hearing. The goal for these sessions was to make them more challenging than the actual hearing itself, ensuring that the nominee would be over-prepared. Failure to prepare is often why nominees do poorly during their hearings and get off to a poor start, even after confirmation.

To elaborate on the expertise of the prep team, Rhett Dawson had also served as a top official in the Reagan White House, had run a major industry association, and brought a keen understanding of legal and policy issues. Rudy DeLeon had also served as chief of staff to a secretary of defense, under secretary of the Air Force, under secretary of defense for personnel and readiness, and deputy secretary of defense. He had a deep grasp of key past and current issues. Kim Wincup had served as an assistant secretary of the Army and assistant secretary of the Air Force in the personnel and acquisition areas. He specialized in prepping nominees on some of the most controversial issues. Jonathan Rue and Irina Plaks, from my staff, were also instrumental throughout. Without their expertise and willingness to respond on short notice, our work would not have been recognized and awarded by Secretary Ash Carter.

Secretary Carter recognized the work of the Department of Defense Confirmation Prep Team on January 5, 2017. From left to right: Jonathan Rue, Rhett Dawson, Ash Carter, Arnold Punaro, Rudy DeLeon, Irina Plaks, and Kim Wincup. Rhett, Rudy, Kim, and I—all former staff directors of the HASC and SASC, as well as senior DOD officials—supported the DOD confirmation process and preparation for decades, with assistance from Jonathan and Irina.

At various times, we would add key subject matter experts, such as Roger Zakheim, former HASC general counsel; Samantha Clark, former SASC general counsel; Ann Sauer, former SASC staff director; and Michael Bayer, former House staffer, to participate on the murder boards as well. The team made all the difference.

The murder boards are grueling and intense, but if done right, they elicit every issue and provoke every controversy likely to come up at the hearing. These sessions have proven invaluable to successful nominees. For example, Secretary Gates took part in three murder boards for 3-4 hours each with us. As a result, he was over-prepared for his hearing, and his performance was stellar.

To prepare Acting Secretary of Defense Patrick Shanahan for his hearing to be secretary of defense, OSD set up an entire mock hearing room with a raised dais for us "senators." It was set up in the secretary of defense's main conference room.

I've found that, in addition to formal murder boards in which the nominee stays in character as if it was the actual hearing, informal discussion sessions help work through the toughest issues. For instance, the prep team will pose a tricky question in very general terms, and the nominee will discuss how he or she might answer. Working together, the group fine-tunes the answer with the nominee's "on the spot" input. These informal discussion sessions help the nominee think through and practice answers before the crucible of the hearing.

At these sessions, we always had one staffer who understood the administration's position, so the nominee didn't veer off course. If a nominee needs to create daylight between his or her views and the views of the administration, it is far better to know that in advance and work out a suitable compromise with administration experts. The president does not want to hear about a nominee deviating from the administration's positions on CNN or read about it in the *Washington Post*.

For the nomination of Ash Carter to be secretary of defense, we stood up a "war room," beginning right before Christmas of 2014 when his nomination was announced. The war room was operational until his confirmation vote more than two months later, in February 2015. The war room day started at 6:00 AM and never finished before 8:00 PM; we worked every weekend. We conducted four or five informal sessions on an issue like Syria, ISIL, Russia, sexual assault, and Ukraine. We identified where Secretary Carter's answers were weak and worked as a group to improve them, constructively critiquing the content of each response and Secretary Carter's delivery.

In addition, we ran two formal murder boards, each lasting many hours. Through the murder boards, we identified several areas where Carter needed to deviate from the administration position. We flagged those for senior decision-makers and worked through his answers before his hearing, ensuring there would be no surprises or breaking news from his answers.

While Ash Carter had been through three previous confirmations, he approached his preparation for secretary of defense with the seriousness and total time commitment that shined through during his hearing. He was a hallmark of our nation's most distinguished national security experts.

For Bush's nominee to be VA secretary, Dr. James Peake, we ran several murder boards. Chuck Hagel, when he was the nominee for secretary of defense, participated in one murder board. When we respectfully told him we recommended more preparation, he felt he was ready. The history of his hearing shows that additional preparation would have been helpful, especially considering how he was "ambushed" by some of his former colleagues. The point of saying this is that the type of preparation Secretary Carter and Secretary Peake underwent is vital for a cabinet-level nominee. Secretary Mattis and Secretary Esper also spent the time necessary to be well-prepared.

COURTESY CALLS

Courtesy or office calls are meetings with senators before a hearing (but only once the president formally sends the nomination to the Senate). If the nominee becomes aware of potential controversies or detonation points, courtesy calls provide an excellent opportunity to diffuse those issues in advance. Even if the issue cannot be diffused completely, raising the matter at the courtesy call may give the nominee additional insights to use at the hearing. Courtesy calls also allow nominees to listen to senators' concerns and preview questions that might be posed during the hearing. They can earn support for the nomination by making the most of goodwill based on existing relationships.

Building new connections is important if the nominee is confirmed and begins their service. Senators get to meet the nominee and start building a relationship, apprise the nominee of the policy issues of import to the Senate, and secure promises or commitments (e.g., a visit to the senator's hometown or specific program requests). A half-hour meeting where the senator and the nominee talk one-on-one is excellent preparation for the five to seven minutes of questioning in which that senator will engage with the nominee during the hearing.

A nominee should offer a courtesy call to every member of the committee of jurisdiction. The protocol is to see the chairman and ranking member first. (Even if their schedules cannot accommodate the visit, it will be noted they had first dibs). It would not bode well for the nominee if the Committee chair were to hear that a senator "just had a great meeting with a nominee" if the chair had not been previously contacted and offered the first meeting.

Two Biden Administration nominees ran afoul of this crucial tradition. At a confirmation hearing on March 15, 2023, Senator Markwayne Mullin (R-OK) noted that nobody had reached out to him on behalf of either nominee to schedule a courtesy call. He wondered whether the administration ignored him and the other new members of the SASC. He ended his remarks with, "I had this kind of unwritten rule in my office; I'm not voting for someone that didn't take the time to meet with me because I want to know who I'm voting for." This was a significant unforced error by the OSD Legislative Affairs Office that is hard to explain away other than poor coordination.

To prepare for the courtesy calls, nominees should have their list of hot topics and talking points to help focus the conversation. A one-pager on each senator is helpful. This should include the senator's background (including any military service), the issues he/she cares about and focuses on during hearings, key legislation he or she has sponsored in areas relevant to DOD and the nominee's position, and military bases and critical defense industries in his or her state.

SASC	MEMBER-SPECIFIC VIEWS	
James Inhofe (R-OK) ✓ Voted for DSD SD Nom: "I'm pleased"	• **BCA:** If the Department was held to the Budget Control Act (BCA) level for Defense, how much would that negatively affect Readiness? • **Experience:** In your DSD nomination hearing you noted: "I believe my skill set strongly complements that of Secretary Mattis... a master strategist with deep military and foreign policy experience," implying you did not have those skills. Isn't that basically still true, and shouldn't that be a concern to us? • **POTUS:** At any time have you felt as though you couldn't take a position or push back on the President because it might impact his decision to nominate you? Do you tell the President "NO"? Can you point to a specific area where you've disagreed with the President? • **Space:** Skeptical of Space Force. Isn't making NRO the Space Office a viable option? • **AFRICOM** Major Installations/Equities: Altus AFB; Vance AFB; Fort Sill; Tinker AFB; McAlester Army Ammunition Plant	**A/SD Engagements:** • 02APR19: O/C Space Force • 12MAR19: O/C Pre-Posture • 09JAN19: O/C Meet & Greet **CODELs:** • 15FEB19: Germany; Kosovo; Israel; Djibouti; Ethiopia; Burundi; Rwanda; Algeria; Spain • 24MAY19: United Kingdom; Italy; Cyprus; Jordan; Bahrain; Iraq; Ethiopia; Spain
Roger Wicker (R-MS) ✓ Voted for DSD SD Nom: "Demonstrated that he is capable of managing the needs of our armed forces and protecting our national security."	• **5G:** Eager to see the U.S. lead the way with 5G development and implementation. How is DoD leading in this area and how will you ensure other federal and commercial interest share in the 5G benefits? • **355-ship Navy:** As Chair of the Seapower Subcommittee, was vocal about the need for a national policy that codifies a 355-ship requirement and sets a course to achieve that 355 in the 2020s. Can you provide a status update? • **Sequestration:** On 2 MAY, said "Military sequestration ... would be utterly disastrous and would amount to a reversal of the progress our Armed Forces have made over the past two years." You've said very little about the BCA recently. What are you doing to help avoid this scenario? • **South Asia Strategy:** Please explain how we plan to keep up the same level of pressure in Afghanistan, while withdrawing troops. Major Installations/Equities: Keesler AFB; Columbus AFB; NAS Meridian; Naval Construction Battalion Center Gulfport; Allen C. Thompson Field ANGB (Jackson IAP); Key Field ANGB (Meridian RAP); L-3 Communications; Northrop Grumman; Lockheed Martin; United Technologies; SAIC	**A/SD Engagements:** • 14MAY19: Telecon Space Force • 24APR19: Telecon Space Force **CODELs:** • 15FEB19: Germany; France; Cyprus; Austria
Deb Fischer (R-NE) ✓ Voted for DSD SD Nom: "I've worked with him on a lot of issues, he's always gotten me information, he's always been open, we've had good conversations."	• **Nuclear Triad / Modernization:** Supports continued investment in nuclear modernization. Believes in order to maintain a safe deterrent, the triad must be maintained. • **China:** How are we countering China around the world militarily, technologically and diplomatically? • **Cyber:** At the SASC Posture hearing, asked if cyber operations, their effects and their ability to deter hostile activity is comparable to nuclear weapons. • **INF Treaty** • **Afghanistan progress:** What is the situation on the ground? How are negotiations proceeding? Major Installations/Equities: Offutt AFB (STRATCOM HQ); Northrop Grumman; Raytheon; BAE Systems; Lockheed Martin; SAIC	**A/SD Engagements:** • 02APR19: O/C Space Force **CODELs:** • 16MAR19: Warsaw, Poland; Budapest, Hungary; Kyiv, Ukraine; Brussels, Belgium

✓ Green – Positive   ○ Black – Neutral   × Red – Negative   ⭐ Army   ⭐ Air Force   ⭐ Marine Corps   ⭐ Navy   National Guard/Reserves

This is an example of a detailed summary prepared by DOD's Legislative Affairs shop on SASC senators from the 116th Congress to help prepare Secretary Shanahan for his confirmation hearing.

There are several things to remember for these office calls: first, these meetings are on the record, even if a senator says otherwise. There is no such thing as an off-the-record conversation with a senator. Second, a pleasant office call will not always translate to a pleasant hearing when the cameras roll. And with few exceptions, senators' personal offices are not cleared for classified discussions. Further, the senator may release information and/or a photo of the meeting.

Victorian courtesy also goes a long way with the SASC. Nominees should always begin the meeting by asking about a senator's interests, including family. Another good rule is to send a brief handwritten note after the meeting to thank the senator for their time. Some nominees resist what I call "kissing the Pope's ring," but humility is a welcome and essential virtue here. The nominee must genuflect as a sign of respect for the confirmation process.

Last, since the COVID-19 pandemic, some senators have conducted their office calls virtually. Be prepared for the pitfalls this may entail, such as missing body language cues and distractions. Always have a backup plan in case of technology failures.

After each courtesy call, the nominee and confirmation team must build a list of should-do action items from these meetings. These lists will remind the nominee of follow-up actions he or she must take after confirmation. In an ideal situation, the nominee has a member of the Sherpa team present with him or her during the meetings to take detailed notes. If there is an intent to create a version of the notes to "circulate" to a broader coordination group, be extremely careful what is put in writing. I always prefer a verbal debrief in the daily war room wrap-up rather than notes or emails that could fall into the wrong hands or be misinterpreted. Putting anything in an email about a private meeting with a U.S. senator is a bad idea.

After the prep work and courtesy calls, a nominee should feel ready to handle the hearing day. The week of the hearing, the nominee should stay on top of breaking news and significant issues in the media to prepare for what may be on senators' minds.

8

HEARING DAY

Congress is the world's expert on running hearings. Nominees need to keep this in mind. Congress always has the upper hand and will always get the last word. Many senators also have decades of experience, specific memories, and a host of ready facts and research that can be provided to them by their staff almost instantly during the hearing. Few witnesses can beat them, so to speak, on their own playing field. As a result, nominees should always expect the unexpected and be prepared to handle anything thrown at them. Nominees should not receive notes during their hearing or read from extensive notes. More on this later.

An informal rule in the Senate is that a nomination should be pending for two weeks before a hearing date is scheduled. According to SASC rules, the Committee must provide public notice at least seven days before the hearing. Nominees for appointment to be secretary or deputy secretary of defense invariably are subject to a solo hearing where they are the only nominee present.

The Military Departments' secretaries are also often subject to an individual hearing. Almost every other nominee, regardless of importance, will be one of a panel—several nominees considered together at the same hearing. SASC rarely intermixes civilian and military nominees on the same hearing panel. Still, there is no hard and fast rule, and panel membership can be adjusted to the circumstances.

At one SASC confirmation hearing in the latter half of the 116th Congress, President Trump's nominees for the secretary of the Navy, the deputy under secretary of defense for policy, and the chief of staff of the Air Force were considered together.[83] Nominees have no say over who they will be grouped with. While a grouping might include nominees with similar positions, the opposite could be true.

On the day of the hearing, nominees should arrive well before the start time to go over any last-minute issues, say hello to the senators and the staff, and settle in at the witness table. Nominees should avoid any trappings of power or a large entourage of DOD staffers. (The same is true during the courtesy calls. Nominees should not wander the halls of the Senate office buildings with a slew of "hangers-on" who will be caught in the inevitable photo ops that occur as they make the rounds). Arriving at the hearing in a black government suburban with a cadre of staffers can set the wrong tone. But arriving with one's family and, perhaps, one or two staffers from DOD (like the ASD for Legislative Affairs) tells a different story. It harkens back to that virtue of humility I mentioned earlier. The Committee loves seeing family at the hearings.

Every confirmation hearing in the SASC typically follows a standard sequence. The chairman of the SASC begins the hearing by making brief opening remarks and introducing each nominee in order of seniority based on the DOD position for which nominated. If desired, a member of Congress may introduce the nominee at the hearing. In rare instances, a former SASC chairman can make the introduction.

In 2017, former SASC Chairman Sam Nunn, along with former Sen. Bill Cohen (R-ME), introduced Secretary of Defense nominee James Mattis. Mattis had worked in Cohen's front office when Cohen was secretary of defense. An eminent third-party introduction is not a requirement. Still, it's nice to have, especially when it can help garner bipartisan support for the nominee.

Then the chairman will read the list of standard questions, to which all nominees must answer with a "Yes" or "No." After the nominees have responded to the standard questions, the Committee's ranking member makes brief remarks.

The chairman then invites each nominee to present an opening statement. Because the SASC limits the length of remarks to five minutes, some nominees will present a shortened version of their written opening statement. (The complete written statement will be included in the hearing record). This brief speech is like a statement of intent for the nominee's prospective job. Its primary audience (aside from the senators in the room) is the nominee's future staff and organization, if confirmed. Trust me, they are watching and evaluating the "new boss" from their staff offices in the Pentagon. They are already forming impressions, both positive and not-so-positive. Nominees should also acknowledge their families. In fact, the chairman will sometimes specifically ask the nominee to introduce them.

A question-and-answer period follows. The SASC operates under a so-called "early bird rule," where questioning alternates between senators from the respective parties in the order they arrive in the hearing room before the chairman strikes the convening gavel. Once all "early bird" senators have been recognized and completed their questions, the senators who arrived after the hearing started will question the nominee. Again, questions will alternate between senators of the majority and minority party in order of seniority. The SASC limits each senator's question-and-answer period to a length the chairman and ranking member have agreed to in advance, usually five to seven minutes. Some chairmen can be assertive about cutting a Committee member off if they have gone over their time. If a senator has more questions than fit in their round (and they do not want to just submit those as QFRs), the chairman will sometimes allow a second round after everyone else has had their turn.

Each senator is free to question any or all nominees. Senators' approaches to the panel vary widely. Sometimes, a senator uses the entirety of his or her question-and-answer period in dialogue with only one nominee, never engaging with other panel members. In other cases, the senator will ask each nominee on the panel the same question. Few questions are off-limits. Members' questions of the nominee may concern the nominee's personal background and qualifications and policy and program matters relevant to the position nominated. The question-and-answer period allows senators to clarify assertions made in a nominee's opening statement, during the nominee's courtesy call with the senator, in response to a question from another senator earlier in the hearing, in the nominee's APQs, or in another context, such as during a public speech, as quoted in the news media, or in the nominee's social media posts.

SASC members use the questioning process to impress on nominees the issues the Committee believes they should focus on once confirmed. SASC professional staff and individual senators' military legislative assistants often draft questions or talking points for members to use in questioning a nominee. It's also important nominees realize that given the press of their many duties, senators are free to come and go during the hearing. Many will leave the hearing room as soon as their question-and-answer session concludes.

The chairman and ranking member are typically present throughout the hearing. Still, some senators may not attend a particular hearing at all. All this is to be expected. Nominees should not allow themselves to be distracted by comings and goings on the dais.

HOW TO HANDLE THE HEARING:

1. Identify a minimum number of key points and themes you want to establish, and then stick to them throughout the hearing. You must balance the dual objectives of staying on message and responding to senators' questions.

This is an example of a highly detailed cheat sheet. It includes quick points about the day's hot-button issues, plus helpful reminders, such as saying, "If confirmed...."

2. Create a cheat sheet or one-pager that looks like a placemat. The military often refers to this as a "horse blanket." Do not bring a large binder or take notes passed by the team. (There is no time to leaf through pages, and trying to do so will make one look unorganized and unprepared.) Even for the most accomplished and well-prepared witnesses, I always recommend each keep a cheat sheet in front of them at the witness table. This page includes key topics and the key bullet points for answers. It can include succinct reminders, such as making eye contact with the senators, keeping answers short, and speaking slowly. General Petraeus, General Dunford, and Secretaries

Carter and Gates were some of the best witnesses I had the privilege to work with and see in action before the SASC, both during their confirmations and their many testimonies. They were always well-prepared, and they smartly took advantage of using cheat sheets with key information at their fingertips. Any witness can freeze into a 1,000-yard stare (or sit looking like a "deer in the headlights"). Having a cheat sheet can help to stay on track.

3. Some good phrases to repeat often: "If confirmed..." and "Working with this Committee, I will...."

4. If you don't know the answer to a question, an excellent response is: "Senator, I'm not as up to speed on this issue as I would like. I want to give you the thoughtful answer you deserve. Let me get back to you." Do not make up answers or guess.

5. You will probably get repeat questions because senators frequently come and go from the hearing. Questions should be answered each time as if they were being asked for the first time. Under no circumstances should a nominee say, "As I told Senator ____ earlier."

6. Do not answer questions not asked of you. At a hearing in 2017, a nominee to be assistant secretary of defense for health affairs, Dean Winslow, was asked about the perpetrator of a mass shooting's record of domestic violence in the military. He answered the question, then added that he probably should not say it, but he did not believe anyone in the U.S. should be able to buy an AR-15.[84] This did not go over well with the Republican-controlled Senate or the Republican administration nominating him. He withdrew his nomination shortly after when it became clear he could not receive majority support. He likely would have been confirmed if he had not made that additional comment that extended beyond the question's scope.

7. Avoid taking the bait on hypothetical questions. Senators often try to draw out nominees to gauge their views with hypothetical (usually politically charged) scenarios; it's best to sidestep those questions. This might be a good time to use the tactic of answering the question you want rather than the question you got. I suggest something like this. "Senator, I agree every situation must be reviewed based on its unique facts, but I believe that...." and bring it back to one of the key themes you want to make.

8. Use the 80/20 rule. Allow the senators to talk 80% of the time, and you talk 20%. The Committee does not usually hold a hearing for someone they do not want to confirm. Your goal is to convince the senators you are qualified and to get confirmed. This is not an oversight hearing or a forum for making policy. There will be plenty of time for that later.

9. Look at the forest, not the trees. Stay high-level with your answers instead of getting into too much detail. This can be tough for some nominees who want to appear knowledgeable and responsive. But sometimes, the best approach is to "dumb down" your answers.

10. Make points in layman's language, and avoid the heavy use of acronyms typical in DOD.

11. Do not obfuscate. Be straightforward and tell the truth; it will come out regardless.

12. Do not get hung up on getting 100 "yes" votes. You only need a majority in Committee and in the Senate.

13. Over-prepare, especially on hot-button issues.

14. If a senator's question includes a reference that the two of you met earlier during a courtesy call, this provides an excellent opportunity to recall some aspect of the discussion during that meeting. I suggest this response: "Senator, I appreciated the opportunity to meet with you and hear your views on...."

Confirmation Do's & Don'ts

DO's:

1. Short opening statements – 6 minutes or less
2. This is a confirmation hearing – not an oversight hearing or policy hearing
3. Keep powder dry on issues you need to dodge such as: home state issues, unresolved administration internal food fights -
   - *"Senator, while having some familiarity with this issue, I am not sufficiently informed to give you the thoughtful answer you deserve."*
     OR
   - *"Senator, while the Department is working this issue, it is not in my area. I am not fully informed to provide the thoughtful answer you deserve."* Can add: *"If confirmed, look forward to addressing it at a future date."*
4. *"If confirmed"* – use this term liberally when answering questions about what you might do
5. Follow **80/20** rule – "Senators talk 80% of the time; nominee answers 20% of the time"
6. Have a mental or paper "cheat sheet" with the 3-5 points you want to make on the major issues: defense budget, military ops, Iraq, Afghanistan, world hot spots, acquisition process, DoD management, your acquisition record, personnel costs, future threats, chain of command, industry, interrogation/torture, cyber, guard and reserve, contractors, "hot rocks" from courtesy calls

DON'Ts:

1. Don't make any news or create any new policies
2. This is a confirmation hearing – not an oversight hearing or policy hearing
3. Don't play favorites – if you tilt to one Senator you may be crossing another
4. No notes from staff during the hearing
5. Civilian nominees do not have "personal views"
6. Don't correct Senators
7. Don't say "As I told Senator 'X'"
8. Don't say more than once –
   - *"That's a good question…"*
     OR
   - *"I'm glad you asked that question"*

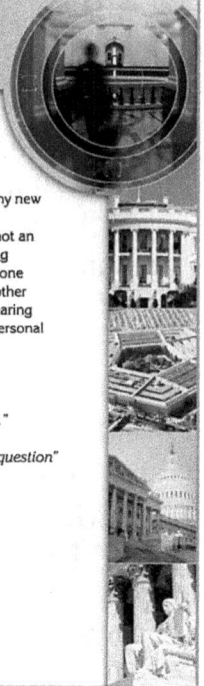

This quick guide contains advice honed over many years of preparing nominees.

OBSERVATIONS ABOUT THE PROCESS

Over many years of helping nominees through their confirmation processes, I have seen many successful and unsuccessful ones. Key features distinguishing these two groups are illustrated well in the different approaches of two secretaries of defense: Ash Carter and Chuck Hagel, both for whom I have the greatest respect.

I'll begin with Hagel, who I've mentioned in his decision to limit the additional preparation recommended for such a high-profile nomination. Hagel was a former Republican senator from Nebraska nominated in 2013 by a Democratic president to be secretary of defense. He had a solid combat record from Vietnam and was a successful businessman and political leader. His confirmation unfolded like that of a federal judge up for lifetime tenure, not like a national security nominee. We saw the same unfair tactics:

smear the individual's reputation with distortions, manufacture problems, quote the nominee out of context, and engage well-funded lobbying groups to spread disinformation and advocate against the nominee. It was the first time in my decades on Capitol Hill that I saw paid opposition ads against a secretary of defense nominee.

Many critical missteps were made:

1. The Obama Administration allowed opponents to operate in a free-fire zone for three weeks without a single rebuttal or defense of Hagel's nomination or long history of distinguished public service, including in combat.
2. The administration did not accept the obvious indications and warning intelligence as serious. It did not discern that what they observed was qualitatively different from far more minor controversies that had dogged past nominees.
3. His confirmation team had several inexperienced individuals, and there was poor coordination between those helping him from his outside office and the administration team.
4. The process allowed "too many cooks in the kitchen."
5. The White House and Pentagon lacked experience dealing with a national security nomination that began unfolding like a politically-charged judicial nomination.
6. Hagel was ambushed by some of his former Senate colleagues, and this should have been anticipated.

A lack of preparation is pervasive among former members of Congress. They believe—mistakenly—that their previous or existing relationships with the senators before whom they will testify will ensure they'll sail through confirmation. Examining the confirmation hearings of Les Aspin and Hagel, both appeared before a Democratic Senate and were nominees of Democratic administrations. Neither was ready for the antagonistic grilling they received from their colleagues. They assumed their colleagues would treat them with the deference they had become accustomed to as senior members of Congress. They were dead wrong. While both got confirmed, neither had a long or very successful tenure as secretary of defense. (Former Congressman Pete Geren, nominated as secretary of the Army, provided a distinct contrast. He prepared extensively and excelled in his confirmation hearing.)

Hagel's nomination was in such disarray that Senate Majority Leader Harry Reid (D-NV) could not secure the votes for cloture on the first vote. Senators were vocal about their disenchantment with Hagel's hearing performance. After his nomination languished for over two weeks on the Senate floor, Hagel was ultimately confirmed. More of Hagel's fellow senators voted no on his nomination than on any other secretary of defense nominee before or after (except for the Senate's rejection of John Tower's nomination during President George H. W. Bush's administration). Before Hagel's 41 no votes, the most no votes for a secretary of defense nominee was two. Regardless, Hagel was successful as the defense secretary. His tenure was marked especially by his care for and commitment to the welfare of our enlisted troops.

By comparison, Ash Carter's nomination to be secretary of defense in 2015, also under President Obama, went much more smoothly. Carter prepared considerably; his team and organizational structure were top-notch. A key decision that proved important to his success was maintaining independence from the Pentagon regarding physical location and his personal team of highly experienced confirmation and transition experts from the outside. Carter worked out of the Eisenhower Executive Office Building. Still, he positioned key members of his Sherpa team (including me) in the Pentagon to enable strong coordination. Every member of Carter's transition team was specifically cleared as a

Special Government Employee (SGE) for the duration of the transition.

Unfortunately, the Pentagon's official team was tough to work with due to the lead from the Hagel front office. During Carter's confirmation, Steve Hedger, who had worked on the Hill, served as the Senate's White House liaison. Hedger's strong ties to top staff leadership in the White House proved a critical advantage. He knew the issues and the hot spots. He knew how to expedite reviews in the National Security Council and elsewhere across the interagency. Every nominee should hope to have a liaison like Hedger on their side—he was that effective. Carter also included Eric Fanning, then the undersecretary of the Air Force, and Maj. Gen. Ron Lewis, then the head of Army Public Affairs, on his confirmation team. Both men had volunteered for the duty and worked the long, hard hours required to ensure Carter's success.

Fanning would become Carter's chief of staff, and Lewis, his senior military assistant. However, Carter hewed strictly to the rules. He took no action that could be construed as presuming the outcome of the confirmation process. Carter also asked me to be the interface with the SASC Staff Director, Chris Brose and then-SASC Chairman John McCain, due to my previous SASC role and my relationship with them. These factors, coupled with Carter's serious and diligent approach to preparing for the hearing, led to as smooth a process as we could have hoped for. Carter sailed through confirmation on a solid bipartisan vote of 93-5.

9

CONFIRMATION FAST TRACK, SLOW TRACK, OR NO TRACK

Regarding confirmations, I have named the SASC's three main tracks: the fast track, the slow track, and the no track. The fast track is the routine pace, with the SASC proceeding through its deliberative and thorough process as described in earlier chapters. The slow track manifests in the Committee prolonging the process because of concerns with the nominee, extending the time usually required to schedule a nominee's hearing date or to vote the nominee out of Committee, for example. Sometimes, the slow track is intentional by the Committee. In others, administration or nominee delays in responding to Committee requests for more information or a meeting to address concerns prompts the SASC to downshift the nomination into slow. For no track nominations, the Committee knows early in the process that the nominee is not likely to be approved, so it goes through the motions—usually without enthusiasm—often to the point of scheduling and holding a hearing, with no intent ever to confirm the nominee. This chapter will cover situations that slow the process and common detonation points that can derail a nominee—either temporarily or permanently. This chapter will outline ways to avoid those detonation points and keep the three-phased confirmation process of nomination, confirmation, and appointment on the fast track.

WHAT SLOWS THE PROCESS WITHIN THE ADMINISTRATION?

The roots of delay in the nomination, confirmation, and appointment processes begin within the administration, well before the president decides who to nominate for a particular position.

Although the SASC and Senate do not confirm every person nom-inated, the Senate cannot confirm a nomination it does not have. Presidents can sometimes be slow to send nominations to the Sen-ate for advice and consent. The Committee and Senate do not re-spond to the White House's issuance of an intent to nominate, with the minimal exception of a small set of cabinet-level national security nominees who are identified between the November elec-tion of a new president and Inauguration Day in January of the following year.

While it can be said the Senate and the Committee appreciate the signal a nomination is on the way, in 99% of cases, they will not act until a nomination is formally transmitted to the Senate. Sometimes, the intent to nominate announcement precedes the nomination's transmission to the Senate by mere days; in others, months elapse between the "intent" and the formal nomination. The short-hand explanation is the Senate does not confirm some nominees they *have*, so you can be darn sure they don't confirm nominees they don't have.

Several factors can help to explain why an administration might be slow to select a nominee formally. For example, compet-ing spheres of influence inside the administration might jockey for the nomination of their own favorite sons or daughters. This was common during the Trump Administration when White House politicals—all with direct access to the president—often had dif-ferent preferences and priorities in selecting nominees than the DOD itself.

Reportedly, the Trump White House announced its intent to nominate Vincent Viola to be secretary of the Army without ever having shared that information with or seeking the views of in-coming Secretary of Defense Jim Mattis. Sources said Mattis be-came angry and threatened to quit if the transition team tried to insert any future DOD appointee into the Pentagon without his involvement. Vice President-elect Mike Pence had to intervene and smooth things over with Mattis.

From that point forward, Mattis appropriately demanded a role in vetting and selecting every DOD nominee. The administration generally honored this demand throughout Mattis's tenure in office. Of course, going forward, White House coordination with Mattis and his consideration of candidates inevitably added additional time to the vetting and nomination process.

In other circumstances, behind-the-scenes political machinations have little to do with the delay. Instead, it's because each administration begins with an almost "blank slate." The policies and standard operating procedures documenting the nomination processes of the well-seasoned prior administration have been swept up and carried away. The experience and expertise honed by the Presidential Personnel Office (PPO) of the outgoing administration are also often lost, as the new administration, comprised almost entirely of new people—many of whom have never worked at such a high level of government—takes the stage.

The sheer volume of national security-related nominations and appointments, particularly at an administration's beginning, is daunting. DOD alone has 65 PAS positions. Hundreds of additional presidential appointees who will occupy senior DOD positions that do not require Senate confirmation also must be identified, screened, and approved by the White House. The incoming PPO has a very tough job with staffing the political apparatus of the Department of Defense—not to mention the entire federal government—so most nominations move more slowly and deliberately until the PPO comes up to speed.

The extensive, complicated, and confusing paperwork and lengthy background investigations required of and for nominees are often a source of delay. Many civilian nominees have never held a high-level government position for which a security clearance or the in-depth cataloging and review of assets, debts, and organizational affiliations for conflicts of interest is required. In administrations that defer publicizing and submitting a nomination to the Senate until all hurdles associated with an FBI background investigation and OGE ethics review have been cleared, it can appear to the Department and the public that nothing is happening.

Not unexpectedly, many nominees have a storied background and a diversified portfolio of financial holdings, including investment funds and other illiquid investments, deferred compensation, equity compensation, and the expectations of large year-end bonuses from a corporate employer. Clearing these hurdles requires the focused attention of several government agencies and the nominee's full and constant participation. Most notably in the ethics domain, a nominee may not know until months have gone by that a conflict of interest has been identified, and mitigating that conflict could require the creation of a blind trust or diversified trust, divestiture of stock or other assets, or resignation from a position in a closely held family business or other organization.

As with Vincent Viola, a nominee may decide—after months of negotiation—that the welfare of his or her family, business, or portfolio outweighs taking the actions required to get through the confirmation process. That this process is rife with delay should surprise no one.

WHAT DELAYS THE SENATE?

After a nomination is submitted to the Senate, a nominee can face a host of additional detonation points that inevitably slow the process and, sometimes, bring it to a complete halt. The vast number of DOD and national security positions that go through the SASC and Senate at the beginning of an administration create a backlog in the Committee, much like at the White House. Such delays usually have one of two primary causes: information of concern about the nominee is revealed, or the nomination is complex and requires a more extensive review. The latter problem almost always puts the nomination further toward the back of the line during the SASC's triage process. The former can foil a nomination, forcing the administration to go back to square one for the position at issue, sometimes grinding the entire system to a halt.

The 1993 "Nannygate" scandal is a perfect example of this phenomenon. On the day before Christmas 1992, President Clinton announced corporate lawyer Zoë Baird would be his nominee to be attorney general. If confirmed, she would be the first woman in the position.

On January 14, 1993, the *New York Times* broke the story that Baird and her husband, a Yale Law School professor, had broken federal law by employing two people who had illegally immigrated from Peru on their household staff.[85] It became public that the couple had failed to pay Social Security taxes for the workers—the so-called "Nanny Tax"—until earlier that same month, when they made a lump sum payment to quickly and quietly resolve the matter with the Internal Revenue Service. Baird had informed transition officials about the matter early on. Still, they had not paid it much attention, deeming it a common "technical" violation.[86]

The Senate Judiciary Committee moved forward with Baird's confirmation hearing on January 19, 1993. President Clinton formally submitted her nomination a day later, hours after he took the oath of office as the 42nd President of the United States. The nomination would stand for only six more days. Public opinion swelled against Baird. Particularly galling to most was the idea that the nominee to be the nation's chief law enforcement officer—who would oversee the Immigration and Naturalization Service—

seemed to have no compunction about knowingly breaking the law herself.

Things went from bad to worse when the public discovered Baird and her husband had an annual income of $600,000—a significant amount—but had paid the undocumented immigrants far less than minimum wage. Congressional support for Baird's nomination plummeted, and on January 26, 1993, President Clinton withdrew her nomination.

The following month, the administration floated the name of Federal Judge Kimba Wood for the attorney general job. Within days, it was discovered that she, too, had employed an illegal immigrant to look after her child. Wood had done so when such hiring was legal and paid the worker's Social Security taxes. But the damage was done, and Wood was immediately removed from consideration. Shortly after that, the nomination process for positions across the federal government ground to a halt when the Clinton Administration announced its intent to examine the household help hiring practices of the 1,000+ candidates for presidential appointments pending consideration.

Baird and Wood may have been the first casualties of "Nannygate," but they would not be the last. In 2001, President George W. Bush selected Linda Chavez as secretary of labor, the first Latina ever nominated to a cabinet-level position. She withdrew from consideration when the media published allegations she had employed an illegal immigrant a decade earlier. George W. Bush ran into trouble again with the nomination of Bernard Kerik in 2004. Slated to head the Department of Homeland Security, Kerik's nomination derailed when he was cited for unpaid taxes on domestic workers of unclear immigration status.

The *New York Times* sagely observed in an op-ed examining the lessons learned from the Baird nomination: "There must be a natural fit between a job and the ethics, background, finances, and talents of a nominee."[87] In all subsequent administrations, PPO has carefully scrutinized any potential nominee's domestic help record. There is no shortage of examples in which disconnects between a nominee and the position requirements for which they were nominated proved fatal.

President Trump's nomination of Cully Stimson as Navy general counsel in 2017 offers one such cautionary tale. Over the years, Stimson, a longtime fellow at the conservative Heritage Foundation, had written extensively on controversial topics, such as military sexual assault, gender integration, and transgender rights.[88] Earlier in his career and well before his nomination, Stimson, a private citizen, wrote an article that negatively reflected on Sen. Kirsten Gillibrand (D-NY), a member of the SASC, and her signature legislation that would remove authority from military commanders on issues of sexual assault.[89]

As Navy general counsel, Stimson would play a significant role in overseeing the prevention of and response to sexual assault in the Navy and Marine Corps. At his confirmation hearing on July 12, 2017, Stimson was required to respond to direct questions from Sen. Gillibrand about this year-old article—an exceedingly uncomfortable situation. Stimson also ran into headwinds with the Committee for what he called a "boneheaded" statement a decade earlier.

In January 2007, at the height of the global war on terror, Stimson—the Pentagon official in charge of military detainees—said during a radio interview he was "dismayed" top U.S. law firms were representing Guantanamo prisoners. He urged corporate clients to cut ties with such firms. Stimson published a written apology in the *Washington Post* but resigned a month later amid the controversy.

At Stimson's confirmation hearing, Ranking Member Jack Reed (D-RI) noted that the U.S. military fights to protect "the right for unpopular people to have a fair hearing in court," implying that Stimson's comments ran afoul of attorney ethics and the ethos of the armed forces. Although Stimson apologized and was later voted out of Committee, his nomination hit a brick wall on the Senate floor, and he was never confirmed.

Similarly, in February 2020, David Patterson was forced to withdraw his nomination to be deputy under secretary of defense for personnel and readiness, the second highest personnel official in the Pentagon, after it was revealed he had co-written a controversial op-ed blaming immigrants' failure to assimilate for mass murders in the United States.[90]

The administration had to return to the drawing board in the Stimson and Patterson cases. It took the Trump Administration over two years to nominate another Navy General Counsel, Robert Sander, who only served for the last year of the administration. The deputy under secretary's position remained vacant until well into the Biden Administration. Administrations that fail to thoroughly vet a nominee or, more commonly, lack the political acumen to discern when a nominee's past words and actions render them a "bad fit" for a high-level position in the present day should not be surprised when those nominations fail.

Nominations of former legislators, tagged with their record of votes taken and legislation sponsored, can prove vulnerable. When word spread in 2017 that Trump considered Tennessee state Senator Mark Green his second choice to be secretary of the Army, opponents pointed to his long list of anti-LGBTQ votes and legislation. Green's nomination didn't have a chance, and he withdrew his name from further consideration. Green later successfully ran for Congress and now serves as chairman of the House Committee on Homeland Security.

Recall my earlier mention about the extensive, complicated, and confusing paperwork confronting a potential nominee as he or she is first being screened by the White House. Once a nomination is forwarded to the Senate and referred to the SASC, the nominee is presented with another stack of paperwork to complete: questionnaires, tax returns, and Advance Policy Questions. Each of these has an essential purpose, to be sure, and a nominee's submissions are carefully reviewed and considered as part of the Committee's process. But there is little transferability between White House paperwork and SASC paperwork. Only the nominee's OGE 278e financial disclosure form is common to both vetting processes. So much of both information collection processes has yet to be automated.

Most times, delivery of completed paperwork continues by human couriers. These processes are antiquated and almost certainly prolong the nomination timeline. A nomination with incomplete paperwork or otherwise lacking in some essential element will be downshifted to the slow track and held in abeyance by the Committee while the request for correction, supplementation, or update is passed from the Committee to the Department of Defense and finally to the nominee. The nominee's answer is passed back through the Department to the Committee, at which point work on the nomination may resume.

The Committee's review of nominees' tax filings is another source of delay. For example, complicated tax histories that include audits, liens, or large charitable deductions take longer to review and clear, particularly if the Joint Committee on Taxation experts are called to consult on a nettlesome return. If an irregularity in the nominee's taxes is discovered, SASC work on the nomination will halt until the nominee files a corrected return. Finally, should a nominee's responses to the Committee questionnaire, APQs, or questions posed by SASC senators during the confirmation hearing prove concerning or controversial, a delay is almost inescapable. The nomination can quickly switch from the slow track to the no track. Recall the case of Trump Administration nominee Dean Winslow's unnecessary comment about gun control policy during his confirmation hearing to be the assistant secretary of defense for health affairs. Even though the matter had nothing to do with the position for which he had been nominated, he was never confirmed.

Once a nomination is favorably reported out of Committee to the Senate floor, it is subject to further delay in the full Senate. Any senator can place a hold on any nominee for any reason, from the merit or suitability of the nominee to reasons entirely unrelated to the nomination. The nominee effectively becomes hostage to the satisfaction of the holding senator's demands. For example, On June 17, 1999, the Senate Foreign Relations Committee began day one of a three-day confirmation hearing for Richard Holbrooke, who had been nominated by President Clinton to be the United States ambassador to the United Nations.

When Holbrooke's nomination had first been floated almost a year prior, it kicked off an investigation into allegations that Holbrooke had violated criminal post-government employment laws. Although the Justice Department found no "willful violation" on Holbrooke's part, he agreed to pay a $5,000 civil fine to settle, allowing his nomination to proceed.

Throughout Holbrooke's confirmation hearing, senators examined and reexamined the allegations against Holbrooke. But on June 30, 1999, Holbrooke's nomination was favorably voted out of Committee to the Senate floor. Then three senators, Charles Grassley (R-IA), Trent Lott (R-MS), and Mitch McConnell (R-KY), secretly put a hold on Holbrooke's nomination, preventing the full Senate from voting to confirm him. None of the holding senators were concerned about Holbrooke's qualifications for the United

Nations position. Instead, they hoped to use Clinton's commitment to the nomination as political leverage to achieve concessions in matters unrelated to Holbrooke or the United Nations.

Grassley was the first to publicly acknowledge his hold, put in place because he did not like how the State Department treated one of its whistle-blowers. Lott and McConnell wanted Clinton to appoint Bradley A. Smith, a law professor at Capital University in Columbus, Ohio, to the Federal Election Commission. Over the ensuing weeks, the Lott and McConnell holds faded with little fanfare (although Clinton eventually would nominate Smith, and Smith would be confirmed to the FEC in May 2000).

Grassley withdrew his hold on August 3, 1999, in an open letter to President Clinton stating he would lift his hold on Holbrooke and vote to confirm him, but only because he had transferred the hold to three new State Department nominees.

Two days later, on August 5, 1999, Holbrooke was confirmed. The absurdity prompted esteemed *Washington Post* political columnist Richard Cohen to coin a new word: "Holbrooked," meaning to put a hold on a person "for reasons that have nothing to do with them."[91]

The United States Senate has long been considered one of the world's greatest deliberative bodies. Whether one agrees with that view, Senate Rules protect the minority party and ensure that neither Democrats nor Republicans do anything without full and open debate. Without unanimous consent to take up a matter, Senate Rules require that 60 of 100 senators agree to vote to end debate on a matter and move forward to a vote on the underlying legislation. This same threshold used to apply to Senate votes to end debate on a nomination.

In the Senate's fancy language, ending debate and moving to vote on a matter is called invoking cloture. Actually passing legislation or confirming nominees has always required only 51 votes. Still, because of the Senate's procedural rules, it took 60 votes to invoke cloture and get to the actual vote.

In 2013, Majority Leader Harry Reid (D-NV) invoked the "nuclear option" during the Obama Administration. Because he could not get 60 votes when the minority blocked nominees, he changed Senate Rules to require only a simple majority to invoke cloture on most nominees (except for U.S. Supreme Court nominees). In 2017, Majority Leader Mitch McConnell (R-KY) returned the favor and changed the rules for Supreme Court nominees during the Trump Administration. Invoking cloture on a nomination now requires only a simple majority of senators present and voting. Given the polarization of national politics and that, in recent years, the majority has controlled the Senate by only a razor-thin margin, the confirmation of a nominee by unanimous consent has apparently (and most unfortunately) fallen out of vogue.

Holds on the Senate floor and use of the "full-up" cloture process to confirm even low-level nominees have become the norm. Even though fewer votes are required to invoke cloture, the process requires a lengthy investment of Senate floor time, sometimes as long as two consecutive weeks. Senate floor time is the chamber's most precious commodity for which many issues compete.

In many cases, majority leaders are loath to allocate the floor time required just to process a DOD nomination—even for a president in their party. DOD nominations lose out to high-profile, "must pass" legislation or the nominations of federal judges and move to the back of the line, where they wait... and wait... and wait. A lengthy delay in DOD nominations is no longer the exception but the norm.

A nomination can be held up because of simple bad timing. The Senate is in session for only about 160 days each year, with extended recesses around federal holidays and a month-long recess in August. When the Senate is in session, senators usually spend weekends in their home states and report to the Senate in the late afternoon or early evening each Monday for a so-called "bed check" vote. They work the following Tuesday through Thursday, then leave Washington for their home state each Thursday night or Friday morning, only to repeat the process the following week. Further, the many weeks the SASC dedicates to generating and marking up the annual National Defense Authorization Act are also a terrible time for the Committee to focus on nominations. Nominations caught up on the wrong side of Senate work periods or the NDAA cycle can suffer lengthy delays.

The end of an administration can also be challenging to move a nomination through the Senate, even for a president whose party also controls the chamber. Ten Trump defense nominees fell victim to this unfortunate timing. Shon Manasco, John Whitley, and Michele Pearce were nominated—all on May 4, 2020—to be under secretary of the Air Force, director of Cost Assessment and Program Evaluation, and Army general counsel, respectively. All three were eminently qualified for their positions.

They appeared before the SASC on August 4, 2020, for a confirmation hearing and were reported out of Committee on September 15. There, the nominations stalled. They sat on the Senate Executive Calendar for the rest of 2020 while the Trump Administration and Majority Leader McConnell singularly prioritized the confirmation of federal judges, most requiring the lengthy cloture process. Not one of the three was confirmed, despite their qualifications. (The Senate had already confirmed Whitley and Manasco for other DOD positions earlier in the administration.) In fact, because of the focus on confirming judicial nominees, not a single Trump defense nominee was confirmed by the Senate after June 2020.

Inspector general (IG) nominations, like Jason Abend's, present a unique case. Unlike most political appointees who serve only for the duration of a presidential administration, the DOD IG and most other statutory IGs are appointed to serve indefinitely, subject to termination only by the president. In the last full year of the Trump presidency, many Democrats and some Republicans rebuked Trump for a string of what they considered politically motivated and self-serving IG removals. On April 3, 2020, Trump removed Intelligence Community Inspector General Michael Atkinson; on April 7, Department of Defense Acting Inspector General Glenn Fine was replaced; on May 1, Trump allegedly fired Health and Human Services Acting Inspector General Christi Grimm.

On May 15 and 17, respectively, Trump terminated State Department Inspector General Steve Linick and downgraded Department of Transportation Acting Inspector General Mitch Behm.[92] In the midst of this turmoil, on April 6, 2020, Trump nominated Abend as DOD IG. But the writing was on the wall: SASC could not muster the votes necessary to favorably report Abend out of Committee. Democrats were not inclined to install a Republican, Trump-era DOD IG, knowing that Abend would continue into the next administration if they did. Under that scenario, new President Biden would be required to fire Abend and appoint a preferable successor. Abend's removal would expose Biden to the same political condemnations that Trump endured. Abend's nomination never moved forward.

The time required for the Senate to act on nominations—both in the SASC and the full Senate—has steadily increased since the Kennedy Administration. The White House Transition Project collects and analyzes nomination and confirmation data for each administration. This data illustrates slowdowns across the board, not simply for defense nominees.

TOTAL NOMINATIONS

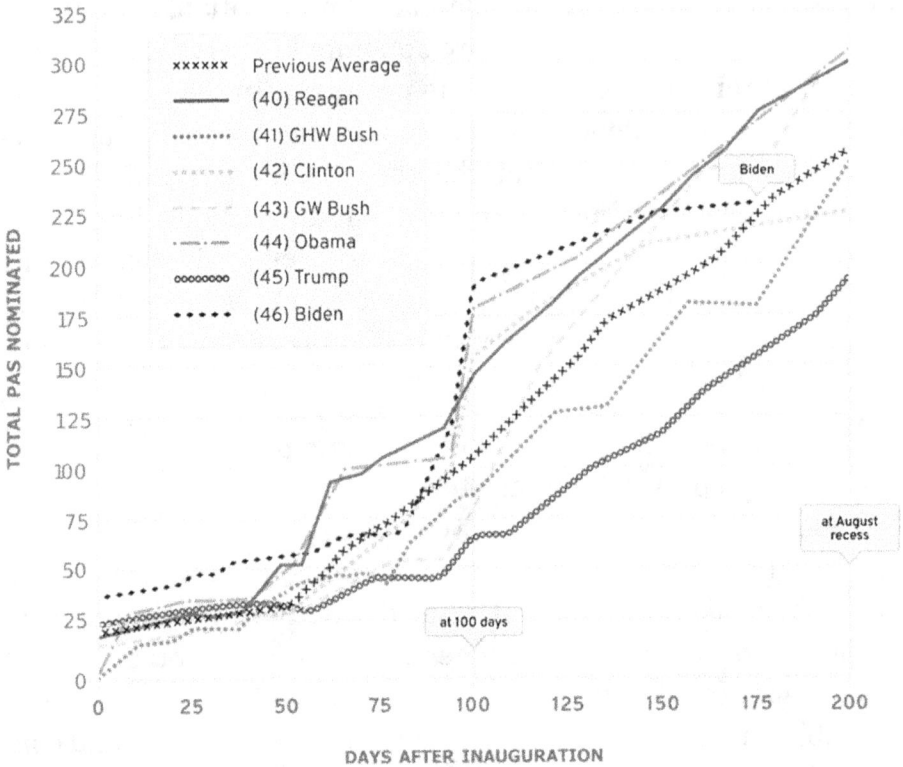

Source: The White House Transition Project
https://whitehousetransitionproject.org/appointments/

The above chart shows that the Biden Administration was on pace with the historical average for the number of nominations made in the first 200 days of a presidential administration. In contrast, the following chart reveals that Biden was far below the historical average in the number of confirmations completed in the first 180 days of his administration.

TOTAL CONFIRMED

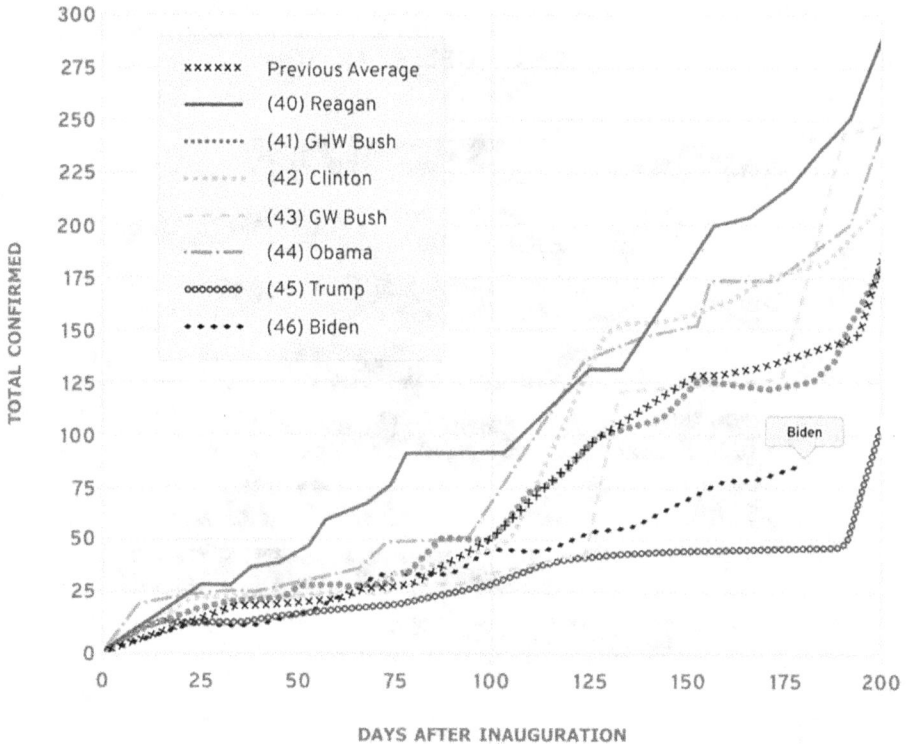

Legend:
- xxxxxx Previous Average
- ———— (40) Reagan
- ·········· (41) GHW Bush
- ········· (42) Clinton
- – – – – (43) GW Bush
- ·—·—·— (44) Obama
- ooooooo (45) Trump
- • • • • (46) Biden

Y-axis: TOTAL CONFIRMED (0 to 300)
X-axis: DAYS AFTER INAUGURATION (0 to 200)

Biden

Source: The White House Transition Project
https://whitehousetransitionproject.org/appointments/

The White House Transition Project also analyzed how long it took administrations to nominate and the Senate to confirm all PAS officials. We can ascertain that Biden is faster than the historical average in time to nominate but has faced significant slowdowns in Senate processing in both time spent in Committee and time on the Senate Executive Calendar. In the Reagan Administration, a nomination spent an average of 24 days in the Senate, from submission by the president to final confirmation. Senate processing times see-sawed between 30 and 39 days across the four presidential administrations that followed, before spiking to 54 days in the Trump Administration, then jumping again to 61 days in the Biden Administration.

PACE OF DELIBERATIONS

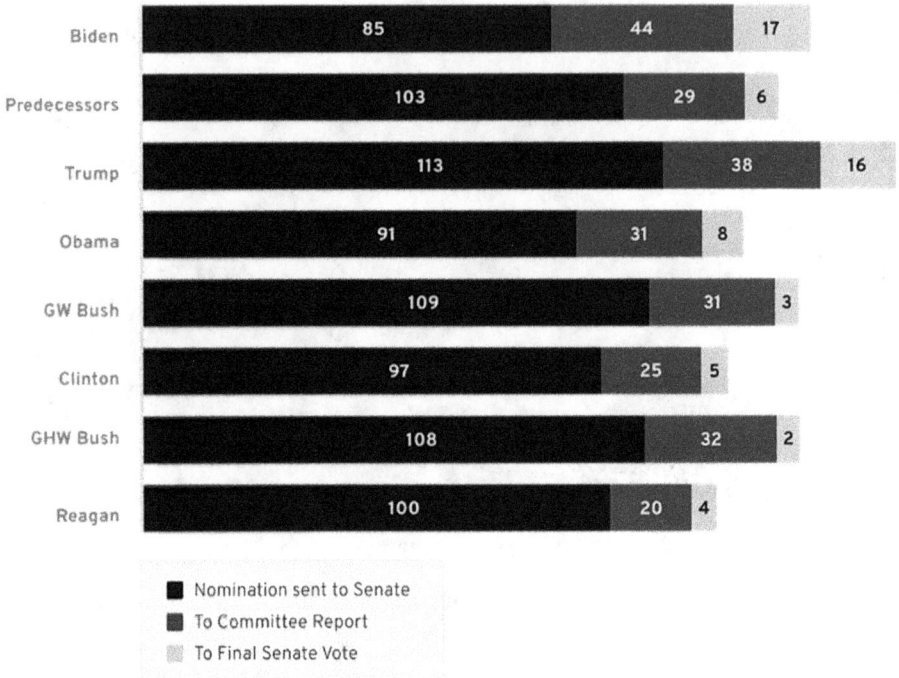

Administration	Nomination sent to Senate	To Committee Report	To Final Senate Vote
Biden	85	44	17
Predecessors	103	29	6
Trump	113	38	16
Obama	91	31	8
GW Bush	109	31	3
Clinton	97	25	5
GHW Bush	108	32	2
Reagan	100	20	4

■ Nomination sent to Senate
■ To Committee Report
▨ To Final Senate Vote

Note: Biden administration numbers reflect the first 180 days of the administration
Source: The White House Transition Project https://whitehousetransitionproject.org/appointments/

Looking at the last two administrations in particular, there has been an increase in the average time defense nominees specifically spend in Committee and on the Senate Executive Calendar:

Administration	Days in SASC	Days on Exec Calendar	Total Days in Senate
Biden (up to Jan. 2023)	74	68	142
Trump (total admin)	59	42	101

Throughout President Trump's term, a nominee spent an average of 59 days in the SASC and 42 on the Senate floor before being confirmed, totaling 101 days. In the first half of the Biden Administration (January 2021-January 2023), nominees spent 74 days on average in the SASC, followed by an additional 68 days on the Senate floor, for a total of 142 days—close to 5 months. By any measure, SASC and Senate processing times have increased significantly over the years.

AVERAGE MONTHS TO CONFIRM TOP DEFENSE OFFICIALS
(below SecDef)

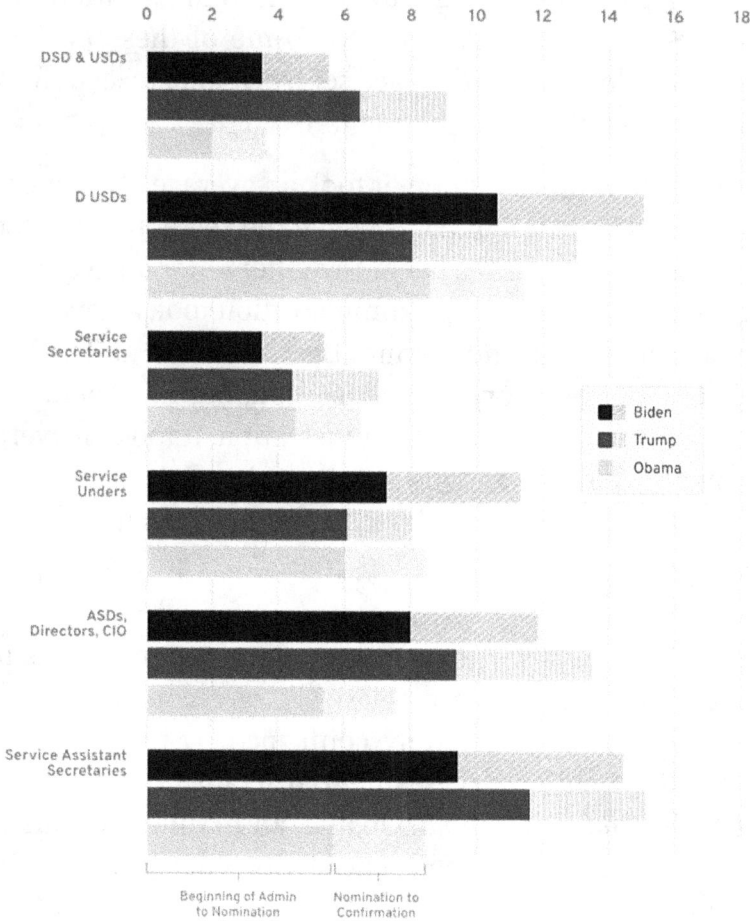

The previous chart compares the average number of months required to nominate and confirm the initial tranche of defense nominees below the level of the secretary of defense (i.e., the deputy secretary of defense, the under secretaries and assistant secretaries of defense, other senior DOD personnel, and the assistant secretaries of the Military Departments) in the three most recent presidential administrations.[93]

Overall, the Trump Administration took significantly longer than the Obama Administration in making nominations and securing confirmations of top defense positions (below the secretary of defense). In its first two years, the Biden Administration's pace shows improvement over Trump's for some of these positions. Still, it remains slower than the pace set by Obama (except for the secretaries of the Military Departments).

In the Obama Administration, it took an average of 5.3 months to nominate all DOD PAS officials below the secretary of defense and an additional 2.4 months to confirm them—for an average total of 7.7 months.[94] The Trump Administration took an average of 7.5 months to nominate and 3.4 months to confirm all DOD PAS officials below the secretary of defense, totaling 10.9 months. In the first two years of the Biden Administration, it took an average of 7 months to nominate and 3.5 months to confirm all DOD PAS officials below the secretary of defense, totaling 10.5 months.

WITHDRAWALS

Although the president's withdrawal of a nomination attracts media attention, withdrawals are relatively rare compared to the number of nominees successfully confirmed by the Senate. An analysis by the Center for Presidential Transition found that throughout the George W. Bush, Obama, and Trump Administrations, only four percent, or 335 nominations out of over 9,500, were withdrawn.[95] As of March 2023, President Biden has withdrawn only 24 of his over 600 nominations—a rate commensurate with his predecessors.[96]

The Center for Presidential Transition undertook to identify the most common reasons underpinning the withdrawal of a nomination.

WHY NOMINATIONS ARE WITHDRAWN

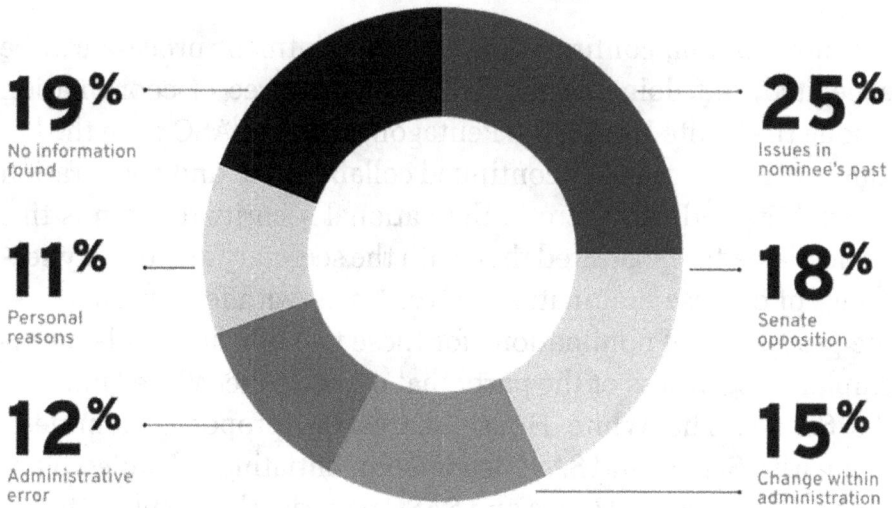

19%
No information found

25%
Issues in nominee's past

11%
Personal reasons

18%
Senate opposition

12%
Administrative error

15%
Change within administration

Source: Center for Presidential Transition analysis of Congress.gov from 2001 to 2020

Nominations are most commonly withdrawn because of an issue in a nominee's past like the "Nannygate" cases discussed earlier. The next most common reason is Senate opposition to the nominee. This may be based on political or policy differences, information newly discovered, or political factors unrelated to the nominee at issue. Another 27% of nominations are withdrawn for reasons internal to the administration, such as an agency reorganization that eliminates the position to which an individual is nominated or an error in paperwork. An additional 11% of nominations are withdrawn at the nominee's request. Most often, this is for personal reasons, ranging from family issues to challenges posed by the increasing time required to complete the confirmation process. Nominees polled cited their frustrations with a process that can sometimes take years. These delays place undue burdens on nominees and present a significant deterrent that frightens others away from public service altogether.

AN EXPEDITED PROCESS FOR SECRETARY AND DEPUTY SECRETARY OF DEFENSE NOMINEES

The nomination, confirmation, and appointment process can be expedited, but doing so requires a high degree of coordination among the White House, the Pentagon, and the SASC from the beginning. It also requires continued collaboration and cooperation through its end. Nowhere in the national security domain is this principle better illustrated than with the secretary and deputy secretary of defense nominations. Over time—with few exceptions—the processing of nominations for these two officials has been exemplary, regardless of the party that controls the White House or the Senate. The White House shares the proposed nominee's name with Senate and SASC leadership, initiating a detailed planning process. White House and SASC paperwork are submitted to and worked on by the nominee simultaneously.

The notional date of the confirmation hearing is set, all well before the president formally submits the nomination to the Senate. Typically, the White House shares any concerns derived from the presumptive nominee's background investigation or ethics compliance review in real-time as they are identified. The Senate and SASC openly discuss with the Pentagon and the White House any concerns or controversies identified through their own vetting processes, from constituent reports, or in political discussions among senators. To the greatest degree practicable, the parties work together to develop strategies to resolve such matters.

As the nominee completes essential paperwork, it is expedited through DOD and White House reviews and transmitted to the Senate on a rolling basis. The Committee immediately reviews such paperwork on receipt. It does not wait in abeyance pending receipt of all required submissions.

The nominee undergoes a robust hearing preparation process led by a specially selected Sherpa who, optimally, is an expert and experienced in Executive and Legislative Branch procedures. The Sherpa regularly updates both the White House and Senate staff on progress and emerging issues and works with officials in both branches of government to resolve them.

The hearing occurs, and SASC stands ready to report the nominee to the Senate floor, often on the same day. The Senate party leaders have agreed on the timing and nature of action on the Senate floor. Once reported out of Committee, the nomination is almost always expedited for confirmation and appointed by the president shortly after.

The following two charts show the timelines for the deputy secretary of defense and secretary of defense nominations, from the day the nominee's name was first floated (the trial balloon) to final confirmation. The record shows almost every deputy secretary of defense and secretary of defense nominee was processed through and confirmed by the Senate within a month of nomination.

The data plainly illustrates that the White House, DOD, and the Senate can move through the constitutional process quickly and efficiently, when necessary, and when the process is coordinated and prioritized by all. Sadly, this expedited process is not currently used for the rest of DOD's PAS officials. Addressing these steadily increasing confirmation timelines should be a major priority for Congress and the Executive Branch.

DepSecDef	Nomination	Hearing	Confirmation
Carlucci*	Jan. 22, 1981	Jan. 13	Feb. 3
Thayer	Dec. 7, 1982	Dec. 14	Dec. 16
Taft	Jan. 23, 1984	Jan. 24	Feb. 2
Atwood*	Mar. 17, 1989	Apr. 5	Apr. 19
Perry*	Feb. 24, 1993	Feb. 25	Mar. 5
Deutch	Feb. 22, 1994	Mar. 10	Mar. 10
White	May 9, 1995	Jun. 13	Jun. 21
Hamre	Jul. 15, 1997	Jul. 24	Jul. 24
de Leon	Mar. 7, 2000	Mar. 21	Mar. 29
Wolfowitz*	Feb. 15, 2001	Feb. 27	Feb. 28
England	Apr. 7, 2005	Apr. 19	Apr. 6, 2006**
Lynn*	Jan. 20, 2009	Jan. 15	Feb. 11
Carter	Aug. 2, 2011	Sept. 13	Sept. 23
Work	Feb. 10, 2014	Feb. 25	Apr. 30
Shanahan*	Jun. 7, 2017	Jun. 20	Jul. 18
Norquist	Jul. 23, 2019	Jul. 24	Jul. 30
Hicks*	Jan. 20, 2021	Feb. 2	Feb. 8

* Nominated at beginning of new presidential administration
** England was held up in the Senate and was recess appointed by President Bush on January 4, 2006

CONFIRMATION FAST TRACK, SLOW TRACK, OR NO TRACK

SecDef	Trial Balloon	Announcement	Nomination	Hearing	Confirmation
Weinberger*		Dec. 11	Jan. 20	Jan. 6	Jan. 20
Carlucci		Nov. 2	Nov. 5	Nov. 12	Nov. 20
Cheney**		Mar. 10	Mar. 14	Mar. 14	Mar. 17
Aspin*		Dec. 22	Jan. 20	Jan. 7	Jan. 20
Perry		Jan. 17	Jan. 26	Feb. 2	Feb. 3
Cohen		Dec. 5	Jan. 7	Jan. 22	Jan. 22
Rumsfeld*		Dec. 28	Jan. 20	Jan. 11	Jan. 20
Gates		Nov. 9	Dec. 4	Dec. 5	Dec. 6
Panetta	Apr. 7	Apr. 27	May 26	Jun. 9	Jun. 21
Hagel	Dec. 12	Jan. 7	Jan. 22	Jan. 31	Feb. 26
Carter	Dec. 2	Dec. 5	Jan. 7	Feb. 4	Feb. 12
Mattis*	Dec. 1	Dec. 6	Jan. 20	Jan. 12	Jan. 20
Esper	Jun. 18	Jun. 21	Jul. 15	Jul. 16	Jul. 23
Austin*	Dec. 7	Dec. 9	Jan. 20	Jan. 19	Jan. 22

* Nominated at beginning of new presidential administration
** Cheney was nominated at the beginning of the Bush administration after John Tower's nomination was not approved

SECTION 4: Military Nominations and Confirmations

10

THE SASC TOUCHSTONE

This section comprising Chapters 10-14 is intended as a standalone guide for military personnel (and others interested) to better understand the nomination and confirmation process for military promotions. Accordingly, there is some overlap between these chapters and previous chapters on the civilian nomination and confirmation process.

INTRODUCTION

In 2023, almost 216,500 commissioned officers were on active duty[97] in the Army, Navy, Marine Corps, Air Force, and Space Force, combined with almost 123,500 commissioned officers[98] in the Military Services' reserve components. Each year, the Senate Armed Services Committee (SASC) considers the nominations of approximately 50,000 commissioned officers for promotion to or federal recognition in the next higher grade and for appointment to statutory roles and positions of importance and responsibility in the armed forces.[99]

The role of the Senate in confirming military officer appointments, promotions, and federal recognition stems directly from the U.S. Constitution, just as for the civilian nominations discussed in Chapter One. Article II, §2, Clause 1 of the U.S. Constitution provides that the president "shall nominate, and by and with the Advice and Consent of the Senate, shall appoint Ambassadors, other Public Ministers and Counsels, Judges of the Supreme Court, and all other Officers of the United States, whose appointments are not otherwise provided for, and which shall be established by law...." Clause 2 states, "but the Congress may by

Law vest the Appointment of such inferior Officers, as they think proper, in the President alone, in the Courts of Law, or in the Heads of Departments."

Military commissioned officers are considered "Other Officers of the United States."[100] Invoking the constitutional prerogative of Article II, §2, Clause Two, Congress enacted laws granting the president the authority to make certain original military appointments[101] and to promote and federally recognize certain commissioned officers while retaining the requirement that others be Senate-confirmed.[102] The president subsequently delegated his authority to the secretary of defense via Executive Order.[103] Accordingly, officer appointments, promotions, and federal recognition actions are approved by the secretary of defense or the president and confirmed by the Senate.

Senate confirmation is required for the promotion and appointment of all active-duty officers to grades O-4 (major or lieutenant commander) and above (including to general and flag officer grades) and for the federal recognition and other appointments of reserve component officers to the grades of O-6 (colonel or captain) and above (including general and flag officer grades). The three-phase process of nomination by the president, confirmation by the Senate, and appointment by the president or his designee also applies to these officers. In any month, the president nominates, and the SASC considers between several hundred and several thousand military officers for Senate confirmation.[104]

Historically, the SASC has held confirmation hearings only for general and flag officers nominated to certain key 4-star positions: the five Military Service chiefs, the chief of the National Guard Bureau,[105] the chairman and vice chairman of the Joint Chiefs of Staff, and the 11 combatant commanders. During the conflict in Afghanistan, the commander of forces there also received a hearing. Most of these positions turn over every four years. Still, a few—particularly combatant commanders—change out on a 2- to 3-year cycle.

Although most officers other than those listed above are confirmed without a hearing, it is the Committee's prerogative to require that *any military officer* appear before the Committee for a confirmation hearing. Under several past chairmen, the SASC held confirmation hearings for positions of particular significance to Military Service members and their families, including the Military Service personnel chiefs (e.g., Air Force A-1, Army G-1) and medical leaders (i.e., the surgeons general). These hearings underscored to both the nominee and members of the military community of all ranks that the SASC was keenly interested in and exercised dynamic oversight of military personnel and family policy matters and the quality of the military health care benefit.

Past SASC chairmen, Senator Nunn foremost among them, also attached importance to holding a confirmation hearing for the Navy officer nominated to be dual-hatted as the director of the Naval Nuclear Propulsion Program in the Department of the Navy and deputy administrator for the Office of Naval Reactors in the Department of Energy's National Nuclear Security Administration —a 4-star appointment. This is the position Admiral Hyman Rickover, considered the father of the nuclear Navy, held for decades. Rickover was a flag officer for 30 years and served on active duty for 63 years—a length of service never equaled by anyone else. Because of this officer's responsibility for critical national security aspects of the U.S. nuclear energy program and, given that, if confirmed, the officer would be appointed to an eight-year term, the SASC was fully engaged in assessing the nominee's technical background and experience, as well as his judgment and temperament.[106] However, the current incumbent of this position, Admiral James Caldwell, was confirmed in 2015 without a hearing.

General Norman Schwarzkopf, USA, Commander of the U.S. Central Command during Operation Desert Shield-Desert Storm, prepares to testify before the Senate Armed Services Committee (SASC) in 1991. Schwarzkopf had to be confirmed by the Senate to be commander of U.S. Central Command. In addition, the SASC requires combatant commanders to testify at least annually on the posture of their commands. From the left: SASC Staff Director Arnold Punaro, Chairman Senator Sam Nunn, General Schwarzkopf, and Committee Counsel Rick DeBobes.

In addition, although the National Security Advisor (who also serves as head of the National Security Council) is appointed by the president and *not* subject to confirmation by the Senate, several past presidents have nominated military officers to that position: in 1987, George H. W. Bush nominated sitting Lieutenant General Colin Powell to the role, and in 2017, Donald Trump nominated Lieutenant General H. R. McMaster.

In each case, the general officer concerned elected to remain on active duty while so serving. Each officer was required to appear before the SASC for a confirmation hearing as part and parcel of his appointment to a new position of "trust and responsibility" and reappointment in the 3-star grade associated with the National Security Advisor's role.[107] Several other presidents appointed a senior retired military officer as their National Security Advisor. Namely President Obama's appointment of retired

Marine General Jim Jones and President Trump's short-lived appointment of retired Army 3-star Mike Flynn to the position. No confirmation hearing was required or conducted for them because each officer was retired and in civilian status at the time of the appointment.

There are many myths about how the SASC deals with military nominations, but these "myths" are neither accurate nor show an understanding of the constitutional responsibilities of the Senate and the Committee. Although many military officers perceive the confirmation process as opaque, most military nominations are not as challenging as the civilian nominations discussed previously. This is because of the level of deference the SASC and the Senate afford the military officer promotion process, anchored in a series of prescriptive statutes created and shaped by Congress over many years.

One wonders how the Senate comes to bipartisan agreement on the confirmation of hundreds, if not thousands, of military officers each month and as many as 50,000 military nominations each year when it seems unable to agree on much else and so many of the president's civilian nominations languish.

The bipartisan consensus on military nominees seriously eroded when, in February 2023, Senator Tommy Tuberville (R-AL) placed a hold on hundreds of general and flag officer promotions because of the Biden Administration's policy on reimbursing service members for travel related to abortion services. While Tuberville is personally opposed to abortion, he publicly justified his hold by asserting that the new DOD policy runs contra to the longstanding Hyde Amendment–a legislative provision barring the use of federal funds to pay for abortion, except to save the life of the woman, or if the pregnancy arises from incest or rape.

Sen. Tuberville claimed that in deviating from Hyde, DOD improperly substituted its own judgment for that of Congress and usurped the prerogatives of the Legislative Branch, in which the Constitution vests the lawmaking function.

When Sen. Tuberville's hold had been in place for over eight months, and neither he nor DOD showed any sign of relenting, DOD mounted a significant campaign to inform the public and the Senate of the disastrous effect this hold was having on national security. Sen. Tuberville countered by asserting that "these [are] promotions that the majority leader can bring to the floor at any time" (referring to the ability of the Senate to consider and confirm each nomination individually, through the "full-up" cloture and recorded vote process).

The Congressional Research Service calculated that it would take over 700 hours of Senate floor time to confirm the 300 nominees on hold at that time. That meant the Senate would need to spend several months working on nothing but those confirmations just to get through the backlog. Despite the impracticality of such a solution, more importantly, it risked politicizing the sacrosanct military promotions system. As seen with the politicization of federal judges' confirmations, opening that pandora's box leads to further issues.

Because Tuberville's hold was going to preclude General C.Q. Brown from becoming chairman of the Joint Chiefs on Oct. 1, 2023, the Senate majority leader did use the cloture process (on Sept. 20, 2023) to confirm him. He also used the cloture process to have General Randy George (Chief of Staff of the Army), General Eric Smith (Commandant of the Marine Corps), General David Allvin (Chief of Staff of the Air Force), Admiral Lisa Franchetti (Chief of Naval Operations), and Lt. Gen. Christopher Mahoney (Assistant Commandant of the Marine Corps) confirmed.[108]

SENATORS APPROACH THEIR ROLE WITH GREAT SERIOUSNESS

Tuberville's unprecedented hold notwithstanding, most military nominations move, like clockwork, through the advice and consent process and ultimately to Senate confirmation. Senators take seriously their constitutional duty to review and provide advice and consent on military nominations, even for military nominations that, at first blush, appear to be a "shoo-in." Senators view their role as ensuring military leaders at all levels reflect the professional competence and values essential to the important positions they will hold in our nation's armed forces. In a 1966 letter to Senator Carl Hayden (D-AZ), Senator Richard Russell, a Georgia Democrat who served as SASC chairman from 1951 to 1969 and for whom the Russell Senate Office Building is named, defended the SASC precedent of carefully scrutinizing military nominations, stating, "[y]ou will probably recall... where a motion picture actor named James Stewart was denied promotion for failure to accumulate the necessary points."

The best illustration of the SASC's purposeful approach to military nominations is the Committee's deliberate and sustained focus on officers involved in the Tailhook scandal. The September 1991 Tailhook convention, held in Las Vegas, Nevada, has gone down in history as a drunken free-for-all, in which a "gauntlet" of Navy and Marine Corps aviators sexually assaulted as many as 83 women and seven men, or otherwise engaged in "improper and indecent" conduct in so-called "hospitality suites" hosted by various military units. News of the disgraceful affair—attended by many a Navy flag officer and senior civilian appointee—exploded in the media a month later. Senator John McCain (R-AZ), a member of the SASC, immediately took to the Senate floor to castigate the Navy and call for a high-level investigation. When the Naval Investigative Service released its investigation in April 1992, Senator Sam Nunn (D-GA), then-SASC chairman, flanked by Senators

John Glenn (D-OH), Barbara Boxer (D-CA), and Pat Schroeder (D-CO), publicly expressed his dismay at the limited scope of the investigation, which had failed to inquire into the role of squadron commanders who had sponsored the "hospitality suites" in which much of the misconduct had occurred, or the actions of the 35 flag officers who had attended the event.

Senator Glenn was vocal about his concerns. Glenn and McCain were the chair and ranking member of the SASC personnel subcommittee, and both were combat naval aviators. Glenn and McCain requested Chairman Nunn and Ranking Member John Warner (R-VA) place all Navy and Marine nominations on hold until a full investigation was completed and any individual attending Tailhook be "cleared" before the SASC considered their nomination. Nunn and Warner agreed with this approach.

Shortly after that, on May 27, 1992, SASC froze all pending Navy and Marine Corps officer promotions until the DOD provided the Committee a list of every officer who had misbehaved at Tailhook. This was consistent with the SASC requirement developed during the Reagan Administration to require the Pentagon to submit any adverse information on a military nominee. The Committee required every promotion package submitted to the SASC for confirmation to include a letter—signed at the level of an assistant secretary of defense—stating whether each nominated officer had been questioned about or "identified as potentially implicated in the Tailhook incident or in any coverup, failure to cooperate or interference with the Tailhook investigation." As to any nominee connected with Tailhook, DOD was required to provide the officer's complete investigative and disciplinary files for Committee review.

Motivated by a desire to ensure officers who had engaged in Tailhook misdeeds or misled investigators were not rewarded with promotion to the next higher grade, by July 1996, the SASC had painstakingly reviewed the promotion recommendations for 39 Tailhook-linked officers, ultimately approving 31 of them while rejecting eight.

Not even Admiral Frank Kelso, who had attended Tailhook as chief of Naval Operations, was spared. In February 1994, Kelso announced his intent to retire from the Navy two months early, asserting he had become a "lightning rod" for criticism over the Navy's handling of Tailhook. Although no longer required in the present day, in 1994, the retirement of an officer in a 3- or 4-star grade required Senate "confirmation."[109] The Senate hotly debated whether Kelso should be permitted to retire as a 4-star admiral or be downgraded to rear admiral (upper half), a 2-star grade.

Some argued that testimony and other evidence showed Kelso had been aware of the lewd behavior at the Tailhook convention, had done nothing to stop it, and later lied about events to a military judge presiding over the trial of three junior officers accused of sexual assault and obstruction of justice. Others asserted Kelso had been lax in integrating women into the Navy. Kelso vehemently disputed these assertions, but the Committee was unsure. Chairman Nunn required Secretary of Defense Bill Perry, Secretary of the Navy John Dalton, and Chairman of the Joint Chiefs John Shalikashvili to testify before the SASC to support Kelso's retirement at the 4-star grade before recommending it to the Senate. With DOD support, the Senate voted 54-43 to allow Kelso to keep his four stars, and he retired on April 30, 1994.

As the years went by, the SASC continued to carefully parse the promotion recommendation for any officer known to have attended Tailhook '91. In a few cases, the secretary of the Navy removed an officer's name from the promotion list rather than subject the officer and the Navy to anticipated SASC pushback. Most of those implicated in Tailhook never made it to the Senate. The Senate confirmed most nominees, and those from the Navy and

USMC were treated fairly, as over 35,000 Navy and Marine Corps nominations were approved in this period. The SASC's process during this time was meticulous, thorough, and discerning—requiring enhanced review of only those nominees who had attended the convention, a stark contrast to the Navy's internal procedures, which treated every Naval and Marine officer—regardless of their actual attendance at Tailhook—with suspicion.

I know at least one 4-star admiral who was unfairly treated by Senate members and DOD leadership. In April 1994, President Clinton nominated the sitting Vice Chief of Naval Operations, Admiral Stan Arthur, as commander of U.S. Pacific Command. Arthur, an aviator, had flown hundreds of combat missions in Vietnam and was the senior naval commander during the Persian Gulf War. He was highly regarded and well qualified for this new position of "importance and responsibility."

The ink was barely dry on the Senate clerk's referral of the Arthur nomination to the SASC when I was notified Ranking Member Warner had placed a "hold" on Arthur's nomination "in support of opposition from Senator David Durenberger" (R-MN). Durenberger was not a member of the Committee but had reached out to Senator Warner for help. This was a very unusual development. I learned Senator Durenberger's concern stemmed from Arthur's determination that officers at a Navy flight school had correctly dismissed a female Ensign from helicopter training. The Ensign, Durenberger's constituent, alleged she had been flunked out in retaliation for bringing harassment charges against one of her instructors a year earlier.

All agreed the Ensign had been harassed; her instructor was verbally reprimanded and later left the service. But Arthur concluded the Ensign's problems in flight school resulted from her subpar performance rather than any retaliation by other instructors. The Navy and Defense Department inspectors general agreed with this. Complaining the Navy refused to respond to his direct inquiries, Senator Durenberger threatened to hold Arthur's confirmation until he received the information he sought.

Additionally, Senator Bob Smith (R-NH) showed he was not keen on Arthur based on his lack of support for POW-MIA efforts in Vietnam. Finally, some of the SASC staff heard Arthur did not meet military weight standards—an assertion not based in fact.

At the outset, the Committee was unaware the new Chief of Naval Operations, Admiral Mike Boorda, did not support Arthur, primarily because Arthur had been chosen by Boorda's predecessor, Admiral Frank Kelso. We would learn the Chairman of the Joint Chiefs, General John Shalikashvili, also preferred another officer for the Pacific Command job. Arthur himself thought I was supporting a hold on his nomination, allegedly because my position in the Marine Corps reserve made me privy to perceptions by several Marine general officers that Arthur had been unsupportive of key Corps initiatives that required Navy approval. This, too, had no basis in fact.

Arthur's nomination stalled. Finally, I hosted a meeting in my office where Secretary of the Navy John Dalton, Admiral Boorda, Chairman Nunn, and Ranking Member Warner participated. Senator McCain, a powerful supporter of Admiral Arthur, attended at Senator Nunn's invitation. I should note that General Shalikashvili asked for a private conference with me before this meeting. Of course, I honored the general's request, and when we met, he asked for my best estimate of how long it would take the Senate to confirm Arthur. I replied I was confident Arthur would be confirmed. Still, it could take several months, given the issues swirling around the nomination. General Shalikashvili responded he "didn't think he could wait that long," which was the end of the conversation.

In the meeting with Chairman Nunn and the others, Secretary Dalton advised he intended to have the president withdraw Arthur's nomination, partly because the Navy did not want to become ensnared in yet another sexual harassment controversy in the wake of Tailhook. Senator Nunn pushed back hard—calling the plan to pull Arthur's nomination a "serious mistake"—and urged Dalton to reconsider. McCain supported Senator Nunn's position. But Admiral Boorda said it was "time to move on," and the Navy had identified a better candidate.

On July 1, 1994, shortly after our meeting, the president withdrew Arthur's nomination and immediately submitted the name of Vice Admiral Richard Macke for the position. Macke was then serving as the director of Shalikashvili's Joint Staff. Macke was confirmed to be commander of U.S. Pacific Command in record time, slightly over two weeks later, but he didn't last long. He was relieved of his command in November 1995, hours after making inappropriate remarks to reporters about the case of U.S. sailors and a Marine accused of kidnapping, beating, and raping a 12-year-old Japanese girl. He later retired as a 2-star rear admiral upon discovery he had engaged in an extramarital affair with a female officer in his chain of command.

The day after Arthur's nomination was pulled, Senator Daniel Inouye (D-HI) criticized the Navy for the decision. He stated, "Have we come to this—where facts no longer matter, where appearances and imagery rule, where symbolism and symbolic value drive out realism and truth? We were appalled by the Navy's Tailhook scandal. But we must stop this cycle of character assassinations by insinuation."[110]

Senator Nunn, too, was very concerned about how unfairly Admiral Arthur had been treated. In a lengthy letter to the Pentagon, he concluded all concerns would have been resolved in Arthur's favor, and Arthur would have been confirmed easily. Even

Admiral Boorda would later state that failing to support Arthur's nomination was the biggest mistake he had ever made. In short, the Department should never have withdrawn Arthur's nomination. In contrast to Macke, Arthur would serve out his tour as vice chief of Naval Operations with honor, retiring with all four stars to his name.

To this day, Senate scrutiny of the leadership record of senior military officers remains vigorous. In March 2003, during SASC hearings on the sexual assault scandal at the U.S. Air Force Academy, Senator John Warner noted the situation "demand(s) a deliberate critical examination and appropriate measure of accountability when a command fails in some key aspect of its mission, particularly when personnel charged to a commander's care have been harmed."[111] In the following years, the SASC would undertake an extensive review of the promotion nominations of military officers at all levels who were perceived to have acted inappropriately or used poor judgment in exercising convening authority in sexual assault cases.

The practice began with Lieutenant General Susan Helms—a highly decorated female Air Force officer and NASA astronaut—nominated to be vice commander of the Air Force Space Command. SASC Senator Claire McCaskill (D-MO) ultimately put a permanent hold on Helms's nomination when it came to light that, against the advice of her military lawyers, Helms had set aside a court-martial panel's conviction of an Air Force captain on charges of aggravated sexual assault. Ultimately, the nomination was withdrawn, and Helms retired. But over the years, the Committee has declined to confirm several officers found to have maintained a hostile command climate, who failed to take action in response to a report of sexual assault, sexual harassment, or other crime, or who failed to provide requisite victim services or treat victims with dignity and respect.

Looking back, I recall many situations where the Senate and the SASC used the military confirmation process to educate the Executive Branch about the Senate's unique role in the constitutional "advice and consent" process. I am reminded of General Mike Dugan, nominated by President Bush in April 1990 to be chief of staff of the Air Force on the retirement of General Larry Welch. The secretary of defense at the time was Dick Cheney, and Don Rice was secretary of the Air Force.

General Dugan came to my office in the Russell Senate Office Building for a standard pre-hearing review of his nomination paperwork, Advance Policy Questions, and other materials. Several other Air Force officers were with General Dugan, including Major General Brett Dula, the Air Force legislative liaison. Everything proceeded as usual until I mentioned to General Dugan the SASC had not yet received all the required paperwork, namely his financial disclosure filings.

General Dugan said I was incorrect and he had submitted all the paperwork required. Whenever I met with a nominee, I made sure I had the most recent update from our Nominations Clerk, Marie Dickinson. She maintained meticulous records of what we had and had not received for each nomination. I asked Marie to come back to my office. In front of General Dugan, I asked her whether we had received all of his financial disclosure forms. Marie verified we had not received all the required forms. Incredulous, Dugan accused us of having misplaced his paperwork. Dugan turned to Major General Dula and said something like: "[b]ecause we certainly turned in all the paperwork, did we not, General Dula?"

As expected, Dula replied, "Yes, sir... every bit of the SASC paperwork was turned in." I then turned to Marie and asked her to please retrieve Dugan's nomination file for my review. She readily brought it to me. Opening the file, I immediately discerned the

issue. Dugan had submitted the Executive Branch financial disclosure paperwork but failed to complete a SASC form, which required additional information. I explained the situation to General Dugan, and he, again, pushed back, asserting the form he had
submitted sufficed to satisfy the Committee requirement.

I stood up from my desk and crossed the office to my bookcase.
I located and pulled out one of my "go-to" references, a book titled
The Constitution and What it Means. I began leafing through the
book, deliberately making quite a show of my search. Finally, General Dugan barked in exasperation, "What exactly are you looking
for?" I replied, "General, I'm looking for that provision in the Constitution stating that you, as an Executive Branch nominee, can
decide how the Senate confirmation process works. And how we,
as a separate Legislative Branch, should best do our jobs. Since I
am not finding this information anywhere, this meeting is over.
Your hearing is canceled until you meet the Senate requirements."

I knew that a report of our meeting would quickly make its way
to Air Force Secretary Rice, so I resolved to speak with Senator
Nunn immediately. I called my minority counterpart, told him
what had happened, and that I was heading to Senator Nunn's office. We walked across the hall together to ask Ranking Member
Warner to join us. We briefed Senator Warner as we walked to the
Dirksen Building, where Senator Nunn kept his personal office.
We were immediately admitted to see Senator Nunn, who supported our approach. Senator Warner commented that in his
meeting with Dugan, the general had come across as one of the
most arrogant people he had ever met. As the four of us spoke together, Senator Nunn's executive secretary, Rose Johnson, entered the room to announce, "Air Force Secretary Don Rice is on
the phone." Senator Nunn took the call with us in the room. On
our end, we could hear only: "He did what? Don, let me check with
Arnold and see what the situation is. If he said the hearing is

canceled, it's canceled for now, and we will get back to you once I am fully updated."

After the call, we agreed to not reschedule the hearing immediately but would let General Dugan cool his heels for about a week. We also decided not to tell the Air Force for a day or so. Later that afternoon, General Dula came to my office with the additional financial information the SASC required of Dugan in hand. Dula said, "I guess we can schedule the hearing now." I replied I would get with Chairman Nunn before letting Dula know "since we are concerned about General Dugan's suitability to be chief of staff of the Air Force." I hoped that comment might get back to General Dugan and spark some self-reflection on his part. After letting the Air Force "stew" for a few days, we scheduled General Dugan's hearing. He was confirmed by unanimous consent of the Senate on June 22, 1990.

Interestingly enough, Dugan lasted only 79 days as Air Force chief. Secretary of Defense Dick Cheney, who had warned Dugan previously about speaking with journalists because he was "loose-lipped," fired him because he had shown "poor judgment [in making comments to reporters] at a sensitive time." Dugan was replaced by Merrill McPeak and retired from the Air Force, effective January 1, 1991; his arrogance had gotten the best of him.

11

MILITARY NOMINATIONS ARE
GENERALLY NOT POLITICAL MATTERS

Senators on both sides of the aisle recognize military confirmations are generally not political matters. A failure to timely confirm officers will unduly delay their promotions and eligibility for increased pay and benefits associated with advancement to a higher grade. Also, delay for delay's sake impedes officer rotations to key military command and staff positions and adversely affects not only the officers involved but the welfare of their families. In line with this approach, the SASC staff takes great pains to ensure the military confirmation process is timely and efficient, mindful that each nomination is significant to the individual officer and the Military Service involved.

That's not to say Committee priorities never enter the picture. Past Committee chairmen and ranking members have leveraged White House and DOD commitment to a particular nominee or the need for an expeditious confirmation to prompt other desired and relevant actions by the administration or DOD. Chairman Nunn, in particular, used the confirmation process—both as a scalpel and a baseball bat—to advance Armed Services Committee legitimate priorities.

One provision of the Goldwater-Nichols Department of Defense Reorganization Act of 1986 changed the chairman of the Joint Chiefs of Staff's (CJCS) statutory tour from one four-year to two two-year terms. This change allowed a new president to select a new chairman in whom the president had personal trust and confidence, given it was almost impossible to remove and replace a senior military officer incumbent before the completion of his tour. Colin Powell was the first CJCS affected by the new law. Because it is germane to my point here and involves General Powell, one of the most well-respected military officers in modern history, I'll retell a narrative I first detailed in my book *On War and Politics.*

Arnold Punaro visits with Chairman of the Joint Chiefs of Staff General Colin Powell, USA, as Powell was completing his second two-year tour as chairman in September 1993. Punaro served as staff director of the SASC during Powell's Senate confirmations and two tours as chairman.

Powell was chairman during the Gulf War and was widely popular, so it seemed unthinkable he wouldn't be tapped for a second term. No one was surprised when, in late June 1991, the Committee received Powell's nomination for reappointment as chairman. Senator Nunn and I had worked with Powell since early in his career, and his intelligence and ability were unquestioned. But there was a hiccup. Bob Woodward's latest book, *The Commanders,* was number one on the bestseller lists for its "behind-the-scenes" account of the first President Bush and his military high command as they wrestled with questions of the use of military force in the run-up to the invasion of Panama and Operation Desert Storm.

In classic Woodward style, he purported to tell the story through the eyes of the key participants, revealing insights that could have come only from then-Secretary of Defense Cheney or General Powell. The book first hit newsstands on New Year's Day 1991, meaning that Cheney and/or Powell had talked to Woodward while deciding to go to war against Saddam Hussein more than a year prior. This concerned many senators on the Committee, notably Senator Warner and other senior Republicans, primarily because the account in Woodward's book differed from what Powell had told the SASC. Based on several senators' requests, Senator Nunn had added questions about Woodward's book to Powell's Advance Policy Questions. Candidly, Powell's responses to those APQs had been perfunctory, satisfying no one. Senators raised the matter again at Powell's confirmation hearing on Friday, September 27, 1991, but remained unsatisfied by his rather vague responses.

With tensions brewing on the SASC and an influx of requests from Democratic and Republican senators—notably Robert Byrd, the Senate majority leader, and Warner, the Committee's ranking member—Senator Nunn asked me to let Powell know he would need to come in for an additional closed hearing to get to the bottom of his cooperation with Woodward. I didn't consider this unusual, so I telephoned Colonel Paul Kelly, USMC, Powell's legislative liaison, to let him know. I was shocked when Kelly replied he didn't think Powell would make a second appearance before the Committee. I asked Kelly to "make sure," given that it was highly unusual for a senior military officer, particularly one with Powell's political savvy, to refuse such a request. Kelly called back in short order and affirmed General Powell would not answer any more questions on the Woodward book. I told Kelly I would inform Chairman Nunn and Ranking Member Warner immediately, and I did not expect Powell's response to be well-received by either. I shared the Kelly conversation with Pat Tucker, the minority staff director, and he had the same reaction: "Uh-oh." We told Senators Nunn and Warner together. After checking with several other senators with concerns, they authorized me to call Kelly again.

I was instructed to ask Kelly to inform General Powell the SASC would not vote on his confirmation for a second term as chairman until he agreed to answer the Committee's additional questions. This was Friday, and Powell's current term as CJCS was set to expire at midnight on Monday, September 30, three days hence. That weekend saw a flurry of calls back and forth between the Pentagon and Chairman Nunn, with the Pentagon callers becoming more senior with each round of calls. Ultimately, Secretary Cheney called Nunn personally but made no headway. Nunn's next call came from National Security Advisor Brent Scowcroft. In the end, it came down to who would blink. The Executive Branch insisted Powell would not and should not have to answer the SASC's additional questions; the Committee should confirm him immediately and move on. Senator Nunn was equally adamant Powell needed to explain why he had cooperated with Woodward and provided a journalist with information contradictory to what he had told the SASC. Colonel Kelly called me repeatedly, incredulous we would let Powell's tenure simply fizzle out on such a negative note.

About midmorning on Monday, September 30, Senator Nunn received what sounded like a final call from Scowcroft. "Senator, you need to understand. General Powell is comfortable letting his tour expire at midnight tonight and going home. The nation will no longer have a Joint Chiefs of Staff chairman." Without missing a beat, Nunn retorted, "That's why we have a vice-chairman."

That's when the administration finally understood Senator Nunn and the Committee would not yield. Within the hour, Kelly called to say Powell was willing to come in. That afternoon, the SASC's closed session was well-attended. The concerned senators essentially took Powell "to the woodshed" for his poor judgment. But the session revealed nothing that would have cast aspersions on Powell's integrity or candor with the Committee. The matter was now closed. There were no leaks or news stories from this hearing. After Powell departed, the SASC approved Powell's nomination before adjourning the closed session, sending it to the Senate floor. He was confirmed by unanimous consent with a few hours to spare before the expiration of his term. It was never about General Powell's qualifications or leadership abilities. He remains one of our most accomplished military and civilian leaders. He belongs in the unique pantheon of five-star officers like Dwight Eisenhower, Omar Bradley, and George Marshall. But the Executive Branch learned again it could not infringe on the Legislature's constitutional responsibilities, which it still needs occasional reminding of.

Another time that a chairman of the Joint Chief's nomination was also delayed by the SASC was specifically by Chairman Nunn, when President Clinton nominated General Shalikashvili to be CJCS in early September 1993. General Shalikashvili was then serving as the Supreme Allied Commander Europe (SACEUR), the top North Atlantic Treaty Organization (NATO) military job, and commander of the U.S. European Command (EUCOM). The administration wanted the Senate to process the CJCS nomination quickly so Shalikashvili could take over immediately on General Powell's retirement on September 30.

But Senator Nunn was extremely concerned about the turbulent situation on Europe's borders. The United States had only recently deployed 300 troops to join the UN peacekeeping mission in the former Yugoslav Republic of Macedonia. The North Atlantic Council had approved operational options for air strikes in Bosnia and Herzegovina. Elsewhere, Russian President Boris Yeltsin's administration was in chaos; he had suspended parliament and called for fresh elections later in the year, but his vice president urged the armed forces to resist Yeltsin's orders. Hardliners were occupying the Russian White House.

Meanwhile, the Senate had not yet received a nomination for Shalikashvili's successor in EUCOM. At the crux of Senator Nunn's disquiet was his knowledge that if the Senate confirmed Shalikashvili as chairman, it would leave a vacuum in U.S. leadership in Europe and NATO. Senator Nunn made it plain to the administration that he would not support that approach, particularly given the nasty turn in current events in-theater. The administration at the time seemed to suggest this was not Senator Nunn's call and that he should simply get about the business of confirming the president's choice for the chairman's job.

Senator Nunn promptly explained that until the Senate acted on Shalikashvili's nomination, he could not and would not take over as chairman of the Joint Chiefs. Senator Nunn emphasized he intended to see to it the Senate *did not* act on Shalikashvili's nomination until his replacement in NATO was nominated and confirmed. The administration countered that filling the position of the chairman of the Joint Chiefs of Staff was a far greater priority than the SACEUR, USEUCOM nomination. Senator Nunn calmly replied, "Not to me."

The stalemate continued. Powell retired as planned and was succeeded temporarily by Vice Chairman of the Joint Chiefs of Staff, Admiral David Jeremiah, while General Shalikashvili remained in Europe. Finally, on October 4, 1993, the SASC received the nomination of General George Joulwan to be SACEUR and Commander EUCOM. A day later, the Shalikashvili nomination was reported out of Committee and confirmed almost immediately by voice vote on the Senate floor.

Two days later, on October 7, General Joulwan appeared before the SASC for his confirmation hearing. Senator Nunn immediately reported him to the Senate floor with a favorable recommendation; Joulwan was confirmed by voice vote only hours later. The Shalikashvili–Joulwan change of command took place on October 22. Immediately after that, Shalikashvili assumed his new role as chairman of the Joint Chiefs. Senator Nunn had scored another significant victory for the Committee and its process.

Senators are sometimes concerned about nominees' backgrounds and whether they fit the position best. In September 2004, Air Force General Gregory "Speedy" Martin was nominated for commander, U.S. Pacific Command (PACOM), the first non-Navy nominee for the prestigious post. However, at Martin's October 6th confirmation hearing before the SASC, he ran into headwinds from Senator John McCain, a retired Navy officer whose father, Admiral John S. McCain, Jr., had served as PACOM commander between 1968 and 1972.

Martin had the distinct misfortune of having been assigned with Darleen Druyun from 1998 to 1999: he as the principal military deputy to the Air Force assistant secretary for acquisition, and she as the principal civilian deputy. In April 2004, mere months before Martin's nomination, Druyun had pleaded guilty in federal court to felony corruption charges. In 2002 and 2003, Druyun had inflated the price of an Air Force lease of tanker aircraft in favor of the lessor, Boeing Corporation, and passed procurement-sensitive information to Boeing on a competitor's bid. Druyun wanted to curry favor with Boeing, who had employed two of Druyun's close family members and with whom Druyun became employed when she left government service in late 2003.

It was undisputed that Martin had moved to another Air Force assignment in Europe before Druyun had committed her crimes. Still, Senator McCain questioned Martin pointedly why he had overlooked Druyun's deceit.

Martin replied, "I'm not an expert in contracting," and "I saw nothing that she was doing that was inappropriate or in any way illegal."[112] Senator McCain also complained—vocally—about the delay he encountered in receiving access to copies of General Martin's emails, both from the period of Martin's assignment with Druyun and subsequent assignments in which Martin had worked on issues related to Air Force tanker readiness. Ultimately, McCain told Martin, "I'm questioning your qualifications for command."

McCain called Druyun's Boeing deal "a national disgrace" and vowed to hold Martin's nomination in the SASC "until we get all the emails and all the answers."[113] Committee Chairman John Warner, who had previously served as Navy secretary, supported McCain. Only hours after the hearing concluded, Martin requested his nomination be withdrawn. He returned to his regular duties as commander of the Air Force Materiel Command, where he would remain until he retired on September 1, 2005.

It took Senator McCain almost a year to complete his review of all the emails related to the Boeing tanker scandal, Martin's included. But the outcome of that review was clear. There was no indication General Martin knew of Druyun's improprieties. It has long been speculated McCain and Warner, with their professional and personal ties to the Navy and PACOM, did not support any general officer outside of the Navy to serve as the commander of PACOM. It is the only combatant command (now called Indo-

Pacific Command) with a history of only Navy commanders, although there are many non-Navy officers qualified for the position.

The Defense Department's concern about senior military nominations and their timely processing by the SASC has always given the Senate no small leverage over the Pentagon, even in matters unrelated to the nomination. It was predictable that the conversation would end with an implied threat when a senior DOD official "stopped by" my office or called to press me about the Committee moving more quickly, even though these nominations were not being held up as the SASC had not processed them, and the individuals' promotion date had not passed. "If you can't commit to a specific timeframe, the chief [meaning the service chief] is going to have to call the chairman [meaning Senator Nunn]." I would always respond, "Chairman Nunn welcomes calls from the service chief, and he [the chief] should call the senator whenever he feels the need to do so."

I had an understanding with Senator Nunn's executive secretary, Rose Johnson, that if anyone from the Pentagon called for Senator Nunn, I needed to know before the senator returned the call. Sure enough, the service chief would place the "threatened" call to Senator Nunn, and without fail, Rose would call me. I would ask Rose to be sure that when Senator Nunn returned the call, he had on hand the standard briefing card on which I detailed all the documents and items of information each service owed the Committee.

The Committee's ability to request and receive documents and information from the Pentagon was critical to our oversight and legislative responsibilities. So, I diligently ensured the briefing card was continually updated. Rose would schedule the return call and ask me to join Senator Nunn for the call. Inevitably, what I would hear on the senator's end of the call was something like, "General, I will check with Arnold on the status of that nomination. But while I have you on the phone, we have five items we have asked the Army to provide to the Committee, and we have gotten no response. Can you tell me when we are going to get this material?" Unsurprisingly, any recalcitrance in responding to SASC's requests quickly became complete cooperation. Almost without fail, the requested documents and information were provided to the SASC within a day or two. At that point, I would call the Service to let them know the nomination would move within the next week, usually in the Committee's ordinary course of business. The Services never seemed to catch on, and we used this tactic to our advantage all the years I was staff director.

SENATORS GENERALLY TRUST THE MILITARY PROMOTION PROCESS

Senators trust the military promotion selection process. It's a process anchored in law that relies on the military selecting those best qualified for promotion to the next higher grade or appointment to a position of "trust and responsibility." In part, Congress trusts the system because it is of its own making. Congress legislated a rigorous but fair, meritocratic process that, over time, has been further perfected by numerous amendments. And given that our military's continued strength and professionalism are essential to national security, Congress believes current military leaders have an inherent interest in ensuring their successors are the best qualified to lead America's sons and daughters. There have been some exceptions over time, in which Congress's trust has been broken and the rules violated. But in each case, the SASC clapped back with a swift and robust response, almost always new legislation designed to prevent future bad acts and ensure every officer had a fair opportunity for promotion based on merit.

In late July 1987, the SASC refused to confirm two Marine Corps officers recommended for promotion to major general because former Navy Secretary John Lehman and former Marine

Commandant P.X. Kelley interfered with the promotion selection process. On a Sunday afternoon, I received a call at my home from retired USMC Commandant and 4-star General Bob Barrow. I had first worked with General Barrow as a second lieutenant when he was the 1-star commander at Camp Butler, Okinawa. He had also served as the 3-star head of Marine Manpower and as the 4-star assistant commandant. I knew him well.

He told me he had information that the USMC major general promotion board had been compromised by the secretary of the Navy and commandant of the Marine Corps and gave me the details. I quickly told General Barrow I was honor-bound to report this to Chairman Nunn and Ranking Member Warner. I could not protect the Marine Corps from the fallout. He replied: "I know that, and that's why I called you."

Chairman Nunn and Ranking Member Warner called Secretary of Defense Caspar Weinberger. They told him he could investigate the matter or that SASC would. Weinberger assured the senators the Department would look into the matter internally. The DOD general counsel determined the October 1986 Marine Corps major general promotion selection board had concluded its work, initially recommending eight officers for promotion, the number first set by Lehman. When Lehman reviewed the board's report and realized an aviator he favored (a preference he had communicated to the board president in advance) and a ground officer Kelley preferred, Sheridan and Meade, were not among the eight selected, he directed the board to reconvene and choose two additional officers, one of them "his" aviator. Kelley then spoke to the promotion board president and "commented favorably" on the ground officer he favored. The board reconvened and returned reluctantly to its task of selecting two additional officers. After several ballots, the board selected Lehman's aviator, who had been a strong contender from the outset. It was only after six rounds of voting that the board also chose Kelley's favorite ground officer.[114]

The Pentagon's report of inquiry documented that seven of the nine board members believed increasing the number of officers to be selected by the board from eight to 10—after the fact—was a bald effort by Lehman to "force" them to promote the aviator. Four of nine board members said Kelley's comments about the ground officer affected their votes. The SASC was appalled by Lehman and Kelley's behavior but divided on whether the two officers selected due to Lehman and Kelley's interference should be promoted with the eight officers originally recommended by the board. Senator Nunn finally announced the SASC had favorably reported to the Senate floor the eight Marine brigadiers initially endorsed by the board but had taken no action on the two officers preferred by Lehman and Kelley. Those two nominations would be returned to the Marine Corps. Senator Alan Dixon (D-IL), then a member of the SASC, referred to the two officers as "innocent and distinguished members of the Marine Corps" and urged the Corps to select them again for promotion at the next earliest opportunity. While acknowledging there was no evidence or suggestion of impropriety on the part of the two officers whose nominations had been set aside, the Committee ultimately united behind the principle that if a promotion is improperly influenced by the actions or communications of senior officials, outside of authorized channels, all officers in the zone before that board could be denied a fair chance at selection.

The SASC legislated its rebuke of Lehman and Kelley's breach of board integrity. In July 1987, the FY 1988 NDAA was already well on the road to completion, but the Committee acted decisively the following year.[115] The NDAA for FY 1989, signed into law on September 29, 1988, added a new provision of law specifically targeted to preclude a future Lehman-Kelley type situation. The new law stated:

> Information or guidelines furnished to a selection board [including the maximum number of officers the board may recommend for promotion, as determined by the secretary of the Military Department concerned] may not be modified, withdrawn, or supplemented after the board submits its report to the secretary of the Military Department concerned....[116]

Perhaps the most egregious and sustained breach of promotion board laws and regulations came to light after Dick Cheney fired General Dugan. The president nominated General Merrill McPeak as chief of staff of the Air Force in September 1990. On October 23rd of that year, the day before McPeak's scheduled confirmation hearing, I found myself again in my office reviewing nomination paperwork, this time with General McPeak and his handlers. McPeak's paperwork was in order. I asked him about the Air Force brigadier general promotion selection board, which I knew he had presided over. Two officers on that promotion list, pending before the SASC, had adverse information: Colonel Peyton Cole and Colonel Eldon Joersz. I knew Cole because he was the head of the Air Force Senate liaison office and worked in the Russell Senate Office Building close to the SASC offices.

The Committee was always interested in nominations with adverse information, particularly whether it had been disclosed to the promotion selection board, which could then recommend an officer for promotion—or not—with a complete understanding of the issues. I asked McPeak if the promotion board had been aware of the adverse information on Cole and Joersz. Without missing a beat, McPeak replied *he* had known about the adverse information but *had not shared it with the board* because he did not want to hurt the two officers' chances of promotion.

This prompted a lengthy and somewhat heated discussion about the Committee's view that such adverse information should be shared with the promotion selection board and the officer to whom it pertained. Every officer should know with certainty what information about him or her will be considered by a board. McPeak told me—almost proudly—the Air Force did not run its boards that way, preferring to rely on a "secret" fitness report written on any colonel considered for promotion to brigadier general. All Air Force 4-stars were encouraged to submit to the board a list of the colonels they wanted to see promoted.

I was floored when McPeak said he understood this "secret" process was contrary to laws and regulations, but he thought it yielded the best results. Given that the Air Force was running an illegal promotion system, I told General McPeak I intended to advise Senator Nunn to put everything McPeak had told me "on the record" at his confirmation hearing the following day. McPeak appeared unfazed and left the office. I consulted with the minority staff director and the Committee general counsels, who agreed with my conclusions and that it was essential to get McPeak on the record. Immediately following the open confirmation hearing the next day, the Committee moved into a closed Executive Session. McPeak repeated all he had told me the day before for the entire Committee. The senators were aghast, and the following year, they took corrective action in the next NDAA, ensuring that nothing like this could ever happen again.

Section 504 of the NDAA for Fiscal Years 1992 and 1993, enacted in law on December 5, 1991, put in place a comprehensive set of requirements to standardize the promotion process across all Military Departments. It also established the secretary of defense as the ultimate guardian and guarantor of the system's fairness and independence. Under the heading of "Integrity of the Promotion Selection Board Process," the new law required the secretary of defense to prescribe regulation governing the types of information that could be provided to promotion boards. It specified these regulations would apply uniformly to all Military Departments, with no more *ad hoc* Air Force promotion systems. The law also stipulated *no* information concerning an eligible officer could be furnished to a promotion selection board except:

1. information in the officer's official military personnel file (to which the officer under consideration always had access);
2. consistent with the regulations promulgated by the secretary of defense, information determined by the secretary of the Military Department concerned to be "substantiated, relevant information" that could reasonably and materially affect the board's deliberations—the SASC's first effort at *legislating* a requirement that adverse information about an officer under consideration be considered by the board in the course of its deliberations; and
3. information communicated to the board by the officer under consideration.

The information in these approved categories—solely—was provided to all board members and made part of the record of the board. No more "secret" Air Force evaluation reports.

Finally, the legislation required the affected officer to be given notice of any adverse information the board would consider and afforded the opportunity to make comments on that information. The board would consider the adverse information and the officer's input, reinforcing the SASC's belief every officer must have the right to review and comment on any information provided to the board regarding them. Considering both the McPeak and Lehman/Kelley debacles, the new law prohibited the secretary of a Military Department and any other official from "attempting to coerce or, by unauthorized means, influence any action of a selection board or any member of a selection board in the formulation of the board's recommendations." There would be no more dodgy Air Force 4-star lists of "favorite sons."[117]

With this single piece of legislation, the SASC made the most significant change to the promotion system since the 1980 Defense Officer Personnel Management Act. It ensured promotion boards were independent and without deception. Military officers at all grades could have confidence they would be impartially considered for promotion on a careful, fair, and equitable basis.

I later discerned, over lunch with former SASC Staff Director Carl Smith at the Pentagon Ritz Carlton, Air Force leadership was unhappy with these changes. At a table near us was retired General Russ Dougherty, head of the Air Force Association, and General Bennie Davis, the former head of Air Force personnel. Apparently, they did not see Carl and me because they spoke loudly and did not hide the subject of their conversation. The whole discussion was about how that "expletive" Arnold Punaro had ruined the Air Force promotion system. I took it as a compliment, satisfied the promotion system was now protected from undue influence. As Carl and I finished our lunch and walked out, we stopped briefly at their table to say "hello."

But the 1994 debate over the retirement grade of Air Force Lieutenant General Buster Glosson illustrates so well that some people will never learn. No matter what happens, they will continue to believe that even the laws established by Congress simply do not apply to them. In December 1993, Glosson, the Air Force deputy chief of staff for plans and operations, had received a letter of admonishment from the then-Secretary of the Air Force Sheila Widnall for improperly intervening in the major general promotion board earlier in the fall. Before the board convened, Glosson had contacted three general officers who would later sit on the board. Those three officers subsequently disclosed Glosson's actions to the board president, who reported the matter to Secretary

Widnall. Although Glosson claimed when he approached these officers that he had "no idea" they would be board members, the three officers stated—and the Air Force and DOD inspectors general agreed—that Glosson had attempted to influence the board's decisions by criticizing one particular promotion candidate, an Air Force brigadier general whom Glosson labeled a "weak leader."

To my thinking, Glosson had clearly violated Title 10 provisions that had been so carefully crafted by SASC and enacted by Congress to stop this sort of thing from happening again. He should have been dropped a star in retirement. But Glosson was a colorful and popular figure in the Air Force and a favorite of former Secretary of Defense Les Aspin, who had left office in February 1994. In addition, Glosson had been the principal architect of the Allied aerial bombardment of Iraq in the Gulf War. All that to say, he had strong supporters in parts of the Committee. His retirement in the grade of 3-star was approved by the Senate in October 1994 by a vote of 59-30. Post-retirement, an extensive legal process involving the bankruptcy of Glosson's company would again call his character into question.

The changes the SASC made in the military promotion process were designed to ensure that all military officers had confidence their performance and potential would be considered comprehensively, fairly, and objectively. The SASC rebuked favoritism. "Thumbs on the scale" would not be permitted in the promotion process.

12

THE PROCESS IN THE DEPARTMENT OF DEFENSE

The military officer promotion system is designed to be competitive, selecting only the "best qualified" officers for service at the next higher grade. With limited exceptions applicable to few officers, it is straightforward. An active-duty officer may not be promoted to a higher grade unless considered and recommended by a promotion selection board.[118] Subject to regulations promulgated by the secretary of defense—that standardize the promotion system across DOD—the Military Department secretary administers the Department's promotion and federal recognition board processes.[119] The laws and regulations even give the secretaries of the Military Departments the authority to establish procedures for promoting all "fully qualified" officers to the grades of O-2 and O-3 without convening a promotion selection board.[120]

For promotions to each grade from O-4 through O-8, however, the secretary annually convenes a centralized promotion selection board.[121] Each board consists of at least five (but usually more) senior commissioned officers charged with evaluating all eligible officers and recommending for promotion only those who, in the opinion of the majority of the board members, are "fully qualified and best qualified" to meet the needs of the Military Service concerned.[122] The secretary of the respective Military Department is also responsible for ensuring the information furnished to the board about eligible officers is limited to that expressly authorized by law and regulation and that the board operates free from coercion or improper influence.[123]

The role of adverse information in the three-phase nomination, confirmation, and appointment process has become increasingly important. The SASC and Congress as a whole have taken deliberate steps to ensure "credible information of an adverse nature"[124] about an officer under consideration by a board for promotion to or for federal recognition in specific grades is provided to and considered by that board at every stage of its proceedings.[125] The secretary of the Military Department is included in making adverse information available to the board in conjunction with the inspector general of the Department of Defense. The secretary of the Military Department and the inspector general of the Department of Defense are responsible for screening all Military Department and DOD investigative files for adverse information attributable to an officer expected to be considered by the board. If adverse information is identified, it must be provided to the affected officer for review and comment. Then the adverse information and the officer's comments are provided to the board as part of the officer's file. Chapter 14 provides more detailed information about adverse information and its role in the nomination, confirmation, and appointment processes.

Once proceedings conclude, the board prepares, signs, and submits its written report to the secretary of the Military Department, including the names of officers recommended for promotion to or federal recognition in the next higher grade. As part of the board report, the board president, each board member, and administrative personnel supporting the board must certify in writing the conduct of the board complied with all applicable laws, regulations, and guidance from the secretary.[126] Board reports are handled confidentially; the board's recommendations may not be disclosed to the officers considered or to the public until later in the process.

The date board members sign the board report "starts the clock," accounting for the time required for the DOD to approve the board report. In its oversight role, Congress has taken great interest in the timeliness of the officer promotion and federal recognition processes. OSD must notify both the Senate and House Armed Services Committees when 100 calendar days have elapsed since the adjournment of a promotion selection or federal recognition board, the results of which have not yet been approved. OSD's "100-day" notification letter must address the reasons for the delay and provide a date by which the Department anticipates approval of the board report. Concerned about the untoward lag in approving National Guard officer federal recognition board results, Congress recently directed a study of the National Guard promotion system. Such a study is sorely needed. It will identify the reasons for delay in processing these actions and propose improvements in "policies, procedures, workflow, or resources to reduce the processing time for federal recognition of state promotions."[127]

The secretary of the Military Department reviews each board report for compliance with laws, regulations and the secretary's guidance. Presuming the board follows regular order, the secretary's next step is to forward a board "package" through the under secretary of defense for personnel and readiness to the secretary of defense for review and action.[128] As required by law or regulation, promotion and federal recognition packages are also submitted to the chairman of the Joint Chiefs of Staff for review.[129]

A Secretarial Board "Package" Includes:

1. The board report.
2. One or more "scrolls." A scroll is a document used by the DOD and the White House that lists the names of officers recommended for nomination, appointment, promotion, or federal recognition. A scroll may contain the name of a single officer,

or it may include a list of names. Usually, all officers recommended by a particular promotion selection or federal recognition board are included on a single scroll.

3. A forwarding memorandum signed by the secretary of the Military Department concerned. The memorandum must include the secretary's recommendation the board report be approved and certification that all officers listed on the scroll are qualified for appointment, promotion, or federal recognition and meet the exemplary conduct provisions set forth in law.[130] In making this certification, the secretary must consider any adverse or reportable information about a recommended officer. DOD is expected to *withhold* an officer's name from a scroll whenever facts support a determination the officer may not be qualified for promotion or when an officer is facing a pending investigation into alleged adverse information or the adjudication of substantiated adverse information not considered by the promotion selection board or federal recognition board.[131] For officers recommended for promotion or federal recognition in the grade of O-6 or below, the duty to determine whether an officer's name should be withheld falls to the secretary of the Military Department. In the case of a package on officers recommended for promotion or federal recognition in a general or flag officer grade, only the secretary of defense may withhold an officer's name from a nomination scroll.[132] When the secretary of the Military Department submits a package that withholds an officer's name from the scroll (or, in the case of general or flag officer, recommends the secretary of defense withhold an officer's name), the secretary's forwarding memorandum must identify the affected officer by name.[133] In this context, "withhold" means only that an officer's name is removed temporarily from a nomination or appointment scroll pending review of his or her eligibility, while other individuals on the scroll proceed for secretary of defense approval or

presidential nomination and Senate confirmation. The officer whose name has been withheld is still on the board report and promotion list until the officer is removed by presidential authority or operation of law or is promoted. In a preponderance of cases, the latter occurs. Although delayed, once the investigation and follow-on disciplinary action (if any) are completed and subject to the favorable recommendation of the Military Department secretary and the secretary of defense, the officer's name will be scrolled separately and forwarded through the regular process for nomination, confirmation, and appointment.

4. The secretary's report of and comment on any adverse or reportable information attributable to an officer listed on the scroll. Although adverse or reportable information will subject an officer to enhanced scrutiny throughout the process, it *does not* preclude an officer's appointment, promotion, or federal recognition. If an officer listed on the scroll has adverse or reportable information, the package must include an Adverse Information Summary (AIS) or Reportable Information Summary (RIS), as appropriate. An AIS/RIS comprises a summary of the information at issue; the investigative agency; the findings of the investigation and corrective action taken; justification of how and why the officer merits promotion notwithstanding the adverse or reportable information; and a statement evaluating the officer's judgment and his or her potential for future service.[134] The AIS/RIS will remain a part of the officer's nomination package throughout the nomination, confirmation, and appointment process.

5. If the package pertains to nominating one or more officers for appointment, promotion, or federal recognition to any general or flag officer grade, their professional career resume and color photograph must be included.[135]

Although rare, there are some cases in which the chain of command determines an officer selected by a board does not meet the exemplary conduct standards or is not qualified for appointment, promotion, or federal recognition, whether because of adverse information that has come to light or for some other reason. In that case, the officer may be removed permanently from the list of officers recommended by the board. This decision is never made lightly, however.

To protect the sanctity of the board process, the secretary of the Military Department may recommend an officer's name be removed from a board report. But the final decision is always made at the highest levels of authority. Officers recommended for promotion or federal recognition to the grade of O-6 or below may be removed from the board report only by the president or secretary of defense.[136] The law reserves to the president the authority to remove an officer's name from a selection board report that recommends that officer for promotion to general or flag officer.

Nominations to the grades of O-9 (lieutenant general and vice admiral) and O-10 (general or admiral) are generated differently. The grade of O-8 (2-star, major general or rear admiral (upper half)) is the last grade to which selection is made by a promotion selection board and the most senior permanent grade in the military structure. By contrast, 3- and 4-star grades (lieutenant general and vice admiral and general and admiral) are temporary and associated only with key duty positions established in law: the chairman and vice chairman of the Joint Chiefs of Staff, combatant commanders, the top two officers of each Military Service, the commander of U.S. Special Operations Command, and chief of the National Guard Bureau.[137] 3- and 4-star grades also attach to other positions of "importance and responsibility" specially designated by the President of the United States to carry such a grade.[138]

Nomination packages involving appointments to the grades of O-9 or O-10 are based on recommendations by the secretary of the Military Department from which the nominated officer hails and the chairman of the Joint Chiefs of Staff. It is within the secretary's or the chairman's discretion to institute an advisory board or process to consider and make recommendations on the relative merits of one or more candidates for a 3- or 4-star position, but this is not required. Even when an advisory process is used, the resulting recommendations are just that—advisory—and do not bind the secretary or chairman's recommendation to the secretary of defense. In making their respective recommendations for nomination to a 3- or 4-star position, the secretary of the Military Department, the chairman, and the secretary of defense must consider any adverse or reportable information associated with the officer or officers under consideration. During Secretary of Defense Don Rumsfeld's second stint, he brought in retired Navy Admiral Staser Holcomb, who reviewed and interviewed all considered for nomination to 3- and 4-star rank. While this non-traditional approach was not well-received by those who did not think there should be an additional review or whose recommendations were not approved, it was within Rumsfeld's authority. In fact, the process underscored that per Title 10, almost every DOD action and process is "subject to the authority, direction, and control of the secretary of defense."

The secretary of defense considers the recommendation of the secretary of the Military Department and the chairman before making a final recommendation to the president.

Once the secretary of defense decides who he will recommend to the president, the action returns to the appropriate secretary of the Military Department, who generates the nomination package and submits it through the Joint Chiefs of Staff chairman and the under secretary of defense for personnel and readiness to the secretary of defense for review and action. The components of a 3- or 4-star nomination package are generally the same as those required for lower-level nominations:

1. The scroll. A nomination to a 3- or 4-star position and the associated grade is always scrolled individually. A 3- or 4-star scroll must include the officer's name and the title and grade of the specific position for which the officer will be nominated. The duty title provided must mirror the specific duty title approved by the president when last designating the position as one of "importance and responsibility." If the position is being recommended for initial designation as one of "importance and responsibility," the nomination must include a request and justification for presidential action. Presidential re-designation of the position is required when there is a change in the grade, title, or significant duties of a previously approved position.

2. A forwarding memorandum signed by the secretary of the Military Department. The memorandum must include the secretary's certification the officer meets the exemplary conduct standards set forth in Title 10 after checking all Military Department and DOD investigative files and considering any adverse or reportable information on the officer. The memorandum must also specify the number of joint duty assignments the officer completed, whether the officer has been designated a joint-qualified officer, whether the officer has attended Senior Service School, and information indicating the proposed action's effect on statutory grade ceilings for that grade. Also detailed are the officer's date of birth, initial date of federal commissioned service and total federal commissioned service; current Mandatory Retirement Date, the basis for the Mandatory Retirement Date (time in service or age); previous extensions of the officer's Mandatory Retirement Date and any waivers required; and whether frocking is anticipated. The

memorandum must include the specific date the Military Department projects the officer will be promoted to the next higher grade (PDOP) and/or assigned to the new position (PDOA) (if the new position's grade and the officer's current grade are the same).

3. If applicable, an AIS or RIS of any adverse or reportable information about the officer.

4. The professional career resume and color photograph of the recommended officer.

The chairman of the Joint Chiefs attaches his own evaluation of the officer's performance in joint billets to the nomination package.

An officer must be nominated by the president and confirmed by the Senate for appointment to a specific 3- or 4-star position and promotion to the grade it carries. Sometimes, an officer already serving in a 3- or 4-star position may be nominated for another position in the same grade. Still, the Senate must confirm the officer for appointment to the new position and reappointment in grade. As to the president's designation of positions of "importance and responsibility," Congress can review the rationale for this designation as part of its oversight function. The Senate retains the power to confirm or reject the nomination of an individual to fill such a position should it deem that rationale inadequate.

The confirmed officer continues to hold the grade of 3- or 4-star only for so long as he or she encumbers the specific position with which that grade is associated. At the end of a 3- or 4-star tour, an officer may be recommended for another 3- or 4-star position, which requires a new presidential nomination and confirmation by the Senate. Or they may revert to their "permanent grade" or request retirement if otherwise eligible. When a 3- or 4-star officer is no longer serving in a position of "importance and responsibility," they can continue to hold that grade for only 60 days before reverting to their highest permanent grade, usually a 2-star. The authorized bridge period between release from one 3- or 4-star position and appointment in another such position or retirement used to be 90 days. The SASC cut the bridge period back to 60 days in the FY 1992 NDAA when senators learned the Air Force had permitted disgraced General Mike Dugan to keep his 4-star grade for 90 days after being fired by Dick Cheney. That allowed Dugan to remain on active duty through January 1, 1991, and to avail himself of the annual military pay raise that takes effect on the first day of each new year—an increase that applied to the amount of retired pay Dugan would receive.[139]

The Department of Defense has no standard time frame within which it will submit a military nomination to the president for approval and transmission to the Senate. Upon nomination and confirmation, some officers will immediately be ready for promotion, federal recognition, or appointment to a 3- or 4-star position. Others—usually the most junior officers on a list of names recommended by a promotion selection board or federal recognition board—will not be eligible for promotion for more than a year. However, there is one limitation on timing to which the Department and the Senate have agreed. The Department will not send, and the Senate will not accept a nomination earlier than nine months before the officer's Projected Date of Promotion (PDOP) or projected date of appointment (PDOA)—the month, day, and year on which the Department anticipates the officer will be promoted or appointed.[140] The PDOP/PDOA is readily ascertained for officers nominated individually. For officers nominated as part of the list, the 9-month limitation is calculated vis-à-vis the anticipated date of the first promotion from the list or scroll. Provided the projected date of the first promotion is within nine months, the entire list may be submitted, even if the other officers on the list are expected to promote much later in time. The secretary of the Military Department must keep DOD (and subsequently the SASC) advised of any changes in an individual officer's or list's PDOP or PDOA.[141]

USAF Commander of U.S. Northern Command and NORAD General Lori Robinson and Arnold Punaro discuss NORTHCOM's major role in civil-support in the homeland and the increased use of the guard and reserve components.

The Office of the Under Secretary of Defense for Personnel and Readiness is responsible for quality assurance of all military nominations. It facilitates a legal review of each secretarial package submitted—regardless of the grade of the officers to whom the package applies. After the steps are completed and any required modifications made, the package is submitted to the secretary of defense for approval, or if presidential nomination and Senate confirmation are required, for endorsement and transmission to the White House Military Office, a component of the Office of the Secretary of Defense established to provide military support and liaison to the White House.

Unlike the civilian nomination process in which the Presidential Personnel Office and the agency White House Liaison Officer often play a role, neither office plays a part in military nominations. Instead, the White House Military Office reviews each package for accuracy and completeness. Then it works through the National Security Council in the Executive Office of the President, where each package is again reviewed to obtain the president's original signature (required by the Senate) on each nomination scroll. The White House clerk forwards the presidential nomination scroll to the executive clerk of the Senate (which must be in session to receive it) no later than 48 hours after presidential signature. For general and flag officer nominations, the White House Military Office notifies the DOD the president has signed the nomination scroll and delivered it to the Senate. Shortly after, the assistant to the secretary of defense for public affairs office coordinates with the Military Department concerned and publicly announces the nominations. For nominations to the grade of O-6 and below for which Senate confirmation is required, the secretary of the Military Department may make a public announcement, including the names of the officers on the newly approved promotion list, after the secretary of defense approves the board report and forwards the accompanying scroll to the president for signature and nomination. For nominations for which Senate confirmation is not required (active-duty O-1 through O-3 promotions and the federal recognition of reserve component O-1s through O-5s), the secretary of the Military Department may make a public announcement after the under secretary of defense for personnel and readiness forwards the scroll to the secretary of defense for signature.[142]

For a select few 3- and 4-star nominations, the president's signature on the nomination package triggers an additional step to complete before the nomination scroll is transmitted to the Senate and a public announcement made. For example, after the president's signature, DOD must coordinate with the Department of State to solicit Canadian government approval of the nomination of an officer to be commander U.S. Northern Command and commander North American Aerospace Defense Command (NORAD). Similarly, the NATO Peacetime Establishment document specifies the president's nominee to be commander U.S. European Command and Supreme Allied Commander, Europe (SACEUR) must be approved by the North Atlantic Council (NAC). The president formally requests the NATO secretary general release the incumbent SACEUR from the position and that the NAC approve the nominee he has selected. Once the NAC concurs, the nominee is informed, the nomination is transmitted to the Senate, and a joint press release is issued.

Despite this comprehensive coordination process, the president decides on every nomination. Although rare, sometimes the president disagrees with the DOD's recommendation and chooses someone else, which is a decision that upsets the DOD applecart but one that is well within the president's constitutional authority. Examples include President Carter's choice of Gen. Edward Meyer to be chief of Staff of the Army, President Trump's decision to name Gen. Mark Milley as the chairman of the Joint Chiefs of Staff, and President Biden's decision to nominate Admiral Lisa Franchetti as chief of Naval Operations.

13

THE PROCESS IN THE SENATE

Presuming the Senate is in session and available to receive nominations, the military nomination packages signed by the president are received and processed by the Office of the Executive Clerk. The executive clerk assigns each nominated officer—whether presented as an individual nomination or a list of names—a Presidential Nomination Number (PN). The first nomination received in any new Congress is designated as PN1. Each nomination thereafter—military or civilian—is assigned the next available PN in sequence, in the order it is received by the executive clerk, through the end of the Congress. Each nomination, with its PN, is added to the publicly accessible Senate website, listed as "pending." Then the executive clerk refers every military nomination (except members of the Coast Guard) to the SASC.

SASC professional staff begin processing a nomination as soon as it is received in Committee, usually within 24 to 48 hours. SASC professional staff first provide the names of each officer nominated to each SASC senator (usually via email to the senator's military legislative assistant) and to every other member of the SASC professional staff. This gives each senator a meaningful opportunity to review each nomination and to raise concerns, if any. For any nominee for appointment, promotion, or federal recognition in a general or flag officer grade, the officer's professional career resume and photograph are disseminated with the nomination. SASC will cease processing a general or flag officer nomination without a career resume or photograph. Processing will resume when DOD or the nominee makes these items available to the Committee.

Major General Arnold Punaro, USMC (Ret.), receives the Commandant's Award in 2017 for exceptional leadership, service, and sacrifice. From the left: Lt. Gen. George Trautman, Secretary of Veterans Affairs David Shulkin, Chairman of the House defense Appropriations Subcommittee Rodney Frelinghuysen, Commandant of the Marine Corps General Robert Neller, Arnold Punaro, Secretary of Homeland Security John Kelly, Marine Corps Scholarship Foundation CEO Margaret Davis.

At the same time, Committee professional staff requests the Office of the Under Secretary of Defense for Personnel and Readiness provide the Projected Date of Promotion (PDOP) or Projected Date of Appointment (PDOA) for each nominee. For nominees on a promotion or federal recognition list, only the anticipated date (month, day, and year) of the first promotion from the scroll is required.

The SASC, acting through Committee professional staff, also requires DOD to provide a "Certification Letter" or "Cert" for any nomination for appointment, promotion, or federal recognition in a general or flag officer grade. Most Cert Letters document no adverse information concerning the nominated officer or officers. The standard Cert provides that:

All systems of records... maintained in the DOD that pertain to this/these officer(s) have been examined. The files contain no adverse information about this/these officer(s) since his/her/their last Senate confirmation. Further, to the best of my knowledge, there is no planned or ongoing investigation or inquiry into matters that constitute alleged adverse information on the part of this/these officer(s).

Some Certs will indicate there *is* adverse or reportable information about an officer or one or more officers. If the Certification Letter for a general or flag officer nomination list identifies one or more officers with adverse or reportable information, it must specify the names of the officers to whom the information applies. Of equal importance, the Cert must specifically affirm there is no adverse or reportable information for the other officers on the list. As to any officer with adverse or reportable information, a summary of that information is included in an AIS or RIS attached to the Cert.

For nominees to grades O-6 and below, the SASC does not require a Cert Letter in every case. DOD must provide such a letter only when necessary to flag for the Committee's attention any adverse or reportable information that meets specific DOD criteria.[143] Said another way, when DOD provides a Cert on an officer nominated for promotion or federal recognition to a grade below 1-star, adverse or reportable information exists and must be considered in the confirmation process.

THE SASC PROCESS FOR ROUTINE MILITARY NOMINATIONS

Most military nominations are routine, and this section details the SASC's process for those routine military nominations. All nominations for appointment and promotion to 3- and 4-star positions, even those free of adverse or reportable information, require enhanced review and processing. A nominee for appointment and promotion to a 3- or 4-star position may be required to participate in a confirmation hearing before the Committee. All nominations with adverse or reportable information, regardless of the grade of the nominee, require significant additional review and processing. Accordingly, the processes attending 3- and 4-star nominations and nominations with adverse or reportable information are discussed in greater detail in Chapter 14.

The Committee usually acts on military nominations monthly, in the third or fourth week. The timing is such that the Committee can vote on and favorably report military nominations to the Senate floor for confirmation by the full Senate before the last business day of the month. This allows the Military Services to promote some confirmed officers on the first day of the next month, consistent with DOD policy and practice, and to minimize the unnecessary loss of time in grade or the deferral of the increased pay and benefits associated with a promotion. Only occasionally will the Committee vote on military nominations more than once a month, and only in exceptional circumstances. The Committee's process and timing are geared toward affording DOD and the White House the greatest opportunity to submit nominations for confirmation in that month. And to ensure that, consistent with Committee rules and precedent, the greatest number of nominees are cleared and ready for the Committee's vote on the date and time selected for that month. Committee rules and precedents provide that:

1. The Committee will vote on a nomination only after it has been in the Committee for seven days. This gives each SASC senator a meaningful opportunity to review each nomination and to raise concerns, if any. This 7-day requirement can be waived, but this is rarely done.

2. The Committee will vote on only those nominations whose PDOP or PDOA is within 120 days. The Committee will vote on a promotion or federal recognition list provided that the anticipated date of the first promotion from the list or scroll is within 120 days, even if other officers will not be promoted for many months or years after that. The 120 days is calculated from the last day of the current month. For example, regardless of the date SASC will vote nominations in February—even if early in the month, and presuming all other requirements are met—the Committee will act on the nomination provided its PDOP or PDOA is on or before the last day of the following June. But under the 120-day rule, the Committee would not vote on nominations with a PDOP from July 1 until March. This practice minimizes delays between confirmation and promotion, federal recognition, or appointment. Because the Senate has no legal authority to recall or reverse its confirmation of a nominee, this ensures SASC retains, for as long as feasible, the ability to consider, as part of the confirmation process, a nominee's new or recently discovered misconduct, poor judgment, or other discreditable acts. In addition, the 120-day rule provides a control on the Office of the Secretary of Defense and Military Department authority to "frock" an officer, a process and status disfavored by the Committee.[144]

3. The Committee will vote on only those nominations with no adverse or reportable information from DOD (e.g., a clean Cert) or from other sources or that has been cleared by the Committee to proceed after full consideration of the adverse or reportable information attributable to the nominee.

As the end of the month nears, SASC majority and minority professional staff review all military nominations present in Committee and clear for a vote those that meet the above three criteria. Notice of the upcoming vote on military nominations, noting the number and name of nominations that have been cleared for a vote and the date, time, and venue (i.e., full Committee hearing or off-the-floor vote) is provided to all SASC senators, usually via an email to their military legislative assistant.

SASC practice has precluded individual SASC members from holding a nominee in Committee. If any SASC member brings to the chairman or ranking member's attention a substantive concern about a nominee, the chairman and ranking work through Committee professional staff to inquire into the matter and resolve it. In many military nomination cases, this may require coordination with the Department of Defense or the nominee's Service. Often the extent and duration of this coordination will remove the military nominee from consideration for a vote in the month the concern is brought to light. Once the concern has been resolved to the satisfaction of the chairman and ranking, and presuming the nominee has met all other Committee criteria, a vote is likely to proceed the following month. That said, before a Committee vote, any SASC member may advise the others of his or her ongoing concern about a nominee. Any member is free to vote "no" on any nominee at any time or place a hold for any reason if and when the Committee reports the nomination to the Senate floor.

As required by Senate Rules XXVI, a Committee quorum must be present to vote on any item to be reported to the Senate floor, including nominations. SASC has long believed—and Senate Parliamentarians agree—that rolling voting, where senators "drop in" to a voting location, provide their vote to Committee staff, then immediately depart, does not meet the Senate Rules. SASC insists a quorum of senators be physically present for a vote. Even during the COVID-19 pandemic, rolling or "virtual" voting was not permitted by the Senate or the SASC.

In the 118th Congress, a quorum is achieved when over half, or 13 of 25 SASC members, are physically present and voting. SASC practice is to assemble the requisite quorum of SASC members in a room off the Senate floor in conjunction with a series of scheduled Senate roll call votes or to vote on military nominations during a scheduled Committee hearing on another matter once enough SASC members attend. It is not uncommon for the chairman—advised by Committee professional staff a quorum is present—to halt the ongoing hearing mid-sentence, proceed with the nomination vote, and return to the hearing at hand—all within a few minutes and with minimal disruption.

Senate practice recognizes three possible motions for Committee action on nominations. These are:

1. Voting the nominations out of Committee with a favorable recommendation (that the nominations be confirmed by the Senate);
2. Voting the nominations out of Committee with an unfavorable recommendation (that the Senate decline to confirm the nominations) or
3. Voting the nominations out of Committee without recommendation.

Given that the nominations subject to vote have been cleared under the Committee's established criteria and processes, the Committee chairman or his designee invariably moves to vote the nominees out of Committee with a favorable recommendation. Presuming the existence of a quorum, a simple majority of senators present and voting must vote in favor of the motion for it to succeed. A tie vote or a majority of votes against the motion leaves the nominations in Committee.

Most Committee votes on military nominations are voice votes. Still, any SASC member may request a roll call vote, in which each senator's name is called, and his or her "Yes" or "No" vote on the motion recorded. Most votes are *en bloc*, meaning the

Committee votes on all cleared nominations in a single vote. Any senator may request a separate "by name" vote on one or more individual nominations, but this is extremely rare.

If a majority of senators present vote in favor of the nominee's confirmation, the Committee reports the nominations to the Senate floor with a recommendation for confirmation. In certain instances, the Committee may file a report on one or more nominees. Shortly after that, a copy of the list of nominees on which the Committee just voted is emailed to DOD. Senate Rules require any nomination reported out of Committee to "lay over" on the Senate floor for one business day before the nominee or list of nominees can be confirmed. This allows all 100 senators, most of whom are not members of the SASC, to review the nominations and raise any concerns. The decision to call up a nomination for consideration by the full Senate resides with the Senate majority leader.

Almost every month, one or more of the Military Services asks the SASC to request a waiver of the "1-day layover" rule to permit the full Senate to consider the pending military nominations as soon as they have been voted out of Committee. In almost every case, a rule waiver is unnecessary because the SASC routinely reports out military nominations well before the month's end. Although the Senate majority leader has the authority to ask for all senators' unanimous consent to waive the 1-day rule and move military nominations on the same day they are received from the Committee, the SASC chairman and ranking member take great pains not to deviate from established Senate processes. SASC leaders will request such a waiver only in extraordinary circumstances and with solid justification. The Committee *is not* impressed by pleas to hurry the confirmation process so changes of command, promotion ceremonies, and promotion parties can proceed or permit the confirmed officer's frocking. In fact, such requests may prompt the Committee to caution that DOD and the officers at issue take care to avoid the "presumption of confirmation." The principle that nominees who have not yet been confirmed by the Senate must avoid actions and statements that presume confirmation or appear to do so also applies to military nominees. A military officer who, before confirmation, sends invitations for a promotion party or change of command ceremony or engages with officer management personnel to reassign a trusted military subordinate to the unit he or she will command, once confirmed, risks derailing a confirmation that would otherwise be routine. Military leaders at all levels must remain vigilant against presumption missteps. They should instead take opportunities to reinforce—in word and deed—their understanding of the Senate's constitutional role in the confirmation process.

The Senate tries to avoid adverse effects on officers' promotions. It almost always confirms pending military nominations by the first day of the following month. In most cases, military nominations are confirmed *en bloc* by voice vote or unanimous consent as the Senate prepares to adjourn for the evening. Before the majority leader's motion for unanimous consent, all military nominee names are "hotlined." Hotlining is a system of telephonic and email messages transmitted to all senators' offices advising them of the military officers under consideration for confirmation by name and allowing each senator to object or withhold consent.

As discussed previously, a hold is a request by a senator to his or her party leader (either the majority or minority leader) to prevent or delay action on a nomination. A standing order of the Senate aims to ensure that any senator who places a hold on a nomination (or any other matter) publicly specifies his or her objection to the nominee. Still, enforcement of this order has proven challenging.[145] Senators may place a hold on a nomination for many reasons. Often the senator merely wants more time to review a nomination or to consult personally with the nominee. Should a senator place a hold on a military nomination, SASC professional staff are informed and immediately reach out to the staff of the holding senator to ascertain the basis for the hold and try to resolve it.

Sometimes, this requires additional coordination with the individual officer involved or with DOD and the Military Departments and Services. But senators have the discretion to continue a hold for as long as they deem appropriate. Some holds continue for many months or may never be lifted at all.

If no senator objects to a nomination, it will be approved. Routine nominations are grouped and brought up on the Senate floor *en bloc* and approved unanimously. I want to emphasize that if even one senator places a hold on a nomination, the unanimous consent process is scuttled for that nominee. However, other nominees will almost always go forward. In the absence of unanimous consent, the only remaining option by which a nominee can be confirmed is through the full-up invocation of cloture on the nomination. After the requisite interval, this would be followed by a vote on the individual nominee. This is incredibly rare concerning military officer nominations, in part because the thoroughness of the SASC process screens out at the Committee stage those officers who simply cannot make it through the full Senate. Such officers' nominations are usually held in Committee without further action, then returned to DOD at the White House or Department's request, upon withdrawal by the president, or at the end of a session of Congress per the Standing Rules of the Senate.[146]

Once confirmed, the nominations are returned to the Office of the Senate Executive Clerk, who transmits them to the White House with documentation of the Senate's action. The executive clerk updates the Senate website, and the SASC staff notifies DOD. At the appropriate time, the president, the secretary of defense, or their designee completes the final stage of the process by issuing official orders promoting and appointing the officer in the grade and/or position to which confirmed or granting federal recognition.

One more comment about congressional focus on the timeliness of the nomination process. I mentioned the "100-day" reports required by longstanding congressional policy. Under this policy, OSD must advise the SASC and the House Armed Services Committee (HASC) when promotion selection and federal recognition board reports are not approved by the 100th day after the board members sign the board report. The 100-day report must include the board's name, an explanation for the delay, the date the board report was approved, or an estimate of when the board report is projected to be approved. A follow-up report, including the same information, must be provided to the SASC and HASC every 30 days after the 100th day following board adjournment until the board report is approved.[147]

3- AND 4-STAR GENERAL AND FLAG OFFICER NOMINATIONS

Positions that carry with them a grade of 3- or 4-stars are the most important and visible in the Department of Defense. Unsurprisingly, nominations to these positions and grades attract the most public interest and are scrutinized by the Senate and the SASC. At the DOD and White House levels, nominations for appointment to 3-and 4-star positions are always individually recommended by the secretary of defense, individually selected by the president, and individually scrolled. These nominations are never submitted as part of a promotion list. These nominations are also processed individually by the SASC.

As discussed, SASC requires a nominee to any general or flag officer grade to submit a professional career resume and a color photo. And DOD must provide the Committee with a "Certification Letter" or "Cert" documenting any adverse or reportable information related to the nominee or affirming there is no such information. These exact requirements apply equally to 3- and 4-star nominees. But officers nominated to 3- and 4-star positions must also submit the following additional documents to the SASC to support their nominations:

1. Office of Government Ethics (OGE) Form 278e, Executive Personnel Public Financial Disclosure Report. Completing the 278e requires the nominee to disclose detailed information about his or her financial assets, debts, and positions held in organizations outside the federal government, as well as the assets, debts, and affiliations of the nominee's spouse and minor children.

2. A cover letter from the Designated Agency Ethics Official (DAEO). In the case of a military officer nominee, this is usually the senior ethics official of the Military Department of which the officer is a member. The DAEO's cover letter attests to the review of the officer's OGE Form 278e for actual or perceived conflicts of interest; assesses the officer's compliance with law, ethics regulations, and SASC divestiture standards; and spells out the steps the nominee must take—including the divestiture of certain assets or resignation from certain outside positions—to eliminate or mitigate any conflict or correct any violation. The letter concludes with the DAEO's certification that subject to the officer taking these steps, the nominee does not have a conflict of interest, or the appearance of one, for the position for which he or she is nominated.

The DAEO is available to guide the officer in completing the 278e. Unlike civilian nominees for whom the nomination process may be the first time they have been required to complete a financial disclosure form, nominees for military 3- and 4-star positions are "old hands." Most have been filing the 278e since first being promoted to general or flag officer grade. Some—depending on their career field—long before that. In short, all general and flag officers must complete a financial disclosure and undergo some level of review for conflicts of interest.

SASC's pre-hearing role in vetting 3- and 4-star military nominees includes a rigorous scrub for compliance with Executive Branch ethics rules and the Committee's ethics policy for nominees. Effective February 22, 2021, the SASC revised its policies concerning the divestitures required of military nominees for promotion to general and flag officer grades. The SASC has long differentiated between nominations for "designated acquisition positions" and nominations for "non-acquisition positions." Designated acquisition positions include, among others, the principal military deputy to the assistant secretary for acquisition, logistics, and technology of each Military Department, usually a 3-star position; the commanding generals of the service materiel commands, usually a 4-star position; and the director of the defense logistics agency, historically a 3-star position. The duties and functions of these positions vest significant acquisition and procurement responsibilities and authorities in the incumbent. Each officer nominated for a designated acquisition position is subject to heightened scrutiny for conflicts of interest that may affect or appear to affect the integrity of the DOD acquisition system.

Under current SASC policy, officers nominated for designated acquisition positions must divest holdings in the "Top 10" companies on the General Services Administration (GSA)-published Top 100 Contractors list for DOD over the most recent five fiscal years.[148] This new policy subjects military nominees for designated acquisition positions to the exact requirements enacted in law in Section 921 of the National Defense Authorization Act for Fiscal Year 2021 and puts nominees for some of the most senior military positions on a level playing field with civilian PAS nominees and members of the Senior Executive Service serving in key acquisition positions.[149] Before February 2021, the SASC required such nominees to divest holdings in companies in the "Top 10" DOD contractors in the previous fiscal year. Although the "Top 10" list rarely changes, the new 5-year timeframe was chosen to promote transparency and longer-term predictability in identifying prohibited holdings.

Individual stock holdings of less than $15,000, even in the "Top 10," are considered by OGE and the SASC as *de minimis* and need not be divested.[150] This same threshold applies to all Executive Branch nominations—military and civilian. It is a nominee's responsibility to ensure such investments do not grow to exceed the $15,000 threshold. Should an officer's investment accrue value above the *de minimis* level, the officer has the option to divest of the holding in full or to partially divest in an amount sufficient to return the value of the shares to or below the threshold. Although the $15,000 Executive Branch threshold has been static for decades, SASC policy will automatically adjust to any new *de minimis* standard should OGE increase the threshold. Nominees are required to divest only direct stock holdings. Divestiture of Excepted Investment Funds (EIFs) or mutual funds is not required unless the OGE of the DOD or Military Department DEAO deems any to be a "sector fund," where ownership could present an actual or perceived conflict of interest with the position's specific duties for which the officer is nominated.[151] These limitations on specific holdings, types of holdings, and the values of same apply throughout the officer's service in the specific position for which nominated.

In February 2021, SASC eliminated any unique SASC-mandated divestiture requirement for nominees to general and flag officer grades, including 3- and 4-star nominees for non-acquisition positions. Nominees are no longer required automatically to divest holdings in any company on the "Top 10" list in the prior year, as they were before that date. Instead, SASC expects DAEOs to continue their robust scrutiny of nominee holdings and outside positions for compliance with ethics law and policy. Officers nominated to non-acquisition positions may avail themselves of the $15,000 OGE *de minimis* exception to the same extent as nominees to designated acquisition positions. These changes in policy notwithstanding, SASC will continue to review all 3- and 4-star financial disclosure reports diligently and to monitor military nominee divestitures required to mitigate a conflict of interest or related ethics issues.

The OGE Form 278e and the DAEO's cover letter must be signed by the officer nominee and the appropriate ethics official, respectively, not more than 60 days before the date the nomination is received in the Senate. The Military Services will occasionally submit an older OGE 278e for the nominee. The SASC will then require a new, more recent OGE 278e or a letter from the nominee certifying the nominee's financial holdings and outside positions, as recorded in the older 278e, have not changed. If a new 278e is submitted, it must again be reviewed by the DAEO, who must also sign a new cover letter. A nominee's failure to comply with SASC's strict standards inevitably delays the SASC's processing of his or her nomination. If, for any reason, SASC believes additional divestitures beyond those described in the DAEO's cover letter are required, it will send a letter to the Department describing the required action. The senators will not consider the nomination until the Department demonstrates to the Committee's satisfaction why such divestiture should not be required under the specific facts and circumstances applicable to the officer's nomination or the nominee certifies he or she will comply.

In the extremely rare case when a military nominee is required to sell or otherwise divest an asset to avoid a conflict of interest or the appearance of one, and selling the asset will cause an unwelcome capital gain, they may be eligible for an OGE Certificate of Divestiture under the same terms and conditions as their civilian counterparts. Detailed information about the prerequisites, process, and timeline for obtaining a Certificate of Divestiture and completing the divestiture requirement is outlined in Chapter Five on Civilian Nominations.

Another area of acute interest to the SASC is the service of senior military officers on the boards of directors of companies doing business with the DOD or focusing their business principally on military personnel—USAA and the Navy Federal Credit Union, for example. Beginning in 1996, the SASC required as a condition of confirmation that officers nominated for appointment to 3- or 4-star grades resign from service, paid or unpaid, on the boards of such companies, including for-profit and non-profit entities and charitable organizations. The Committee was and remains concerned about military officers—particularly 3- and 4-stars—using the status of their positions for personal gain, whether compensation or resume building, or for the gain of entities that do significant business with DOD or military personnel or their families.

This policy had its origins in the nomination of Admiral Jay Johnson. On June 5, 1996, President Clinton nominated Admiral Johnson, then serving as vice chief of Naval Operations for only four months, to be chief of Naval Operations. Johnson would succeed Admiral Jeremy "Mike" Boorda, whose suicide a month earlier had rocked the Navy to its core.[152] Just hours after the White House announced Johnson's nomination, SASC Chairman Strom Thurmond (R-SC) raised concerns about the nomination based on Johnson's position on the board of USAA, an insurance company that serves military personnel. It was a paid position that had netted Johnson more than \$33,000 over several years. Although the issue had not come up when SASC confirmed Johnson for the vice chief's job only months earlier, Senator Thurmond publicly stated he would "withhold [his] opinion of the nomination" until he examined the DOD policy allowing active-duty personnel to hold paid corporate posts. Soon after, the secretary of defense changed the DOD policy to prohibit 3- and 4-star officers from holding such positions. Johnson resigned from the USAA position. After a closed session and a public hearing on July 31, he was favorably voted out of Committee by unanimous vote and confirmed days later by voice vote on the Senate floor.

Years later, in September 2011, DOD voluntarily expanded the SASC policy to a broader class of personnel. In November 2021, it expanded it further. Today the DOD policy applies to officers nominated to *all* general and flag officer grades in active and reserve components.[153] The purpose of this expansion was to preclude "any suggestion of impropriety that a military leader's participation in the management of certain outside businesses suggests governmental endorsement or sanction of the business." Given the scope of the DOD policy, this issue rarely raises its head today. Still, the Committee remains attentive to this concern.

3. A letter from the officer nominee to the chairman of the SASC addressing conflicts of interest and other sensitive matters. Like other SASC-required paperwork, the nominee's letter must be signed personally by the officer no later than 60 days

before receiving the officer's nomination in the Senate. A template letter, which sets forth all issues the SASC requires the nominee to address, is in Appendix D. Note: this is only a template. SASC expects each nominee to change the letter to reflect his or her unique personal circumstances. Nominees are also expected to use the letter to elaborate on sensitive matters or concerns, such as past misconduct allegations or disciplinary actions. Anything that may be revealed in their financial disclosure forms or responses to the SASC Questionnaire for Military Nominees should be included.

4. A completed SASC Questionnaire for Nominees for Certain Senior Military Positions. Part A of the questionnaire elicits the nominee's biographical information and commitments in furtherance of congressional and Committee oversight. Part B of the SASC Questionnaire requests additional personal information and information about employment relationships, potential conflicts of interest, legal matters and prior discipline, foreign affiliations, and financial data. The questionnaire must be completed and personally signed by the nominee no more than 60 days before the date the officer's nomination is received in the Senate. SASC professional staff reviews the responses to ensure all questions are answered and to identify any potential controversy or concern or an item of interest to any senator.

Some requirements applicable to civilian nominees do not apply to the military or may apply only in particular circumstances. Unlike civilian nominations, for which the submission of paperwork is required to start a full-field FBI background check, this is not required in the case of military nominations. Most general and flag officer nominees first completed the SF 86 paperwork required to initiate a background investigation before being authorized to attend a Military Service Academy or participate in Reserve

Officers' Training Corps or Officers' Training School. They have held security clearances for many years and have been re-validated many times through periodic 5-year reinvestigations or continuous monitoring.

Although the SASC Questionnaire for Military Nominees requires the nominee to disclose whether he or she has filed all required federal tax returns and paid taxes on time, there is no automatic requirement to submit copies of recent tax returns to the Committee. Civilian nominees must provide the Committee complete copies of their last three federal tax returns. Military nominees are advised only that their tax returns *may be requested.* I am unaware of a single situation when the Committee made such a request.

Finally, military nominees are not required to provide the Committee with copies of publications they have authored or speeches they have delivered. General and flag officers are subject to close public attention in the ordinary course of events. The Committee presumes their public statements, subject to advance screening by Departmental public affairs experts and legal personnel, will be readily available from public sources. As in all cases, the Committee reserves the right to request such documentation from any military nominee should the need arise.

Unlike civilian nominees, military officers are not subject to the White House's "intent to nominate" announcement. That's not to say there isn't plenty of back-and-forth between the DOD, the White House, and the Committee when considering an officer or several officers for a high-profile military position. Similar to civilian nominations, particularly regarding 3- and 4-star positions, there can be great confusion among DOD, the White House, and the individual officer involved whether a nomination and all paperwork have been received in the Senate and by the Committee.

The SASC chairman or ranking member often must remind a Military Department secretary, eager for the Committee to push forward the nomination, "I cannot process a nomination I do not have." More commonly, the Committee has received the nomination, but the officer's paperwork, which usually filters into the Committee incrementally, is incomplete, à la General Dugan. It also frequently happens the SASC is awaiting a response to posed questions to the Department about some aspect of the nominated officer's submissions to the Committee. Then processing is on hold until all paperwork is "in-house" and questions about a nominee's OGE 278e, Letter to the Chairman, or SASC Questionnaire have been addressed to the Committee's satisfaction.

All the information submitted by the president, the military officer nominee, and the Military Department is made available to the senators comprising the SASC, the SASC staff director, the minority staff director, majority and minority general counsels, and other specially designated members of the Committee's Professional Staff. Any senator and Committee professional staff member is authorized to raise questions associated with the nominee and his or her nomination package. Questions that cannot be answered "in-house" are redirected to the Department or the nominee for response or clarification.

Again, the SASC cannot and will not clear a nomination until it has received and reviewed all required documents and information and satisfactory responses to all questions posed to the nominee and the Department. Nominees can rest assured that because these nomination files contain confidential and very personal information, they are maintained under lock and key. It is available only to Committee professional staff with a demonstrably official "need to know." To my knowledge, over many years of experience with the Committee, the contents of these files have never been breached or improperly disclosed by SASC senators or Committee professional staff.

After all required documents are submitted to, received, and reviewed by the Committee, the Committee staff director and/or general counsel may request the nominee participate in an interview or meeting. These are commonly known as "courtesy calls," during which additional questions arising throughout the Committee's nomination review may be addressed. The minority staff director and minority counsel may request a similar interview. It is also common for 3- and 4-star military nominees to meet with individual members of the SASC at their request. However, not every 3- or 4-star nominee, particularly those slated to fill Military Service command billets, will be asked to meet with the Committee.

If the Committee intends to conduct a hearing on the nomination, the following procedures apply:

A hearing date is selected by the Committee chairman in consultation with the ranking member. Soon after a hearing date is selected, the Committee's majority and minority counsel provide Advance Policy Questions (APQs) to the nominee. APQs can run into hundreds of questions, addressing every policy and program over which a nominee will exercise authority and responsibility if confirmed. For example, when Chief of Staff of the Army Gen. Mark Milley was nominated to be chairman of the Joint Chiefs of Staff, the Committee presented him with 41 pages of APQs. They ranged in subject from civilian control of the military to the military relationships with countries in every regional combatant command to the impact of environmental contaminants on military installations. Milley responded to every question. In most cases, nominees have only 3-5 days to provide their completed APQ responses to the Committee. A 3- or 4-star nominee's APQ responses are almost always reviewed and, in some cases, adjusted by the DOD general counsel. In 2023, General C.Q. Brown received 339 APQs for his confirmation to be CJCS.

Under SASC rules, public notice of the date and place of the hearing and the name of the nominee who will testify must be issued at least one week before the hearing. Although this deadline for public notice may be waived, this is rarely done. Other deadlines also loom. The nominee's APQ responses and the text of any written statement the nominee plans to deliver at the hearing must be provided to the Committee no later than 48 hours before the hearing (not including holidays and weekends).

The nominee's responses to Part A of the SASC Questionnaire, the letter from the DAEO, the officer's letter to the chairman of the Committee, and the nominee's responses to APQs are made available for public inspection in the Committee office before the hearing. After the hearing, this same information will be entered into the record, which is also available to the public. The nominee's responses to Part B of the SASC Questionnaire, financial data, and other confidential information are not publicly available. They will be kept in the Committee's executive files.

A Committee hearing is conducted and chaired by the chairman or his or her designee. Nominees for appointment to 3- and 4-star positions (though 3-stars rarely have hearings) may be subject to an individual hearing and may be the only nominee present or on a panel with other nominees. SASC rarely intermixes civilian and military nominees on the same hearing panel. Still, there is no hard and fast rule, and the Committee will adjust panel membership to the circumstances. All confirmation hearings are open to the public. Although, matters relating to conflicts of interest or other confidential matters may be heard in a closed Executive Session that, if required, usually takes place immediately before or after the public hearing. Classified information may also be discussed in closed hearings or briefings in properly cleared spaces in the Capitol reserved for this purpose. Such off-the-record sessions are infrequent, having occurred only once or twice in the last five years. The chairman of the SASC begins the hearing by making brief opening remarks and introducing the nominee. If desired, the nominee may be introduced by a current or former member of Congress at the hearing. Unlike other committees, the SASC does not require nominees to testify under oath. I cannot recall a single instance where a nominee was sworn in during my tenure as staff director.

The chairman of the SASC begins the hearing by asking the nominee to respond on the record to standard questions designed to ensure the nominee has not taken actions or decisions that might reflect a "presumption of confirmation." These questions, originated by Chairman Nunn during my service as staff director, are also intended to secure each nominee's commitment, once confirmed, to comply with SASC requirements for providing information to assist the Committee in its oversight of DOD. The questions are generally the following or some variation thereof:

1. Have you adhered to applicable laws and regulations governing conflicts of interest?
2. Have you assumed any duties or taken any actions that would appear to presume the outcome of the confirmation process?
3. Exercising our legislative and oversight responsibilities makes it essential that this Committee, its subcommittees, and other appropriate committees of Congress receive testimony, briefings, reports, records, and other information from the Executive Branch on a timely basis. Do you agree, if confirmed, to appear and testify before this Committee when requested?
4. When asked before this Committee, do you agree to give your personal views, even if they differ from those of the administration?

5. Do you agree to promptly provide records, documents, and electronic communications when requested by this Committee, its subcommittees, or other appropriate committees? And to consult with the requester regarding the basis for any good faith delay or denial in providing such records?
6. Will you ensure your staff complies with deadlines established by this Committee for producing reports, records, and other information, including timely responding to hearing Questions for the Record?
7. Will you cooperate and provide witnesses and briefers in response to a congressional request?
8. Will those witnesses and briefers be protected from reprisal for their testimony or briefings?

Question four is a matter of particular interest for most military nominees. Unlike civilian nominees who are always deemed to be representatives of the current administration, it has long been SASC policy to secure a public, on-the-record commitment from 3- and 4-star nominees that, if confirmed and when asked by the SASC or other appropriate committees of Congress to provide their personal views on an issue, they will do so, even if those views differ from the position of the administration in power.

This will be at least the third time the military nominee has been required to respond to such questions and make such commitments. Similar written questions, including those related to personal views, are contained within the SASC Questionnaire that all 3- and 4-star military nominees must complete, whether slated for a confirmation hearing or not. In addition, the same questions are set forth in each nominee's APQs. SASC and its subcommittees can leverage this commitment to secure the personal views of senior military officers on controversial and political issues. As was widely reported in June 2021, SASC Ranking Member Jim Inhofe (R-OK) invoked these commitments to request the chairman of the Joint Chiefs, the service chiefs, and the chief of the National Guard Bureau provide their personal views on the potential effects of a pending legislative proposal to shift the prosecution of sexual assault and other serious crimes out of the traditional chain of command, a proposal that Inhofe opposed.[154]

But over time, not every senior military officer has responded to this question with the conviction desired. On June 14, 1990, during his confirmation hearing to be chief of Naval Operations, Admiral Frank Kelso responded to Chairman Nunn's question about personal views. He stated, "I would check first with the secretary of defense." Nunn replied with complete equanimity, "Admiral, the only acceptable answer is "yes" or "no." You can use either. And if it's "no," I won't support your confirmation." Admiral Kelso replied, "Mr. Chairman, yes."

More recently, during the Trump Administration, nominees began to caveat their written responses to these longstanding questions with lengthy, legalistic answers with words to the effect that the nominee "would provide the Committee with information or testimony subject to all the tenets of executive privilege and other laws and regulations." The Committee was unimpressed. It quickly made plain that a simple "yes" or "no" answer would suffice and was expected. Without a simple "yes," the nominee would not proceed to a hearing.

After the nominees have responded to the standard questions, the Committee's ranking member makes brief remarks. The chairman then invites the nominee to present an opening statement. Because the SASC requests each nominee limit the length of his or her remarks to five minutes or less, nominees typically present a shortened version of each submitted written opening statement. (The complete written statement will be included in the hearing record.) A question-and-answer period follows. The SASC operates under a so-called "early bird rule." Questioning alternates between senators from each party in the order in which they arrived in the hearing room before the chairman struck the convening gavel.

Once all "early bird" senators have been recognized and completed their questions, the senators who arrived after the hearing will begin questioning the nominee, again alternating between senators of the majority and minority parties in order of seniority. The SASC limits each senator's question-and-answer period to a time the chairman and ranking member have agreed in advance, usually five to seven minutes. Each senator is free to question the nominee as he or she sees fit, and senators' approaches to a nominee can vary.

Whichever way a senator might choose to proceed, few questions are off-limits. Members' questions of the nominee during the hearing may concern matters relating to the nominee's personal background and qualifications or policy and program matters relevant to the position for which the officer is nominated. The question-and-answer period allows senators to clarify assertions made in a nominee's opening statement, during the nominee's courtesy call with the senator, in response to a question from another senator earlier in the hearing, in the nominee's APQs, or in other contexts—such as during a public speech or as quoted in the news media.

In SASC's early days, then-Chairman Russell used the confirmation process to put the Committee's policy *preferences* before the nominee. To a significant degree, this practice continues today. SASC members use the questioning process to impress on nominees the issues the Committee believes they should focus on once confirmed. It is important to note Senator Russell still firmly believed SASC's role was to provide oversight and accountability while initiating and implementing policy belonged to the Executive Branch. SASC professional staff and individual senators' military legislative assistants often draft questions or talking points for members to use in questioning a nominee. It's also important for nominees to realize, given the press of their many duties, senators are free to come and go during the hearing. Many will leave the hearing room as soon as their question-and-answer session with the nominee concludes. The chairman and ranking member generally are present throughout the hearing. Still, some senators may not attend a particular hearing at all. All this is to be expected, and nominees should not allow themselves to be distracted by comings and goings on the dais.

After the hearing, each SASC member can submit Questions for the Record (QFRs), to which a nominee will be expected to respond in writing. A nominee's satisfactory responses to all QFRs must be received and reviewed before the Committee votes on his or her nomination.

To summarize, the Committee will vote on a 3- or 4-star nominee:

1. Only after the nomination has been in the Committee for seven days. This gives each SASC senator a meaningful opportunity to review each nomination and to raise concerns, if any. This 7-day requirement can be waived, but this is rarely done.
2. Whose PDOP or PDOA is within 120 days.
3. As to whom there is no adverse or reportable information from DOD (e.g., a clean "Cert") or from other sources, or who has been cleared by the Committee to proceed, after full consideration of any adverse or reportable information attributable to the nominee, as discussed in Chapter 14.
4. As to whom no issues were raised in the nominee's financial disclosure package, Letter to the Chairman, or completed SASC Questionnaire, and provided that any issues raised have been resolved to the satisfaction of the Committee.

5. If the nominee was required to participate in a confirmation hearing, no issues were raised by the nominee's APQs or hearing responses. If issues were raised, they have been resolved to the satisfaction of the Committee, and the nominee's QFR responses have been received, reviewed, and deemed sufficient.

Once these conditions are met, the chairman, in consultation with the ranking member, will set a day and time for the Committee vote. The Committee vote and Senate floor processes mirror those for other civilian and military nominations. From this point forward, 3- and 4-star military nominations will proceed along the same trajectory, process, and timeline as any other civilian or military nomination.

A quick aside. Some military nominees for a 3- and 4-star position may be required to undergo more than one Senate confirmation hearing. Nominations—even military nominations—can be multi-dimensional. They cross the jurisdictional boundaries of more than one Senate committee. Under a process known as "sequential referral," a nomination may be referred to two or more committees for successive consideration, usually under some predetermined time limit. For example, the commander of U.S. Cyber Command is dual-hatted as the director of the National Security Agency. After such a nominee is favorably reported out of the SASC, the nomination is referred to the Senate Select Committee on Intelligence for follow-on review and consideration for 30 days.[155] The nominee must submit to the separate procedures of the SSCI, including a confirmation hearing. However, the SSCI must complete its process within 30 days, or the nomination will be automatically discharged from the Committee to the Senate floor.

Sometimes, however, a military nominee's engagement with other Senate committees as part of the confirmation process is a matter of comity rather than mandate. Because of the civil works program under the Army Corps of Engineers, together with its use of program funding to execute civil works projects in each of the 53 states and territories, all senators have great interest in the military officer nominated to be the chief of engineers and commanding general, U.S. Army Corps of Engineers. In some years—particularly after Hurricane Katrina—the nominee for this 3-star position was first required to participate in a hearing before the Armed Services Committee, then *requested* to stand before the Senate Committee on Environment and Public Works (EPW). Although the nomination is not in EPW's jurisdiction, the EPW exercises oversight responsibility for the Corps' civil works program. Only a short-sighted nominee—one unconcerned about his or her pending consideration by the entire U.S. Senate—would decline such a request from the EPW Committee.

One other matter of interest. At the beginning of the Biden Administration, individual members of the SASC posed their own "questionnaires" to general and flag officer nominees. They required the nominee to sign and return the completed questionnaire to the member's personal office "no later than 72 hours before the Senate votes on your nomination." It posed questions such as "Do you believe that the Declaration of Independence, the United States Constitution, or both are inherently racist? If yes, explain." And "Do you believe race should be a key factor in the military's promotion decisions, job assignments, or other personnel actions? If yes, please explain." It is unclear how nominees' responses are evaluated or the impact on a nominee providing an answer with which the sponsor of the questionnaire may disagree. Nominees should know they may be required to complete such a questionnaire, even though it is not part of the SASC's official confirmation process. A senator on the SASC is certainly well within the Senate Rules to do this.

Given the extensive body of laws, rules, regulations, directives, and processes governing military personnel management, especially selection, confirmation, and promotion, the SASC considers military nominations and promotions a sacrosanct area. The SASC, through history, continues to ensure only the military officers who are highly qualified for the rank and/or position are approved by the Senate in its advice and consent role.

14

THE ADVERSE INFORMATION PROCESS

Although most military nominations are routine, some are encumbered by adverse or reportable information. The SASC considers its review of adverse and reportable information attributable to military officers nominated for appointment, promotion, and federal recognition critical to its "advice and consent" role. Knowing such information allows senators to make informed decisions about whether an officer should be confirmed. Although the nominations of officers for promotion or federal recognition in any grade may be affected by adverse or reportable information, the Committee expressly focuses on officers nominated to general and flag officer grades and positions of "importance and responsibility."

Over the years, some SASC senators have viewed the Committee's consideration of and action on adverse and reportable information as a tool for enforcing strict accountability for an officer's prior bad acts and instances of poor judgment. Most others have come down on the side of considering an instance of misconduct or lapse in judgment in the context of the "whole person" over the entirety of the officer's military career. It's hard to argue with either, given the Committee's solemn constitutional responsibility for oversight of the Department and its duty to ensure the leadership of our Soldiers, Sailors, Airmen, Marines, and Guardians is entrusted to officers of the highest caliber.

SASC employs a robust adverse information reporting and review process, much of which has been enacted in law and formalized in DOD policy. But most important to the process is the trust between DOD and the SASC built up and reinforced over time by

DOD's strict compliance with the formal rules and informal practices around the identification, consideration, and unflinching disclosure of adverse or reportable information attributable to an officer nominee. DOD's long-held practice of informal consultation with SASC on cases of first impression, "close to the line" policy calls, and new policy development in this area has also served the Department, its nominees, and the SASC exceedingly well.

The SASC upholds its part of this bargain by maintaining—to the greatest degree possible in the context of the confirmation process—the privacy of the officer concerned. SASC does this by carefully safeguarding the sensitive adverse and reportable information DOD provides to the Committee, handling all records, documents, and information on the matter with the utmost confidentiality. Only specially designated Committee professional staff with an official "need to know" and SASC senators are made aware of the names of nominees with adverse or reportable information, much less read into the specific facts of these cases. This "close hold" information *is not shared* with most Committee staff or senators' personal office staff. Even senators' military legislative assistants (MLAs)—their direct liaisons to the SASC—are not kept in the loop for purposes of adverse information. In my many years on the Committee and since leaving public service as a careful observer of SASC activities, I am unaware of a single leak of adverse or reportable information that can be laid at the feet of SASC senators or professional staff.

When information about a case gets out, it is almost always attributable to the affected officer. They put their story out there to solicit the support of high-ranking Executive Branch officials or other members of Congress in pushing the nomination through the Committee. This tactic is rarely helpful in achieving the objective.

After the Committee completes its review and action on a nomination with adverse or reportable information, all investigative files provided by DOD are returned to the Military Department concerned. The Committee does not retain file copies.

The SASC ensures every officer's nomination, particularly those with adverse or reportable information, receives full and fair consideration against a backdrop of understanding mistakes are part and parcel of the human condition. And a "zero-defects" approach to eligibility for promotion, federal recognition, and appointment to key senior positions *does not* serve our nation's interest in developing a cadre of competent and caring military leaders.

The fact is that adverse or reportable information *is not career-ending* in the vast majority of cases. Although nominations accompanied by adverse or reportable information are subject to enhanced scrutiny, *most ultimately result in the officer's confirmation.*

Even though most officers with adverse or reportable information are confirmed, these nominations take longer to process. In prioritizing nominations with adverse or reportable information that must be reviewed and cleared before the Committee will act, the Committee may consider the following factors: when the Committee received the adverse or reportable information, including any additional information requested by the Committee; the level of complexity of the case and the issues it raises; the likelihood the Committee will clear the nomination, notwithstanding the adverse or reportable information; the level of senator interest; the level of DOD interest; and the date on which the officer's 30-month promotion eligibility period will end (after which an officer who has not yet been confirmed by the Senate must be removed from the list, re-compete for promotion, and if again selected be renominated by the president).[156]

That said, in each session of Congress, there are a few military nominations not confirmed. The issues that most frequently stand in the way of confirming an officer include:

- Personal integrity. As in so much else in life, it is often not the bad act or mistake that most weighs against an officer's confirmation but the lack of candor, lies, or coverup after the fact.
- Actions reflecting an officer's belief that the laws and regulations simply do not apply to them, including the misuse of junior military personnel and aides and willful disregard of limitations on the use of official travel and time.
- Adverse leadership climate. The Committee and the Senate have long been concerned about senior military officers who failed to promote a proper leadership climate in the organizations they commanded. An example that still holds true today is the SASC's approach to the controversial circumstances of the nomination of Major General Robert Clark as the commander of Fifth U.S. Army (later redesignated as the Army Component Command of the United States Northern Command), a 3-star position. In 1999, Clark was criticized when Private First-Class Barry Winchell was viciously murdered at Fort Campbell, Kentucky, by two other soldiers who suspected him of being homosexual. Clark served as commander of the 101st Airborne Division (Air Assault) and Fort Campbell at the time of the murder. Although an Army investigation cleared Clark of allegations that he had tolerated anti-gay attitudes on post, critics asserted he had permitted an atmosphere of harassment to pervade. In a press release referencing Clark's nomination for a third star, SASC Senator Edward Kennedy (D-MA) stated: "We need to hold senior commanders accountable if they allow a climate of bigotry, intimidation, and fear to exist." Ultimately, Clark was confirmed, but not until November 2003, more than a year after the president first submitted his nomination.

The SASC's vigilance in examining military officer misconduct—senior officers in particular—together with the corresponding requirement for DOD to divulge adverse information about its nominees, first came to a head in the late 1980s through an exchange of letters between SASC Chairman Sam Nunn and Secretary of Defense Frank Carlucci on the matter of Army Lieutenant General John F. Wall. The Tailhook scandal of the early 1990s would put an even finer point on the Committee's efforts to ensure it confirmed only officers who met exemplary conduct standards. But the Wall case is where it began in earnest.

On August 1, 1988, Chairman Nunn and Ranking Member Warner sent a joint letter to Carlucci expressing "deep concern" about the Senate's confirmation of Lieutenant General Wall's retirement in the grade of 3-star only months earlier. Recall that at the time, Senate "confirmation" was a prerequisite to an officer's retirement in the grade of O-9 or O-10. As submitted by DOD and the White House, Wall's retirement package had appeared routine. At the SASC's recommendation, the Senate quickly confirmed Wall's retirement grade without debate. The Army retired Wall in grade on July 1, 1988. A mere two weeks later, in mid-July, a DOD legislative affairs representative somewhat cryptically reported to SASC that a House Government Operations Committee hearing on fraud and abuse in defense procurement had revealed allegations against Wall the day before. The House Committee had gone so far as to question the propriety of his retirement as a 3-star. Purportedly, Wall had used government transportation for personal convenience and released sensitive acquisition information to a defense contractor. In the following days, the Army disclosed to SASC that in March 1988—well before his retirement package had been submitted to the Senate—Wall had received a letter of reprimand from the Army vice chief citing significant allegations of misconduct on Wall's part. The SASC and Senate were not privy to these allegations when they confirmed Wall for retirement almost three months later.

The Nunn-Warner letter emphasized the SASC depended on the good faith of the Executive Branch in providing the Committee with information that might affect the outcome of the confirmation process. In Wall's case, it labeled the process a "failure" and a "serious breach of trust." Nunn and Warner concluded by stating:

> ... until further notice, we must ask that all flag and general officer nominations by the president be accompanied by a statement regarding any adverse action taken or pending against the officer since his or her last Senate confirmation. A simple statement is sufficient if no adverse action has been taken or is pending. If adverse action has been taken or is pending, a summary of the relevant facts should be provided.

Secretary Carlucci responded on August 17, 1988, expressing his displeasure and embarrassment at DOD's handling of the Wall retirement nomination. He implied he, too, had been unaware of the allegations against Wall. Carlucci echoed Nunn and Warner's views of the importance of "good faith" in dealings between DOD and the SASC and assured them he would never intentionally jeopardize their trust. Carlucci promised to report to the Committee on the completion of reviews he had directed into the Wall case and the handling of nominations Department-wide.

Meanwhile, Carlucci directed the Secretary of the Army, John O. Marsh, to conduct a detailed post-mortem of the Wall case, which Carlucci called an "unacceptable aberration" that had seriously jeopardized the credibility of the nomination process and the Department. Carlucci also ordered the other Military Department secretaries to review their departments' internal processes to ensure any potentially adverse information concerning an officer received appropriate scrutiny by the secretaries of the Military Departments, the secretary of defense, and the White House before a nomination was forwarded to the Senate.

After these reviews, in late September 1988, Carlucci wrote again to Nunn and Warner, advising he had established new DOD procedures to ensure the Senate was aware of adverse information regarding general or flag officer nominees. Carlucci committed to advising the Committee when the nominee was the subject of a pending investigation or any disciplinary action had been taken against the nominee or was in process. In appropriate cases, he also agreed to certify DOD had no evidence that a nominated officer had engaged in conduct constituting a conflict of interest, failed to adhere to required standards, misconduct, or was pending investigation. Finally, Carlucci provided the Committee with a thorough, by-name review that showed no evidence of adverse information pertaining to a long list of military nominations pending before the Senate.

These commitments serve as the underpinning of DOD policies and SASC expectations that continue through the present day.

DEFINITIONS:

Although grasping how it all began is important, the next logical step in understanding the modern-day DOD and SASC processes surrounding adverse and reportable information is an understanding of the current "technical" definitions to which the DOD and the SASC have agreed:

Adverse Information:[157] Adverse information is any substantiated adverse finding or conclusion from an officially documented investigation or inquiry or any other credible information of an adverse nature. The information must be resolved and supported by a preponderance of the evidence to be credible. To be adverse, the information must be derogatory, unfavorable, or of a nature that reflects clearly unacceptable conduct, integrity, or judgment on the individual.

The following types of information, even though credible, are not considered adverse:

a. Motor vehicle violations that did not require a court appearance.
b. Minor infractions without negative effect on an individual or the good order and discipline of the organization that were not identified because of substantiated findings or conclusions from an officially documented investigation or did not result in more than non-punitive rehabilitative counseling administered by a superior to a subordinate.

Adverse information does not include information previously considered by the Senate under an earlier nomination of the officer or information attributed to an individual 10 or more years before the date of the personnel action under consideration. The exception to these exceptions is that any substantiated act that, if tried by court-martial, could have resulted in a punitive discharge and confinement for more than one year must be reported, regardless of the date of the incident. The date of the substantiated adverse finding or conclusion from an officially documented investigation or inquiry is used to establish the period, not the date of the incident.

Reportable Information:[158] Information other than adverse information requested to be reported by the SASC or by any member of the Senate or information related to alleged misconduct or impropriety, which is subject to an ongoing investigative, administrative, or judicial process. Typically, a nomination will be delayed pending investigation or administrative process resolution. Credible information related to an individual's involvement or affiliation with a significant event widely known to the public or members of Congress that brings discredit on or calls into question the integrity of members of the DOD, components of the DOD, or the DOD may also be reportable. Ordinarily, information known for more than three years before the nomination process or information previously considered by the SASC as part of a previous nomination of that individual will not be reported.

EXECUTIVE BRANCH PROCESS FOR ADVERSE INFORMATION

Most of the actions required to identify and review adverse and reportable information and weigh how it should factor in the nomination of a particular officer take place at DOD and the White House long before a nomination is submitted to the Senate.

SCREENING AND IDENTIFICATION

Before convening a promotion selection or federal recognition board, the secretary of the Military Department must establish the number and names of the military officers eligible for consideration by the board. In concert with the Department of Defense inspector general, the secretary will screen the names of eligible officers against Military Department and DOD systems of records to identify any adverse information attributable to them.

This screening encompasses a wide swath of investigative files, including files of the DOD, Service, and state inspectors general; Equal Employment Opportunity[159] and Equal Opportunity[160] records; and National Crime Information Center, Central Clearance Facility,[161] judge advocate general, general counsel,[162] and other Service databases.

Information identified in these investigative files or databases and attributable to an officer to be considered by an upcoming board is reviewed against the previously mentioned definitions. Only information that meets the definition of adverse or reportable information is subject to additional review. In general terms, information over 10 years old or that meets one of the exceptions built into the definitions (e.g., a traffic citation for a minor violation) is not usually considered further. Once an officer has been confirmed by the Senate after the SASC is notified of adverse information, that information will usually not be part of any future nomination for that officer. This does not relieve the secretary of the Military Department from advising of other information not reported to SASC during the last confirmation, which might affect the current nomination and confirmation process.

This screening and identification process has been refined over many years. Challenges persist, however, in identifying adverse or reportable information associated with administrative investigations, so-called AR 15-6, JAGMAN, and command-directed investigations. Most of these are conducted and retained in field commands. The SASC has continued to press the Department to centralize the retention of these investigations for adverse and reportable information screening purposes. Although progress has been made in this direction, more work remains.

REFERRAL TO OFFICER

The law also mandates that before adverse information about an officer is furnished to a promotion or federal recognition board, it must be made available to the officer involved. And the officer must be allowed a reasonable opportunity to review the information and submit written comments for the board's consideration. The adverse or reportable information is distilled into a summary (an AIS or RIS).

Going forward, the AIS/RIS will be paired with any written comments the officer provides and considered by the board. If the officer is recommended by the board for promotion or federal recognition, that information will be considered at all stages of the process.

INFO PROVIDED TO PROMOTION BOARDS

Until recently, the Military Departments screened officers for adverse and reportable information *after* a promotion or federal recognition board to ensure each officer selected met standards of exemplary conduct. The Military Departments vastly preferred that post-board screening policy. It reduced the administrative burdens on the Department by eliminating the screening of thousands of colonels eligible for consideration for promotion to brigadier general before the board was convened. For example, the Department was required to screen only the 40-plus officers ultimately recommended by the board. If this post-board screening identified adverse or reportable information attributable to a selected officer, the information would be referred to the officer for comment. After that, the officer's promotion board file, the adverse information, and any written comments the officer submitted would be referred to a promotion review board (PRB). The PRB was an *ad hoc* board comprising three general or flag officers. Cognizant that the officer under consideration had been recommended by a board, the PRB's task was to determine whether the nature of the adverse information was such that it warranted removing the officer's name. The PRB's recommendation to keep the officer on the list or remove the officer's name from the board report was submitted to the secretary of the Military Department, who could accept or reject it. If, after considering the PRB's recommendation, the secretary determines the officer should be promoted or federally recognized, their name would move forward with the secretarial package and continue through the process. Whenever the secretary of the Military Department attributes adverse or reportable information to an officer, the memorandum forwarding the board report for approval must include the following:

1. The AIS or RIS and the officer's written comments.

2. The specific rationale for support of the officer for nomination as it applies to the adverse or reportable information.
3. An explanation of how the officer meets the requirement of exemplary conduct set forth in law, given the adverse information.
4. A statement regarding the officer's judgment concerning the specific information.
5. Documentation of non-judicial punishment imposed, copies of administrative letters or memoranda of counseling, admonition, reprimand, or a statement explaining why such documents are not included in the package.[163]

In contrast, if the secretary determined the officer should not be promoted or federally recognized, the officer's name would be withheld from the board package and processed for removal.

In the last few years, however, the Armed Services Committees and Congress as a whole have taken deliberate steps to ensure that "credible information of an adverse nature"[164] about an officer under consideration by a board for promotion to or federal recognition in specific grades, is provided to, and *considered by the board at every stage of its proceedings*.[165] The grades for which board review is mandated under law are the same as those for which Senate confirmation is required (i.e., active-duty officer promotions and appointments to grades O-4 and above; federal recognition and other appointments for reserve component officers in grades O-6 and above).

Congress also enacted laws that effectively discontinued the PRB process after January 1, 2022. After that date—at the election of the secretary of the Military Department—any officer who went before a board and was later determined to have adverse information not considered by that board must be referred to a so-called Special Selection Review Board (SSRB) or be reconsidered by the next promotion or federal recognition board (which will most likely not occur until the following year), this time with the adverse information and the officer's comments included.[166] If the secretary chooses the SSRB option, the SSRB will gather for a second look at the officer's promotion folder, including the adverse information. The SSRB would not indicate or disclose for which officer or officers it was convened. It would apply the same standards used by the board that initially recommended the officer for promotion or federal recognition and determine whether that recommendation should be sustained. If, after considering the adverse information or for any other reason, an SSRB did not sustain the original recommendation, the officer would be considered to have failed selection for promotion. The SSRB's findings are binding on the secretary of the Military Department. In contrast, an officer whose promotion or federal recognition was sustained by an SSRB could be moved forward and, once confirmed and appointed, guaranteed the same rank date expected under the original board's recommendation.

In my assessment, Congress views the new SSRB as important to ensure the most deserving and best-qualified officers are advanced to higher ranks and responsibilities. I think there is a perception that a competitive process, in which officers to whom adverse or reportable information is attributed compete with peers, who themselves may or may not have adverse or reportable information, as more likely to identify the highest performing officers with the greatest potential for future service. At the same time, the process still allows for leadership development and personal growth in the officer corps. Lacking the crucible of merit-based competition, a PRB's "thumbs up or thumbs down" recommendation, whether adverse or reportable information disqualified an officer advancement for which they were already selected by a prior board, appears in hindsight to be far less likely to yield an outcome of greatest benefit to a Military Service's long-term leadership lineup. One must question whether the PRB was fair to *all officers* considered by the original board, including the officer at issue and those who competed head-to-head but were not recommended for promotion by the original board.

For general and flag officer nominees, adverse and reportable information consistent with the definitions must always be reported to the Senate as part of a nomination package. DOD has far more latitude concerning nominations to the grades of O-6 and below. In such cases, the secretary of the Military Department has some discretion to determine that adverse or reportable information need not be reported to the secretary of defense, the president, or the Senate for confirmation. But the secretary almost always errs in favor of reporting, even if there is no strict requirement.[167]

In addition, over time, SASC has periodically required DOD to disclose certain types of adverse or reportable information to the Committee for all nominations, regardless of grade. For example, in the wake of the scandal at Abu Ghraib during the Iraq War and continuing through the present day, the Department must disclose if the nominee was involved in actual or alleged detainee abuse. Similar mandatory disclosures of information about a nominee's involvement in events resulting in the death of football star turned Army Ranger Pat Tillman early in the invasion of Afghanistan or in the WikiLeaks classified information breach were once required but discontinued.

ONGOING INVESTIGATIONS

Usually, the SASC will not process a nomination subject to an ongoing investigation. This rule is strictly applied, and exceptions are rare. Thus, DOD *will not* normally forward a nomination to the secretary of defense or the president for approval or to the Senate for confirmation if there are planned or ongoing investigations into matters potentially adverse to the nominated officer.[168] In almost every case, a nomination's submission will be delayed pending resolution of the investigation and any follow-on administrative or judicial processes. Even if DOD were to forward such a nomination, SASC would almost certainly decline to process it.

However, there are some extraordinary situations where SASC will consider the nomination of an officer who is the subject of an unresolved allegation. For example, Equal Employment Opportunity complaints often require years to resolve before the Equal Employment Opportunity Commission and the federal courts. Similarly, alleged Anti-Deficiency Act violations go through multiple layers of official review over many months and even years before liability is fixed and the case transmitted to the Government Accountability Office for reporting to Congress. When a completed DOD investigation indicates allegations are unlikely to be substantiated, and where it is plain that the final resolution will probably involve outside agencies and may take months or even years to resolve, the SASC may decide to consider the officer's nomination. The secretary of the Military Department must include in the nomination package the particulars of the complaint, the results of the completed DOD investigation, the opinion of an expert that the probable outcome is likely to favor the accused officer, and the analysis justifying this conclusion; the status of the pending action and the expected time to resolve it; and the impact if the nomination is not forwarded.[169] The Committee may advance the nomination subject to the senators' agreement with the secretary's conclusions.

LEGISLATIVE BRANCH PROCESS FOR ADVERSE INFORMATION

When a nomination package signed by the president and submitted to the Senate contains the name of an officer to whom adverse or reportable information is attributed, OSD transmits a Certification or "Cert" Letter to the chairman of the SASC. That letter advises that such information exists and provides the name of the officer to whom the information applies. The Cert Letter is accompanied by an Adverse Information Summary (AIS) or Reportable Information Summary (RIS).[170] If the nomination is part of a list, the Cert Letter will affirm none of the other officers on the list are the subject of adverse or reportable information.

Within days of the nomination and Cert Letter's arrival in Committee, DOD provides the Committee with two complete and unredacted copies of the Report of Investigation (ROI) (including all witness statements, interview transcripts, and other documentary evidence) underpinning the adverse or reportable information. Any rebuttal or comments submitted by the affected officer and copies of any non-judicial or administrative punishment imposed on the officer are included with the ROI.[171]

In the past, some Military Departments and Services have initially declined to send full ROIs to the Committee and have tried instead to submit a one-page summary or some other lesser document. The Committee will certainly accept these offerings as additional information. Still, it will never settle for anything less than the total ROI on which to decide about the nomination. Bottom line: the nomination will not be considered by the SASC until all required information has been received and reviewed.

A quick aside about the quality of investigations. Investigations are essential, and the SASC carefully reviews every investigation associated with adverse or reportable information attributable to a nominee. Over my many years of association with the Committee, I have heard many complaints about the quality of DOD investigations. The most common is they are incomplete or too narrowly drawn. Whether the investigation was conducted by an inspector general, a criminal investigative organization, or an officer appointed by the command to conduct an administrative investigation, senators want more than narrow findings. They want a full and fair investigation that explains the circumstances in which the violation occurred; the motivation for the action; whether the officer at issue took action "knowingly" and deliberately; whether the officer sought legal guidance before taking action, and if so, whether the officer followed the lawyer's advice; and whether the officer received any personal gain from his or her misconduct. Senators want to ensure all key witnesses, including the officer involved, are interviewed. They want to know exactly what the officer said to investigators and whether he or she was forthcoming. And regardless of the allegation that started an investigation, senators expect DOD investigators to follow the facts wherever they might lead, including the investigation of new allegations that might be uncovered along the way. Senators are not interested in a simplistic black-or-white finding that an officer did or did not engage in a criminal act or did or did not violate a DOD policy. Although those determinations are important, senators also want to understand whether the officer at issue exercised sound judgment and good leadership under the circumstances.

A poor-quality investigation is the surest way to draw out an already lengthy SASC process for evaluating nominations encumbered by adverse or reportable information. A poor-quality, incomplete investigation invites senators to engage in a back-and-forth with the Department, asking for this information... and that information... until all questions are answered, with the nominee on hold throughout it all. It's far better to ensure any investigation submitted to the SASC is as high quality and complete as it can be from the start.

Typically, DOD will not report unsubstantiated allegations to the Senate. Some assert this practice prevents full disclosure of multiple unsubstantiated allegations to the Senate and hinders SASC's identification of negative trends that may manifest over time in an officer's performance, conduct, or judgment. In extraordinary cases, most often involving an allegation receiving significant media attention or when the Committee has brought the allegation to DOD's attention, the summary of an unsubstantiated allegation may be provided to the Committee. This is usually intended to quiet destructive speculation and quell senators' concerns they are not receiving "the full story." If the Committee believes more in-depth information might bear on its vetting and confirmation duties, the SASC may ask to review the ROI underlying an unsubstantiated allegation. DOD will protest but almost always cedes to these requests. Over time, DOD has understood that unless the Committee receives the information it requests, it is unlikely to move the affected officer forward for confirmation. Even if the officer has done nothing wrong, SASC has the constitutional right to "check DOD's work" for itself. The Department denies that right at its peril.

If, after considering adverse or reportable information, SASC senators agree the nomination should go forward, it is considered cleared. It will be included in the military nominations on which the Committee will vote that month.

If the senators need additional information, they may occasionally instruct staff to seek it from DOD, the Military Department, or the nominee. In some cases, senators will request the Department of Defense inspector general review a Military Department investigation or conduct a new investigation to determine whether the information in the initial investigation is accurate or to answer additional questions. In other cases, senators instruct cleared professional staff to meet personally with a nominee to discuss the adverse information. This will occur only at the direction of the senators, and the senators will give specific guidance for such meetings. Staff will not meet with a nominee at the nominee's request or as a staff initiative. On rare occasions, a Committee Executive Session, attended only by members and select Committee professional staff, has been held to discuss a nomination marked by significant adverse information. It is rare, but not unheard of, for the military officer nominee to be asked to appear before the Committee in Executive Session.

Sometimes, adverse information—regardless of when or how it becomes known to DOD or the Committee—is of such magnitude or so fraught politically it becomes plain the nominee cannot or will not be confirmed by the Senate. Rarely, if ever, is a nomination voted down by the Committee or on the Senate floor. When SASC senators agree a nomination should not be cleared, the Committee puts its pencils down and takes no further action. OSD is advised the nomination will not proceed and asked whether the president will withdraw the nomination or DOD prefers that the nomination remain in Senate to be returned to the president automatically at the end of the next legislative session.

ADVERSE OR REPORTABLE INFORMATION FOLLOWING THE NOMINATION SUBMISSION TO THE SENATE BUT BEFORE THE COMMITTEE APPROVES THE NOMINATION

Particularly after a nomination is received in the Senate, the SASC is usually made aware of adverse or reportable information about a nominee in one of two ways:

1. *DOD-provided information.* SASC requires DOD to ensure a military officer nominated for appointment, promotion, or federal recognition in a general or flag officer grade remains qualified for promotion and meets exemplary conduct standards, even after the nomination has been received in the Senate. DOD must inform the White House and the SASC of any adverse or reportable information that arises or becomes known concerning a nominee for general or flag officer grade until the officer is confirmed by the Senate or a determination is made the officer will not be confirmed.[172]

The SASC also expects DOD to take proactive measures to uncover such allegations. Every 90 days, the secretary of the Military Department with which the nominee is affiliated and the Department of Defense inspector general[173] check nominees' names against the full battery of DOD investigative files and databases.[174]

Bottom line: should DOD become aware—by any means—of adverse information, alleged adverse information, reportable information, or an investigation not previously reported and attributable to an officer whose nomination has been submitted to the Senate for confirmation, it must report that information expeditiously to the White House and SASC and take appropriate action to investigate it.

2. *Information from Third Parties.* The Committee also may receive adverse or reportable information from non-DOD sources. The very public aspects of the nomination process can subject a nominee to intense personal scrutiny. It is not uncommon for the spotlight cast by DOD's public announcement or a nomination's posting on Congress.gov to generate reports from media, aggrieved members of the public, or watchdog organizations alleging the nominee has engaged in bad acts or misjudgments that render him or her unsuitable for the position for which nominated. In some cases, constituent reports to an individual senator or inquiries undertaken by SASC professional staff as part of the confirmation process yield potentially adverse information about a nominee. Regardless of the source, the Committee carefully reviews each such report. If the Committee deems the information credible (even if anonymous), it will contact OSD requesting information on the allegations. It will hold the officer's nomination until the requisite information is received. In many cases, DOD was aware of, investigated, and unsubstantiated these allegations before

proceeding with the nomination. But if the allegation is new or different from those previously investigated, DOD will examine the matter.

Immediately upon receiving notice by any means—whether from DOD or a third party—of previously unknown allegations, new adverse information, or other matters of concern about a nomination pending before the Committee, SASC will cease processing the nomination.

If the name of the officer at issue is scrolled individually, the Committee will hold the nomination until an investigation is completed and disciplinary action on any substantiated adverse information adjudicated. If the officer's name is part of a list of officers, SASC must decide whether the entire list should be held in abeyance or whether the sole officer of concern should be held back and all others on the list moved forward for confirmation. In the latter case, the Committee votes to recommend the list for confirmation, except for the officer in question. The Committee's decision is documented by "redlining," drawing a red line through the name of the individual not yet cleared by the Committee. The original list is partitioned, and each part is assigned a modified PN number. For example, a hypothetical promotion list at PN1234 contains the names of 40 officers nominated for promotion to brigadier general. A single name is redlined, and the list of 39 officers is redesignated as PN1234-1 and favorably reported out of Committee to the Senate floor. The single redlined name remains on hold under the new designation of PN1234-2 until the Committee receives the information required to resolve the concerns attending that nomination.

Although the final decision rests with the SASC, the Committee typically coordinates with OSD and the Military Department or Service concerned before holding a list or redlining a specific officer and moving the rest of the list forward. Services may take different approaches to this decision. Most Services view some confirmations as better than none and request the Committee red-line the single nomination and allow the remaining "cleared" nominations to proceed. While acknowledging the delay posed by the single uncleared individual will affect all officers on the list, some Services take the opposite approach. They ask the Committee to hold the entire list until the names of all on the list can move forward together. Services that choose the latter course may fear the single redlined nomination will be left behind and forgotten in the press of Committee business, or in standing alone, they will be subjected to harsher scrutiny than warranted. In their view, keeping the list together promotes the spirit of the list's cohort. It incentivizes the Committee to work harder and faster to process all the nominations.

When OSD's investigation is complete or concerns about the officer are resolved in some other way, the secretary of the Military Department will inform OSD and the White House. If the allegation is unsubstantiated, OSD will advise SASC of the outcome. SASC will resume processing the individual officer's nomination or the list of nominations (if the entire list was placed on hold). If the allegation is substantiated and, notwithstanding this new adverse information, the secretary of defense and president still support the nomination, OSD's notification to the Committee will include the AIS or RIS and any written comments by the affected officer; information about disciplinary action taken, if any; an assessment of the officer's overall qualification for promotion or federal recognition and of the officer's judgment as it relates to the substantiated adverse information; as well as complete copies of the underlying ROI and allied papers, in the same formats as described earlier. SASC will resume its consideration of the nomination, according the nominee the same enhanced scrutiny and process applied to any nomination accompanied by adverse or reportable information.

If the new adverse information is such that DOD or the administration *does not* support the nomination, the secretary of defense will advise SASC. All action on the nomination will cease. The secretary of defense may recommend the president formally withdraw the nomination to minimize distraction and embarrassment, or DOD and the White House may simply allow the nomination to remain on hold in the Senate until the end of the legislative session, at which point it will be returned to the president automatically, and without fanfare.

ADVERSE OR REPORTABLE INFORMATION DISCOVERED FOLLOWING APPROVAL BY THE COMMITTEE BUT BEFORE SENATE CONFIRMATION

There are rare occasions when, following SASC's approval and report of a nomination to the Senate floor, OSD advises the Committee that one nominee is now under investigation or that potentially adverse or reportable information about a nominee has come to light. In such a case, the chairman or ranking member will place a hold on the nomination so it is not confirmed along with others awaiting action by the full Senate. Once the investigation and any resulting disciplinary action are complete, the Committee will review any adverse or reportable information attributable to the nominee under the same processes described above. If the nomination is cleared, the chairman will lift the hold. If, considering the new adverse or reportable information, the nomination cannot be cleared by the Committee, the chairman's hold will remain in place indefinitely. No further action will be taken on the nomination.

ADVERSE OR REPORTABLE INFORMATION COMES TO LIGHT FOLLOWING CONFIRMATION

There have been infrequent occasions when—following confirmation by the Senate but before an officer's appointment or promotion—the Committee has been notified the officer was now under investigation or that potentially adverse information had come to light. In each case, the chairman or ranking member wrote a letter to the secretary of defense advising of the Committee's recommendation the officer not be promoted until the investigation was complete and the secretary had fully considered the findings. The letter also requested the Committee be advised before the secretary takes final action on the investigation, deciding whether the officer should be promoted. This is a highly delicate issue. Once the Senate has provided its advice and consent by confirming a nomination, the matter now lies with the Executive Branch. The secretary of defense and the president may promote the officer. Neither the Senate nor the Committee has any formal authority concerning the promotion. But as a political matter, the secretary and the president often consult with, consider, and heed the advice of the SASC chair and ranking member.

We now end this section where we began by considering the three-phased constitutional process required for appointment to senior military office: the president's nomination, confirmation by the Senate, and the president's appointment. No case better illustrates the importance of each of these three phases than that of Air Force Brigadier General Terry Schwalier. The 1995 Air Force major general promotion selection board recommended Brigadier General Schwalier as part of a list of officers for promotion to major general. President Clinton nominated the list, Schwalier included, for promotion.

The Senate confirmed the list in March 1996, and Schwalier's PDOP was slated for January or February 1997. Meanwhile, Schwalier assumed command of the 4404th Wing (Provisional) at the King Abdulaziz Airbase in Saudi Arabia. Many of the Wing's personnel lived in Khobar Towers, a nearby apartment complex. On June 25, 1996, a terrorist group detonated a truck bomb at

Khobar Towers, killing 19 Airmen and injuring hundreds of others.

Schwalier was advised that his promotion would be delayed while Congress, DOD, and the Air Force investigated the attack. The DOD investigation was unfavorable to Schwalier, and the secretary of defense recommended that President Clinton remove Schwalier from the promotion list. Clinton did so on July 31, 1997, and Schwalier retired later that year.

Over the next 15 years, Schwalier filed several applications to correct his military records to reflect the promotion he believed due him. When these proved unsuccessful, Schwalier sued in federal court, seeking retroactive advancement to major general. When the Appeals Court finally decided the case in 2015, it was no surprise that the decision against Schwalier turned on the three-phased constitutional process: nomination, confirmation, and appointment. In Schwalier's case, the president chose not to exercise his appointment power and removed Schwalier from the promotion list. Accordingly, the third and final act required for appointment to major general was altogether missing. Without this essential third step (the president's appointment), Schwalier's prior nomination and confirmation by the Senate had no effect.

SECTION 5: The Need for Change

15

WHY DON'T WE GET
THE PEOPLE WE NEED?

After immersing ourselves in the finer details of the nomination, confirmation, and appointment processes and considering how nominees can navigate each of these phases to increase their likelihood of success (and minimize the issues that can lead to a delayed or derailed nomination), it is patently clear that answering the president's call to serve as a PAS in the Department of Defense is not for the faint of heart. This chapter will discuss the significant disincentives to political service at the highest levels of DOD and why some—whose leadership and technical competence would undoubtedly contribute to good government—choose to forego the opportunity altogether.

The world is more dangerous now than at the peak of the Cold War. America's global dominance and superiority are profoundly challenged. DOD, in particular, desperately needs political leaders with the breadth and depth of management skills, innovation, and technical capabilities to ensure our nation's security. DOD's senior political leadership must be drawn from the very best among us, often individuals from the private sector, business, academia, think tanks, and non-profits. But the road to a PAS appointment in DOD is marked by considerable obstacles that diminish the value proposition of service for the highest performing, highly skilled individuals: the people we need to lead our defense enterprise into the future.

I hope that identifying some of these disincentives to service for our best and brightest will prompt a thoughtful re-examination of the overall process and its underlying rules and limitations. Most of these rules and limitations were created with the best intentions but have become disconnected from today's political and national security environment.

Nominees face several dilemmas when an administration approaches them with a call to public service. As discussed in Chapter Nine, delays in the nomination and confirmation processes have steadily increased and become more unpredictable over the past years. This trend shows no sign of reversing. The Executive Branch vetting process continues to stretch out and be marked by indecision, so a potential candidate often does not know their status. Once in the Senate, the nominees can hang in limbo for many months and, in extreme cases, years. (And this is increasingly becoming more common.) The rest of the nominee's life and livelihood are put on hold during this time. Not knowing when the Executive Branch and Congress might act on their nomination prevents a nominee from seeking other job opportunities, relocating geographically, or making other major life decisions. There is a consensus among former (and currently serving) nominees that the process takes much longer than necessary at every turn and that the White House and the Senate both contribute to inordinate delays.

Feelings of confusion, uncertainty, and embarrassment are increasing among nominees, especially as the Senate confirmation process becomes more politicized. Nominees face the prospect of airing information irrelevant to their nomination or position for all to see. This can be too much for some, such as Patrick Shanahan. After Trump's first Secretary of Defense, James Mattis, resigned in December 2018, Shanahan, a former Boeing executive then serving as Mattis's deputy secretary, assumed the mantle of acting secretary of defense by operation of law. In May 2019, impressed by Shanahan's performance in the Acting role, Trump announced his intent to nominate Shanahan to the secretary's position.

Arnold Punaro and Deputy Secretary of Defense Patrick Shanahan in the Pentagon's secretary of defense conference room.

The following month, old, unflattering news about Shanahan's family (information that was neither material nor disqualifying to be deputy secretary) exploded in the national press. Shanahan, who would have easily been confirmed by the Senate and had been an outstanding leader, withdrew his nomination rather than subject his children to unnecessary public scrutiny. I had been asked to be part of his confirmation prep team and had frequent meetings with him and his team, so I was very familiar with his thought process and decision. His decision was courageous, as he walked away from one of the most prestigious and influential government positions to avoid putting his children in a difficult situation.

The mandatory divestiture of personal financial investments as a prerequisite to confirmation to a DOD position is another significant hurdle. The brilliant, high-performing individuals the Department needs in its senior-most political roles are likely successful in their chosen fields of endeavor—almost always outside government.

In today's economy, these top performers are compensated and rewarded in ways and amounts very different from the era in which the original ethics rules were created over 50 years ago. Wealth is no longer gained primarily through traditional competitive salaries, which go away when you enter government. Instead, it is derived principally from stock options, restricted stocks that vest over time, and other deferred compensation that accrues value over time (and also has tax advantages until one exercises those options). Complicated and costly stock divestiture requirements designed to avoid the appearance or actual financial conflicts of interest put nominees at risk of losing money held in stocks, options, and equity, intended initially to mature over a lifetime and sustain the nominee and their family post-working age. George W. Bush cabinet officials, notably Colin Powell and Donald Rumsfeld, lost significant capital because of the requirement to rapidly divest large stock portfolios—all while the nation found itself in the throes of a severe bear market, for example.[175] Many in the private sector aspire to serve in government, but irreparably degrading the short and long-term financial security of one's family is not a motivating prospect.

I recall firsthand, in 1977, Dr. Bill Perry's sacrifices in the Carter administration as the under secretary of defense for research and engineering, then the top acquisition position in the DOD. He came from a highly successful business position, and it cost him over seven figures in equity and other holdings alone (not even including salary) to serve in government. Years later, in 1993, during the Clinton Administration, in my position as staff director, I handled Dr. Perry's confirmation to be deputy secretary of defense. Again, he came to this position from the business world and would lose double the seven figures he had sacrificed for his first appointment. When he commented on what it cost him, I jokingly said, "Bill, your losses this time are less than inflation."

In the George W. Bush administration, Don Winter, a longtime senior executive at Northrop Grumman Corporation, was nominated as secretary of the Navy. Much of his wealth was in deferred compensation that he would give up if he went into government. Despite being one of the largest financial sacrifices I recall from any nominee, he served without hesitation. When I asked why he would make such a considerable financial sacrifice, he said he saw government service as "giving back" and a much higher cause than his family finances.

As we saw in the cases of Trump Administration nominees Vincent Viola and Philip Bilden, while both were willing to make financial sacrifices, the magnitude of what was required to be divested was unworkable. With Viola, this would have most likely undermined and collapsed the business he had built, and he did not want to do that to his employees. For Bilden, he had some illiquid investments that could not be divested in the needed time frame, even though he was willing.

I had argued for years the SASC's total divestiture requirements (in addition to those required by government ethics laws and regulations) kept promising nominees out of the Department of Defense. The SASC requirements were so strict that when Don Atwood from General Motors went through the confirmation process for deputy secretary of defense in the first Bush administration, the SASC required his wife to give up her "stock club" in which she and others would invest under $100 in various stocks to see how they would perform. Previously, I outlined how the SASC finally has shifted to requiring PAS nominees to divest of stocks in companies in the "Top 10" slots of the GSA-published

Top 100 Contractors listing for DOD over the most recent five fiscal years.

The challenges do not end if and when a nominee makes it through the grueling confirmation process. Political appointments are marked by the lack of a competitive, market-based pay and compensation structure. Often, political appointees are paid far less than some of the career Senior Executive Service (SES) positions they supervise. A vestige of sequestration, political appointees have been excluded from the annual pay raise in most years; a relatively meager cost-of-living adjustment is the best they can hope for. Further, they are not eligible for annual performance bonuses or cash awards. The federal government needs to make key managerial positions in DOD more attractive and financially rewarding to those with the extraordinary talent we need.

PAS appointees, mainly those unfamiliar with government, may find their new DOD jobs less satisfying and more difficult than they had imagined. Once in the job, political appointees are subject to government-specific challenges they may not have faced in their non-government positions: requirements for the protection of classified information; application of the Freedom of Information Act; limitations on the use of official travel and transportation; restrictions on the use of personal assistants and military aides; and constraints on the acceptance of gifts, including meals, from those who seek to do business with the government. All of these rules and regulations are important. All have a sound basis in the overarching policy that the role of government and its officials is to serve the public interest, that public office may not be used for private gain, and that government officials must act impartially without giving preferential treatment to any private organization or individual.

But these rules can prove byzantine to those accustomed to perks designed to free up time for corporate leadership to lead.

Further, these new appointees are now subject to and bound by the laws, rules, and regulations that govern the federal bureaucracy writ large—even the slightest deviation can result in an inspector general or equal employment opportunity complaint. And, of course, the congressional oversight of an appointee's every decision, with the looming threat of being hauled before unhappy legislators to answer questions, lacks appeal for many. Decision-making in government is also much more subject to lengthy reviews and coordination, which is not the norm in the for-profit business world.

As if all this were not enough, appointees face restrictions and prohibitions on their post-government careers at the end of the administration. There have always been strictures to prevent government personnel who made decisions that impacted major companies' programs from profiting from those decisions after leaving government employment. The 1-year "cooling-off period," with which we are most familiar, restricts former senior Executive Branch officials from representing a new employer back to their former agency or component for one year, regardless of their prior government responsibilities. There is also a 2-year ban on post-government involvement in "qualifying matters" pending under a former government employee's official responsibility. Then there's the permanent ban. For example, if you were a decision-maker on a major aircraft acquisition program, you are banned from representing a private entity back to the government on the same program for the *life of that program.*

With the intent of additional restrictions on the so-called "revolving door" (generally described as when someone moves from a particular industry to a position in government that contracts with or oversees that industry, then back to that industry after government service), SASC Chairman John McCain added a provision to the FY 2018 NDAA that, in some cases, prohibits former

PAS, senior civilian executives, and senior military officers from providing even internal or "behind-the-scenes" advice to a new private-sector employer for as long as two years after retiring or separating from DOD.

Interestingly, this provision applies only to former DOD personnel. *I've searched, but I can find no evidence that any other federal agency is subject to a similar law.* This DOD-specific provision is in addition to the longstanding one-year cooling-off period that applies to all federal agencies and Congress. Many in both government and industry view the McCain provision as excessive, placing undue burdens on individuals leaving public office; confusing because it does not integrate clearly and cleanly with the longstanding Title 18 ethics regime; and unnecessary—a "solution in search of a problem." But at this point, there is little chance the provisions will be repealed or amended. No member of Congress wants to be accused of being lax on ethical standards, even though Congress does not apply the same rules to themselves or their staff. The minimal restrictions they place on themselves post-service are much less onerous than those on Executive Branch personnel. For now, former DOD personnel and their industry employers must comply as best they can.

Many companies now refuse to hire qualified former government employees covered by the McCain provision because they don't want to risk non-compliance with a prohibition that is not well-defined. There are examples of both civilian and military personnel turning down promotions so they will not be restricted by the provision when they retire and seek a productive career outside of government.

In particular, Senator Elizabeth Warren (D-MA) has been strident in her belief Congress must maintain a secure firewall between DOD and the defense industry. During Mark Esper's hearing to be secretary of defense in July 2019, Senator Warren pressed him to commit to extending his recusal from matters relating to Raytheon (his former private-sector employer) for twice the time required by law and to promise not to work for any defense contractor for at least four years after his government service—again, a "cooling-off" period far longer than required by law.

Much to his credit, Esper stuck to his guns in a terse exchange with Senator Warren from the dais and refused to abide by an arbitrary timeline. He repeatedly stated he would commit to following the law and nothing more. He set a good precedent for future nominees, avoiding the "requirements creep" that certain members of Congress strive to foster. Interestingly enough, at the beginning of the Biden Administration, Senator Warren put a hold on her own party's nominees for Under Secretary of Defense for Research and Engineering, Heidi Shyu, and Secretary of the Air Force, Frank Kendall, in an effort to push them to "voluntarily" commit to a recusal period above and beyond what the law required. Perhaps those toward the end of their long careers could live with something like this, but those who still have the promise of upward mobility in the private sector could not. We need smart and innovative people to serve in key technical and highly-skilled positions in government. But the smart and innovative people we need may not be willing to subject themselves to arbitrary restrictions on how they transition back to the private sector.

In recent years, the increasingly high hurdles imposed by both the Executive and Legislative Branches have concentrated presidential recruitment of potential PAS nominees in the following areas: 1) lawyers, who typically have few conflicts and generous severance packages, together with the law firm's "handshake," guaranteeing a return to the practice in an ethics-compliant capacity post-government service; 2) academics, who also have few conflicts and are not typically over-encumbered by financial divestiture requirements, and for whom universities typically keep positions open until their return from government service; and 3) current government employees of both the Executive and Legislative Branches, who usually have minimal conflicts and financial burdens (and as to congressional staff, are already intimately familiar with the confirmation process). Not to minimize the skills and expertise of nominees from these three groups, but I believe that limiting ourselves *only* to members of these "user-friendly" groups invariably means we are missing out on other top talent the Department desperately needs, especially those who have considerable experience leading and managing highly complex technical activities.

We can and must eliminate conflicts of interest affecting federal employees. But I am confident that longstanding Title 18 restrictions—with their criminal and civil penalties for violations by former government employees, and sometimes, civil or administrative penalties for the private-sector contractors who employ them—continue to enforce ethical standards of conduct and mitigate so-called "revolving door" considerations. Going overboard hurts our ability to recruit and retain the best people to serve in government.

Unfortunately, some members of Congress and White House personnel shops unjustly believe that working in the defense industry amounts to a scarlet letter for government service and vice versa. In reality, strong business and technological expertise are highly desirable traits needed in the Pentagon. We should do more to incentivize these top performers to serve in our nation's government, not erect roadblocks built of speculation regarding their intent and purpose.

Our government will not function well if only those who have never had industry ties or conflicts of interest are confirmed to serve in high-level positions, especially at the Pentagon. While maintaining ethical standards in government is essential, we are rapidly approaching the other end of the spectrum, scaring off potential recruits because of the many personal, financial, and ethical hurdles associated with government service.

One solution to fix these problems is to maximize incentives for service. The true harm associated with a dysfunctional confirmation process is that talented individuals are likelier to decline a White House invitation to serve in important senior DOD positions. Further, many who survive confirmation find themselves so disillusioned with the process that they are unwilling to suffer it again. In addition to the problems with the confirmation process, factors endemic to government service and post-service are similarly discouraging.

I have discussed at length the asset divestiture requirements associated with accepting a PAS appointment and how they have adversely affected many qualified nominees over the years. The SASC has already taken steps in the right direction here, but more should be done. Outdated and non-market-driven limitations on the salaries and financial incentives for which political appointees are eligible dissuade service, and the plodding pace and lack of transparency in IG investigations merit further attention. Finally, I've advocated that Congress consider the various post-government employment restrictions and recusal requirements unique to the DOD. I'm pleased that Section 1073 of the NDAA for FY 2023 requires a study and report on the effects of certain DOD-particular ethics rules on the Department's hiring, retention, and operations.

This is not to say that vigilance on ethics matters is not important. Serving the American people as a presidential appointee is a privilege, and with it comes the responsibility of maintaining the public trust. But as in all things, we must strike the right balance. Perhaps the most pressing imperative is to work to change the belief prevalent among some in Congress and the American public that government servants are inherently corrupt—that their base instincts must be controlled by enacting restrictive laws and regulations. In my experience, nothing could be further from the truth. In contrast, the vast majority of government servants with whom I have been privileged to work over many years in the national security community have been committed to serving their country and their fellow Americans honorably and selflessly.

Acclaimed leaders like Norm Augustine, Jim Ambrose, Don Atwood, Gordon England, Bill Perry, and many, many more like them over the years made significant sacrifices to come into government and brought with them much-needed expertise, then continued their illustrious careers in the private sector (or in some cases, served multiple tours in government). Given all the hurdles they would face, I doubt these individuals would have made it through the process in today's environment.

16

REFORMING, ACCELERATING, AND STREAMLINING

After exposing the confirmation process's good, bad, and ugly aspects, this chapter will propose solutions for addressing the outlined challenges. It's important to note many individuals, commissions, hearings, and think tanks have made recommendations for improving the nomination and confirmation process over the decades. I have benefited from these materials; in some cases, their recommendations support mine. In some cases, they differ. The sources are too numerous to credit individually but deserve general recognition.

"Fixing" and improving the confirmation process has been studied at length, many times, over many years.[176] There is a consensus that presidents should be able to choose their own teams from among the very best—the most highly qualified leaders, managers, and technical experts—those men and women most committed to and capable of assisting the president in governing well. At the same time, there is agreement around the need to limit a president's ability to install unqualified, unsuitable candidates in positions of governmental power or to use government jobs to perpetuate cronyism, conflicts of interest, corruption, or graft. Alexander Hamilton wrote in the Federalist Papers: "Senate concurrence in executive appointments... [would be a] powerful, though, in general, a silent operation... it would be an excellent check upon a spirit of favoritism in the president."[177] For government to function properly, we rely on the Senate to ensure that, as Hamilton noted, a president's poor choices do not lead to poor governing officials.

We need innovative proposals and bold action to get the current confirmation system back on track.

My top recommendations for fixing the process fall into three broad categories:

1. Decreasing the number of Senate-confirmed positions.
2. Streamlining the Executive Branch and Senate vetting of nominees.
3. Speeding up Senate processes for bringing nominations to a conclusion.

None of these recommendations will be easy to achieve; there is no "low-hanging fruit." It would require the Executive Branch and the Senate to relinquish some prerogatives, practices, precedents, and unilateral powers. But we could see significant improvement by focusing on and implementing even a few reforms.

AN IMPORTANT NOTE: My recommendations focus on nominations in DOD, but they could just as easily apply to any department or agency across the whole government.

(1) Decrease the current number of PAS positions in the Department of Defense and avoid creating new posts subject to Senate confirmation.

The requirement to select, advance, and process the over 1,200 PAS positions government-wide is far too large for either the White House or the Senate to manage in a timely and effective way. Downsizing the overall number is essential, especially in the national security area. Sixty-five positions belong to DOD. (By comparison, the Department of Veterans Affairs—the agency most comparable to DOD in terms of enterprise-scale—has just 11.) The SASC also has five Department of Energy nuclear-related nominations, five Court of Military Appeals judicial nominations, and five Nuclear Facility Safety Board nominations it must consider, for a total of 80. Of course, this doesn't even begin to count the hundreds of senior military nominations and thousands of field grade nominations the Committee confirms, for a total of about 50,000 annually.

We must address the sheer glut of DOD confirmations. DOD's PAS officials include the secretary of defense, deputy secretary, six under secretaries plus their deputies, the secretaries and the under secretaries of the three Military Departments, and an all-time high of 36 assistant secretaries of defense and assistant secretaries and general counsel in the Military Departments. Do not mistake me: the assistant secretaries of defense and the Military Department assistant secretaries and general counsels are crucial positions seminal to civilian control of the military and accomplishment of the DOD's national security missions. But they may also be subject to Senate confirmation for reasons that may no longer make much sense, given that they now function principally as part of a long and complicated chain of accountability. Is it necessary for the Senate to vet and process 36 PAS nominees, each subject to the authority, direction, and control of *at least* two (if not more) other senior Senate-confirmed officials? The SASC has to spend considerable time preparing for and hearing from these 36 nominees, which comprise over one-half of the total number of DOD PAS positions. The SASC does not conduct hearings for their 3-star military counterparts. What is the case for the general counsel of each Military Department to be put up for a vote by the full Senate, not to mention the extensive SASC process? In the past, these were not Senate-confirmed positions.

Reducing the number of positions that require Senate confirmation can be achieved only through legislation. This is a difficult ask, as Congress has been adding Senate-confirmed posts even when passing legislation to reduce the size of OSD and the number of general and flag officers. In consultation with the administration, Congress should pass a bill to modernize and update the list of Senate-confirmed positions, aiming to reduce by at least one-third the number of DOD positions subject to Senate approval. The ASDs and Military Department assistant secretaries and general counsels would be an excellent place to start based on their growth in number and current orientation in DOD's leadership structure.[178] In terms of PAS officials, the number of OSD officials has grown from four in 1949 to 42 today. This leadership and agency growth comes from the substantial increase in lower-level positions, such as deputy assistant secretaries, which total 60 today, as well as hundreds of SES and general and flag officers.[179] The number of PAS in OSD has grown by 35 percent in the last 10 years.

Of course, this reduction should be assessed on a case-by-case basis by examining a position's unique responsibilities and authorities, which the Senate may decide should be subject to its advice and consent. For example, perhaps the assistant secretary of defense for special operations and low-intensity conflict warrants Senate confirmation since, in recent years, the law has vested this position with many authorities akin to a Military Department secretary. At the Military Department level, senators could decide that the assistant secretary of the Army for civil works should remain Senate-confirmed, given congressional interests in civil works projects and funding in their home states.

For those positions eliminated as PAS, to retain the authority, status, and prestige associated with these positions, the legislation should provide that each will keep its current protocol ranking and place in the DOD order of precedence. The Senate should include a provision that a person appointed to any such position, even without Senate confirmation, can use the address of "Honorable" for the period of service while in the job and post-government service.

The legislation should also include provisions to address the genuine concern that the lack of Senate confirmation renders incumbents unaccountable to Congress. First, I would argue that converting these positions to appointments not requiring Senate confirmation enables filling them more quickly and efficiently. That's far preferable to such posts remaining vacant while other unconfirmed appointees or career DOD officials serve as Acting or perform the position's duties—all with little to no visibility on the part of the SASC and HASC. Second, this new system would free the Armed Services Committees to fix their focus where it belongs: on DOD's top civilian and military officers. The SASC and HASC can and should hold USDs and even the secretary of defense accountable for their subordinate ASDs and other senior staff appointed without Senate review. The same principle would apply to the Military Departments. To assuage concerns about accountability, reform legislation could require that an official appointed under the new process certify in writing, before appointment, his or her responses to the same questions SASC poses to nominees for Senate confirmation (as discussed in Chapter Two) to ensure they will testify when requested and will provide the information required by Congress.

While some in DOD may not agree, we cannot have it both ways. Reducing the number of unnecessary confirmations would yield myriad benefits. Broadly speaking, it is reasonable to expect that any reduction in SASC and Senate roles in confirming certain DOD officials would increase other legislative and oversight activities. When viewed through the narrower lens of the nomination process, this change would permit the SASC to focus on vetting, more efficiently and effectively, a smaller (though still significant) number of positions at the highest levels of DOD and the Military Departments for which advice and consent really matters. Nominees to these senior-most DOD positions would take on even greater importance to the Committee because they would now be directly accountable to Congress for leading, managing, and over-seeing the new category of appointees, themselves vested with significant powers. This reduction in the number of PAS would also allow those positions to have a more competitive pay rate equal to the current SES grades, which is an important factor. Currently, PAS officials are often capped at a rate of pay less than their senior subordinates. Those coming into government already face significant financial sacrifices; reducing the number of PAS, coupled with increasing the pay of those remaining, would lessen that burden and increase the appeal of such positions.

Let's not forget the Senate's role in military promotions. Congress should consider reducing the number of active-duty officers whose advancement must be confirmed by the Senate. As discussed in Section Four, Senate confirmation is required for the promotion and appointment of all active-duty officers to grades O-4 and above and for the federal recognition and other appointments of reserve component officers to grades O-6 and above, in total, about 50,000 a year. In this context, I see no reason for differentiating between active and reserve component officers. Except for those officers whose promotion packages include adverse information, all other active-duty officers nominated for promotion to the grades of O-4 and O-5 should not require Senate confirmation. I was the staff director of the SASC when the Senate removed the requirement that 3- and 4-star generals and admirals had to be "confirmed" to retire in those grades (February 1996). This single change has significantly reduced the SASC workload and worked smoothly for 28 years. The same would be true in reducing the number of military officers requiring confirmation. The SASC should centralize its focus on general and flag officer nominations.

In addition to the course of action described above, the SASC could better use the Senate's privileged nomination process.

S. Res 116 established a total of 285 privileged nominations. Only five are DOD: the under secretary of defense (comptroller) CFO (but SASC *never* processes this one as privileged—it always goes through the full confirmation process), the assistant secretary of defense for legislative affairs, and the three Military Department assistant secretaries for financial management and comptroller. Though most privileged nominations are for board appointments, the SASC should consider where it could be appropriate to use them for other DOD nominations.

As discussed in Chapter Five, this process creates a streamlined path to a full chamber vote for the 285 typically uncontroversial positions across the federal government. A privileged nomination bypasses the Committee hearing and moves directly to the Executive Calendar within 10 session days of the nominee's submission of the requisite Committee vetting paperwork unless a senator requests that the nomination be referred to the Committee. The privileged process has not been the panacea hoped for, however. The average time required to confirm a privileged nominee has continued to increase since the process was first established in 2011, and privileged nominees still get caught up in lengthy Senate floor procedures.[180] Although there may be an improvement from the SASC adding more DOD positions to the list of nominees who move via the privileged process to yield optimum benefit, any such action must be coupled with creating a more streamlined Senate floor process, as discussed in greater detail below.

(2) The Executive Branch and the Senate should collaborate to make their vetting processes more streamlined, efficient, and timely.

In an age when technology has transformed almost every aspect of life to move more quickly and efficiently, it is unacceptable that White House and Senate vetting processes remain tied to hard-copy paperwork and its administration that moves at a snail's pace.

Nominees must fill out a mammoth amount of information for their background check, financial disclosure, ethics, and personal data forms, some containing hundreds of questions and under penalty of perjury, just to begin the White House vetting process. Once the president transmits a nomination to the Senate and the SASC, the nominee confronts a new set of questionnaires and document production requirements. The different forms used by the Executive and Legislative Branches in vetting nominees are arcane and redundant. That most must be completed by "stubby pencil" adds insult to injury. This antiquated approach—problematic for more than just the nomination process—deters good candidates from considering government service and places enormous burdens on those who choose to serve. It becomes sand in the gears of the White House and SASC vetting processes, contributing to untold delays in staffing the top tiers of the Executive Branch.

Streamlining nominee paperwork would improve the process dramatically.[181] The White House and the SASC should leverage mainstream technology to develop and implement a single "smart" form—a set of common core questions that address the information needs of both the Executive and Legislative Branches. Repetitive questions would be eliminated, and overlapping questions—that ask for similar information slightly differently—reduced. A nominee could digitally complete, sign, and submit the smart form to the relevant stakeholders with the push of a button.[182] This is not rocket science; smart forms and enabling software, secured for personal privacy and protecting sensitive information against cyber threats, are widely used in academia, industry, financial transactions, and other government entities.

Imagine if we took the next logical step of creating a dashboard to which authorized personnel from the Executive and Legislative Branches and the nominee would be given controlled access. It would be another leap toward efficiency and transparency in the vetting process, showing the status and completion of each step in the nomination, confirmation, and appointment phases. Such a tool would keep the White House, transition teams, DOD, the Senate, the SASC, and the nominee apprised of uncompleted tasks and actions necessary for the nomination to move forward. Today, there is no one source for this information as it resides in the individual stovepipes.

In this same vein, it's time to get past the outdated requirement for the president's "wet" signature on each nomination scroll submitted to the Senate. Laws enacted by Congress provide that an electronic signature may satisfy any need for a signature.[183] Electronically executed agreements can be presented as evidence in court. They are used extensively in critical financial transactions. The president's electronic or digital signature should also suffice in this context. Additional practical tips for improving the vetting process can be found in Appendix E.

We should create, and the FBI should apply, the presumption of a 10-year investigative scope for national security nominees subject to confirmation. While the current approach requires extensive investigations starting with a nominee's high school years, these are not lifetime judicial appointments for federal judges. Where appropriate, if something disqualifying emerged, the individual could be fired (unlike judges who would have to be impeached).

In addition, the Presidential Transition Act, enacted as part of the 2004 Intelligence Reform and Terrorism Prevention Act, allows presidential *candidates* to expedite background checks and security clearances for those who will be members of their transition teams if they are elected; recommends that new administrations submit nominations for national security positions by Inauguration Day; and encourages the full Senate to vote on these positions within 30 days of nomination.

The Act has made it possible for transition teams to prepare a president-elect to make key appointments early in the administration a national security imperative.[184] Presidents-elect simply must do more to ensure the nominations of their national security team are submitted to the Senate for confirmation as early as possible. Both presidential candidates can put in people for pre-clearance starting after the nominating conventions, thereby having a cadre of individuals that could be appointed or submitted for confirmation quickly. Once a candidate is selected, transition team members (who, in many cases, will also be future nominees) can be cleared. The president-elect can also submit names for high-level national security positions through the under secretary level. Unfortunately, many candidates and subsequent presidents-elect have not taken advantage of this ability to jump-start the process.

Finally, the White House should not back a national security nominee who cannot garner a single vote from the opposing party. Senator Arthur Vandenberg's assertion that "we must stop partisan politics at the water's edge" is paramount to a functional national security apparatus. Particularly for DOD, if an administration discerns its nominee cannot gain bipartisan support in the Senate, it should pull the plug on the nomination. A strict application of this principle is essential to containing the politicization of the confirmation process in the Senate. The example of Colin Kahl, as mentioned in Chapter Two, provides ample support for my hypothesis that putting forward a nominee who cannot garner a single vote from the opposing party weakens the bonds of trust and mutual recognition of prerogatives so essential to the SASC-DOD relationship. Nominees who perceive that they don't have to earn the support from senators not of their party think, wrongly, that they need not respond to those senators' concerns once confirmed. This principle has been more than demonstrated through Kahl's relationship, or lack thereof, with the Committee. For example, on March 23, 2023, SASC Ranking Member Roger Wicker complained in a public hearing at which the secretary of defense and the chairman of the Joint Chiefs were witnesses that Kahl had responded dismissively to Wicker's written questions about decision-making in the matter of the Chinese spy balloon earlier in the year.

Besides streamlining processes, the Senate and White House should also consider the effects of their creeping ethics requirements and pay and benefit structures on nominees' willingness to serve in government. As discussed in Chapter 15, addressing the disincentives for government service is paramount to ensuring we get the best outcomes from these processes.

(3) The Senate should revisit its processes to allow regular and predictable paths to a final confirmation vote.

The Senate confirmation process is increasingly long and arduous, even for nominees who are ultimately confirmed. Over time, a president's personnel choices have taken on increased ideological significance. Scott Faulkner, the National Director of Personnel for the Reagan-Bush Campaign of 1980, who served in the Reagan White House, once said, "Personnel is policy." Essentially, Faulkner believed that the course of a presidential administration is set by controlling who is appointed and to which positions. Presidents of both parties would adopt this same mindset as the years passed, prompting even greater scrutiny of nominees by the Senate and giving way to a confirmation process that has become ever more politically charged. Today, confirmation votes for even lower-level agency positions are hotly contested. Both the left and right view each vote as a clarion call for party allegiance.

In an earlier chapter, I outlined the confirmation fast track, slow track, and no track. Historically, the Senate would simply approve or disapprove of a nomination. Nowadays, however, senators often choose the third route, where a nominee is put in nomination purgatory, never told whether he or she is going to get through. This can happen in Committee or on the Senate Executive Calendar, and some nominees have been in limbo for months, or even years. When a senator believes a nominee should not be confirmed yet cannot muster the votes to reject the nomination formally, deferral (nomination purgatory) is one of the few tactics at his or her disposal.

In other cases, nomination purgatory is driven by the belief that the hold will force the Executive Branch to appease a senator–giving into the demands that often have nothing to do with a nominee's qualifications. The increasing use of the full-up cloture process, vice unanimous consent agreements and voice votes is another example of such delaying tactics.

Contrast this with the Senate's recurring grant of unanimous consent to confirm hundreds (if not thousands) of military officers at regular monthly intervals, a long-held practice and custom that, mostly (with one significant exception discussed below) ensures the predictable promotion of military officers to the next higher grade and the rotational manning of critical operational and institutional duty positions.

Each of these delaying tactics, deferrals, holds, and the insistence on time-consuming, full-up voting processes is an inefficient use of the Senate's precious time and discourages qualified individuals from accepting a presidential nomination. And let us not forget the profound inefficiencies in DOD operations created by the dearth of Senate-confirmed senior officials.

The Senate is a 21st-century body operating on a foundation of 18th-century rules.[185] Yet the beauty of the Senate system is that unanimous consent can modify or waive any rule. The Senate makes its rules, and the Senate can change them. To expedite the confirmation process, the relevant committee of jurisdiction (the SASC in the case of DOD) could commit to holding a confirmation hearing within 60 days of nomination and commit to an up-or-down vote on the Senate floor within one month of a favorable committee vote. The result would be more regular and predictable confirmation votes. The practice of letting nominations pile up and pushing through only a few confirmations right before a congressional recess would properly recede.

In addition, the Senate should enforce the rule that requires senators to publicly disclose their holds on nominees and should also require senators to offer clear, public arguments for rejecting nominees.

Senate practices governing the sequential referral of national security nominees could also be streamlined. All implicated Committee processes could be consolidated rather than requiring the second (or, in some cases, third) committee to vet a nominee anew. For example, the primary committee of jurisdiction could include the chairman, ranking member, and key staff of the secondary and tertiary committees in its business meetings on the nomination. Questions particular to follow-on committees could be incorporated into a merged set of APQs. And select majority and minority members of the secondary and tertiary committees could be invited to participate in a single joint hearing.

The Senate should also revisit its rule on returning nominations to the president. Under Senate Rule XXXI, Clause Six, nominations pending when the Senate adjourns *sine die* at the end of a session of Congress are returned to the president.[186] The return of nominations intra-session and the requirement for renomination by the president places an additional burden on the Presidential Personnel Office, the Office of Government Ethics, agency ethics officers, the nominees—who most times must refresh financial disclosures filings and other paperwork—and the committee of jurisdiction, which has to restart its process as well.

The Senate should revisit the rule, which dates back to the 1800s, and consider limiting its application to the end of the 2nd session of a numbered Congress (which brings that Congress to a close) or raising the number of senators required to block waiver of the rule. Conversely, the president and the White House should diligently examine returned nominations; automatic renomination in all cases is imprudent. Fostering a dialogue with the Committee and Senate leadership staff could help the White House identify those nominations returned for legitimate reasons, including when the nominee has no chance at confirmation. Resubmitting such a nomination to the Senate disadvantages the nominee in question. It also diminishes Committee and Senate focus on still-viable nominees and delays the administration's inevitable effort to identify a new nominee likely to be confirmed.

Under the Senate Rules, the minority party and individual senators are granted significant power. So it is that the Rules permit a single senator to place a hold that gums up the Senate's consideration of a nomination or group of nominations by unanimous consent and, in so doing, keep those nominations at a standstill almost indefinitely.

In my view, the confirmation process—especially as it applies to military officers—is in so dire a state that a change to the Senate Rules may be in order. For example, the Senate could enact a new rule that limits to 30, 45, or 60 calendar days, the length of time that any single senator can hold one or more nominees for reasons not germane to their qualifications for the positions to which nominated. At the end of allotted time, the majority and minority leaders could, by mutual agreement, request a ruling from the Parliamentarian—who is well-versed in evaluating and deciding issues of germaneness—as to whether the hold is germane to a nominee's skill, experience, character, or integrity. If the Parliamentarian deems the hold "arguably not germane," then the Senate leadership can set up a mechanism to end that senator's hold via a mutually agreed upon method (either a majority or supermajority vote or simply the ruling of the Parliamentarian). Regardless of the method, the Senate must strike the balance of ensuring a smooth conclusion to the confirmation process and respecting each senator's rights and prerogatives. Of course, were the hold to be lifted, the "holding" senator would have the right to vote against confirmation of the nominee or group of nominees, as well as the right to endeavor to bring other senators around to his or her way of thinking. Certainly, this new rule could and should be invoked very deliberately. This new procedure could be tailored to apply only to military nominations, given their unique role in the national security enterprise, or more broadly to all nominees—military and civilian. In any event, I believe it is critically important that the Senate begin to think creatively about how it might address the arbitrary and capricious actions by a single senator and deter others from adopting this unseemly tactic going forward.

Finally, the White House and the Senate must collaborate to staunch further politicization of the Senate's confirmation process, especially regarding military nominations. As discussed previously, in February 2023, Senator Tommy Tuberville (R-AL) began an unprecedented hold on all general and flag officer confirmations. He openly acknowledged that his hold had nothing to do with the qualifications of any one of these officers but with a DOD policy he disagreed with. Senator Tuberville's use of military nominations as pawns in a pitched political battle was a significant disruption of the Senate's longstanding nonpartisan, non-political military confirmation process and of civil-military relations more broadly. We expect our military to be distinctly apolitical, serving with competence and professionalism without regard for the political affiliation of the commander-in-chief. Yet Senator Tuberville's hold put hundreds of senior military officers and others squarely at the center of a political debate. His suggestion that the nominations could be processed in regular order using cloture would not only take an enormous amount of time but also risk destroying the delicate balance of unanimous consent agreements necessary for the routine and predictable confirmation of military officers of all grades. Military nominations, essential to our national security, were relegated to the same dysfunctional path on which many civilian nominations, especially all federal judges, are now forced to travel.

The Senate needs to pass new rules to safeguard the process of confirming all national security nominees—military and civilian—from overt politicization. This could include rules to limit the time that national security nominations can remain on the Senate Executive Calendar without a vote and, as to military nominees in particular, to prohibit holds unrelated to the qualifications of the individual officer at issue.

As former Secretary of Defense Bill Perry once told me, "Bad processes beat good people every day." The nomination, confirmation, and appointment functions have devolved markedly from the Founding Fathers' vision. They have become riddled with "bad processes" that undercut the efficient and effective operation of our government's Executive and Legislative Branches and undermine the trust and confidence of the American people. We must fix these processes to face the coming decades' challenges.

On the first day of boot camp, Marines are taught to always take the objective, no matter how difficult. The difficulty of this undertaking must not deter us. We must start somewhere. We will significantly increase the number of those willing to serve and achieve good government outcomes by reforming, accelerating, and streamlining the nomination and confirmation processes.

AFTERWORD

There is a broad-based, bipartisan, and longstanding agreement that the authority to provide "advice and consent" on key presidential nominations is one of the most important and essential constitutional roles of the United States Senate and one that is key to our democracy's system of checks and balances. Those who ensconced "advice and consent" in our Constitution had a clear vision of its purpose and process, just as Alexander Hamilton observed in Federalist No. 76.

During his tour as President Clinton's Ambassador to the United Kingdom, former Chairman of the Joint Chiefs of Staff Admiral William Crowe quipped to a roomful of British guests, "In my country, a person is innocent... until appointed by the president."[187] We need this paradigm to shift regarding government service, particularly in our government's most critical national security positions. The process should not be a trial where the presumption is an individual is guilty and should not be confirmed until they can prove they deserve the position to which they have been nominated. Delays unrelated to their personal qualifications should also not beset them.

There is also broad-based, bipartisan agreement that the confirmation process has become far too burdensome, arduous, and lengthy, well in excess of anything Alexander Hamilton and his compatriots envisioned. There has come a point in every recent administration at which the president and other Executive Branch leaders have justifiably lamented the sluggish pace of Senate confirmations and its adverse effects on the administration's ability to perform its essential duties and functions. In March 2022, the Senate Homeland Security and Governmental Affairs Committee, under the chairmanship of Senator Gary Peters (D-MI), even devoted an entire hearing to the subject. However, the Senate has also bemoaned the slowness of recent administrations in nominating individuals to critical positions, especially in the Department of Defense.

As with all government institutions, the Senate's time and resources are limited. Senators' "advice and consent" duties are but one of their many critical responsibilities. There can be little doubt that time spent in processing nominations limits senators' ability to address urgent issues for their constituents. When consumed with the administrative processing and lengthy cloture debates, they can't develop, debate, and enact critical legislation or conduct meaningful, hard-hitting oversight of Executive Branch actions and decisions.

Good government isn't the only victim of this overly onerous and challenging confirmation process. As I emphasized earlier in this book, the present nomination and confirmation process takes an unwarranted toll on nominees and, far too often, on their families and discourages highly qualified individuals from serving in government.

Bold action—beginning with a willingness to bridge divides between the Executive and Legislative Branches and political ideologies—is vital for the DOD, our government's largest organization by almost any metric and unassailably the most critical to our collective national security. I have written extensively about the DOD problem I call the "ever-shrinking fighting force." It is a well-documented fact that we spend more in constant dollars on defense today than at the peak of any previous buildups. But what have we to show for that burgeoning investment? We have bought a force of at least one million fewer active-duty personnel and almost 40% fewer major combat units than at the peak of the Reagan buildup: fewer Army brigade combat teams, fewer Navy battle force ships, and fewer Air Force combat aircraft.

This cannot be attributed to any single administration or decision; it has been coming at us for decades. Addressing and reversing this insidious trend has never been more critical than now.[188] Today, and in the coming "decisive decade," we face a world more dangerous and unstable than ever in recent memory. It will take firm and decisive leadership to address these challenges. Identifying, installing, and putting that leadership to work depends on the confirmation process.

ACKNOWLEDGEMENTS

I have long acknowledged that any success I have had in my career—in the military, government, and industry, in addition to leading boards, commissions, and associations—is because I have been fortunate to have had inspirational mentors and superb help from day one. I have always followed the principle that collective wisdom is better than individual wisdom. I have benefited greatly from that approach. None of us are successful on our own; we all stand on the shoulders of those who came before us and those who work with us in the present.

I come from a family with a distinguished military tradition, as my father, Angelo Punaro, was a 1938 graduate of the Citadel and served in the U.S. Army during WWII, and my mother, Annina Benedetto Punaro, was an Army dietician during WWII. My wife Jan's mother, Anita Cassidy Fitzwilliam, and her father, Albert Fitzwilliam, both served in the Navy during WWII, as did most of Jan's and my uncles: Joe Benedetto, Joe Mulieri, Vincent Punaro, John D. Cassidy, and Edward Cassidy. My older brother, Anthony, served in the U.S. Air Force during the Vietnam era. My two sons, Joe and Dan, went into uniformed service. Joe served in the United States Marine Corps as a platoon commander in the second Gulf War and left as a major. Dan is now serving as a major in the Army reserve with both the signal and cyber military occupational specialties.

In my formative years in the Marine Corps, my company commander in Vietnam was then Captain Jim Van Riper, USMC, a truly legendary Marine from whom I learned the fundamentals of leadership. Soon after leaving active duty and working on Capitol Hill, I met then Majors Jim Jones and Peter Pace, both of whom set the highest examples of what leadership and service is all about.

In my 24 years in the U.S. Senate, the senators from the WWII, Korean, and Vietnam eras were powerful. These included Bob Dole, Danny Inouye, Ted Stevens, John Warner, Barry Goldwater, Mike Mansfield, John Glenn, John McCain, Jim Webb, Chuck Robb, and so many more to whom our country will be forever grateful. After leaving the Senate, I got to know many others whose military backgrounds positively influenced their Senate Armed Services Committee (SASC) leadership, including Chairman Jack Reed and Ranking Members Jim Inhofe and Roger Wicker. In addition to these leaders, there are myriad industry leaders I've worked with who have made an indelible impact on both myself and our country's defense.

As a staffer, as I moved up in seniority and positions, so did the younger officers and civilians I met earlier in my career. I had the good fortune of knowing and working with most of the senior leaders of our Department of Defense and Intelligence Agencies. After I left the Senate, I was privileged to assist many of them with their confirmations.

My immediate office personnel have worked tirelessly on this book. Irina Plaks, who has worked now on all three of my books, has done such a terrific job. A fellow UGA grad, Irina has made unparalleled contributions to both my business and my writing. Irina was recognized by Secretary of Defense Ash Carter for her role on the confirmation prep team; she is an expert in this area as well. Julie Robertson, my older daughter, is an accomplished writer and editor. She has a master's degree in English and has many years of experience in the education and consulting industries. She has also done tremendous work on all three of my books. New to this book, specifically for her tremendous expertise on the SASC confirmation process, is Stephanie Barna, the former general counsel of the SASC, a retired Army colonel and member of the Judge Advocate General Corps. Stephanie has served in key civilian leadership roles at OSD. Stephanie was invaluable in terms of her insights and explanations of the overall process, especially her knowledge of today's SASC operations, as she only recently left the SASC as the day-to-day leader for its confirmation process.

In terms of the book cover and graphics, I went back now for the third time to my good friend and colleague David Tillson and his team in San Diego. David was the head of the SAIC graphic arts department in one of my organizations there and now runs his own highly successful business. He has collaborated with me on all three books as well as providing other support with his San Diego-based firm, VSSL.

We were very fortunate to work with Dennis Lowery of Adducent for all the aspects of writing, editing, and publishing this book under their Fortis nonfiction imprint. Dennis was a pleasure to work with throughout the entire process, sharing his considerable expertise and always had timely and sound advice.

Brittany Bramell Punaro and her team at Steer PR brought their considerable personal and company expertise to impact positively the publishing and promotion of this book.

Anita Kayser, my office manager and executive assistant, made sure everything worked smoothly as Irina, Julie, and I were also engaged in the day-to-day Punaro Group business enterprises. Her hard work and dedication have been invaluable to our success.

I worked for one of the most distinguished, accomplished, and principled senators, Sam Nunn, from 1973 to 1997. I am especially grateful to Sen. Nunn for writing the foreword to this book and for his continuing leadership in our country's national security work, especially as it pertains to reducing the proliferation and risk of nuclear weapons. There is no way I could do justice to his full career in such a brief setting, which, itself, is the subject of numerous full-length books. Suffice to say that it is truly fitting that our government made the decision to name one of our nation's most powerful warships, the *USS Sam Nunn*.

To those who were kind enough to give praise for this book, colleagues I have worked with over the years who have my immense respect—not just for their service in key leadership roles but for their overall continuing contributions to a strong national defense and supporting those who continue to serve their country—thank you.

I would like to thank those Americans who have chosen to serve their country, both in uniform and as civilians. We all recognize the sacrifices and dedication of those who are willing to serve in Senate-confirmed positions in DOD, DOE, and the military courts, either in uniform or in key civilian roles. We need the very best in our country to serve, and we need the Senate confirmation process to be significantly improved so that it matches the excellence of those who go through it.

I am saving the best for last: my own immediate family, now 10 adults and 11 grandchildren. Our grandchildren range in age from 13 years old to 11 months old—Colbie, Reese, Jack, Bryce, Logan, Jordan, Blake, Brooke, Nancy, A.J., and Vincent. I want to thank my wife, Jan, my children—Joe, Julie, Meghan, and Dan—and their spouses, Laura, Sean, Matt, and Brittany, for their constant support and encouragement. I realize how blessed I am.

—Arnold Punaro

APPENDIX

A: PAS LIST

List of all Civilian PAS Officials Considered by SASC (as of 2024):

Department of Defense

1. Secretary of Defense
2. Deputy Secretary of Defense
3. Secretary of the Army
4. Secretary of the Navy
5. Secretary of the Air Force
6. Under Secretary for Policy
7. Under Secretary for Research and Engineering
8. Under Secretary for Acquisition and Sustainment
9. Under Secretary Comptroller
10. Under Secretary for Personnel and Readiness
11. Under Secretary for Intelligence and Security
12. Deputy Under Secretary for Policy
13. Deputy Under Secretary for Research and Engineering
14. Deputy Under Secretary for Acquisition and Sustainment
15. Deputy Under Secretary Comptroller
16. Deputy Under Secretary for Personnel and Readiness
17. Deputy Under Secretary for Intelligence and Security
18. Under Secretary of the Army
19. Under Secretary of the Navy
20. Under Secretary of the Air Force
21. DOD General Counsel
22. Director of Cost Assessment and Program Evaluation
23. DOD Inspector General
24. Director of Operational Test and Evaluation
25. Chief Information Officer
26. Director of National Security Agency

27. Inspector General for National Security Agency
28. Director of National Reconnaissance Office
29. Inspector General for National Reconnaissance Office
30. Assistant Secretary of Defense for Legislative Affairs
31. Assistant Secretary of Defense for Special Operations and Low-Intensity Conflict
32. Assistant Secretary of Defense for Homeland Defense and Hemispheric Affairs
33. Assistant Secretary of Defense for Indo-Pacific Security Affairs
34. Assistant Secretary of Defense for International Security Affairs
35. Assistant Secretary of Defense for Strategy, Plans and Capabilities
36. Assistant Secretary of Defense for Space Policy
37. Assistant Secretary of Defense for Acquisition
38. Assistant Secretary of Defense for Sustainment
39. Assistant Secretary of Defense for Nuclear, Chemical and Biological Defense Programs
40. Assistant Secretary of Defense for Energy, Installations and Environment
41. Assistant Secretary of Defense for Industrial Base Policy
42. Assistant Secretary of Defense for Health Affairs
43. Assistant Secretary of Defense for Manpower and Reserve Affairs
44. Assistant Secretary of Defense for Readiness
45. Assistant Secretary of Defense for Cyber Policy (new position)
46. Assistant Secretary of Defense for Science and Technology (new position)
47. Assistant Secretary of Defense for Critical Technologies (new position)

48. Assistant Secretary of Defense for Mission Capabilities (new position)
49. Assistant Secretary of the Army for Manpower and Reserve Affairs
50. Assistant Secretary of the Army for Acquisition, Logistics and Technology
51. Assistant Secretary of the Army for Financial Management
52. Assistant Secretary of the Army for Civil Works
53. Assistant Secretary of the Army for Energy, Installations and Environment
54. Army General Counsel
55. Assistant Secretary of the Navy for Manpower and Reserve Affairs
56. Assistant Secretary of the Navy for Research, Development and Acquisition
57. Assistant Secretary of the Navy for Financial Management
58. Assistant Secretary of the Navy for Energy, Installations and Environment
59. Navy General Counsel
60. Assistant Secretary of the Air Force for Manpower and Reserve Affairs
61. Assistant Secretary of the Air Force for Acquisition, Technology and Logistics
62. Assistant Secretary of the Air Force for Financial Management
63. Assistant Secretary of the Air Force for Energy, Installations and Environment
64. Assistant Secretary of the Air Force for Space Acquisition and Integration
65. Air Force General Counsel

Department of Energy

1. Director, National Nuclear Safety Administration (NNSA)
2. Deputy Director, NNSA
3. Deputy Administrator for Defense Programs, NNSA
4. Deputy Administrator for Defense Nuclear Nonproliferation, NNSA
5. Deputy Administrator for the Office of Naval Reactors, NNSA

Other Independent Entities

*   Five Members of the Defense Nuclear Facilities Safety Board
*   Five Judges for the Court of Military Appeals

B: Department of Defense Medal for Distinguished Public Service

Citation

TO ACCOMPANY THE AWARD OF THE

Department of Defense Medal for Distinguished Public Service

TO

Arnold L. Punaro

Major General (Ret), Arnold L. Punaro, USMCR is recognized for distinguished public service as Chairman of the Department of Defense Confirmation Prep Team from January 1997 through January 2017. While serving as Chairman of the Confirmation Prep Team, Chairman Punaro provided sustained and outstanding leadership, advice, and guidance to prepare dozens of Department of Defense appointees to assume their positions. Beginning in 1997, he has guided every civilian and military nominee from multiple Defense Secretaries and Chairmen of the Joint Chiefs; Service Chiefs and Service Secretaries; Under Secretaries, and Assistant Secretaries of Defense to navigate the confirmation processes and prepare them for service in positions of national leadership. During this period, General (Ret) Punaro also served as Chairman of the Secretary of Defense Reform Task Force of 1997 and as Chairman of the Commission on the National Guard and Reserve from 2005 to 2008. Since September 2011, Major General (Ret) Punaro has also served as Chairman of the Secretary of

Defense's Reserve Forces Policy Board (RFPB), the first to serve as chairman under the RFPB's statutory independence and authority to report directly to the Secretary. In this role as chairman, he led the RFPB's transformation into an advisory body that has routinely offered highly impactful reports and recommendations that have significantly improved the efficiency, effectiveness, and capabilities of America's Reserve Forces. His leadership has ensured that the Reserve Components remained ready and relevant throughout a period of greatly increased mobilizations and operational deployments. Chairman Punaro is a respected and distinguished statesman and military officer who has contributed immeasurably to the military readiness of the United States and the well-being of the men and women of the Department of Defense. The distinctive accomplishments of Major General (Ret) Punaro reflects great credit upon himself and the Department of Defense.

C: Nominee Checklist

This long and arduous process is not for the faint of heart. But it is the path to one of the most meaningful jobs that one can hold.

Nomination Process:

- Biographical information sheet
- Appointee release and consent for background investigation
- SF 86 security questionnaire
  - SF 86 supplement and SF 86 certification
  - Authorization for release of information required for the background investigation
  - Authorization for Release of Medical Information Pursuant to the Health Insurance Portability and Accountability Act (HIPAA)
  - Disclosure and Authorization to Obtain Consumer (Credit) Report and Fair Credit Reporting Disclosure and Authorization.
- Office of Government Ethics Form 278e Executive Branch personnel public financial disclosure report
  - Take steps or pledge to take steps on confirmation that OGE and the Designated Agency Ethics Official (DAEO) require to avoid conflicts of interest and conform to ethics laws and rules (including Senate Armed Services Committee policy), which may include:
    - Asset divestiture—the nominee may apply for a Certificate of Divestiture from OGE
    - Resignation from certain outside positions
- IRS Form 4506
- Personal data statement

- Fingerprint card
- FBI full-field background investigation (6-8 weeks):
    - Interview with FBI agent
    - Interviews of nominee's family, colleagues, and other references
    - Review of publicly accessible social media
    - Reengagement with nominee to clarify or explain new information that comes to light, ask for additional references
    - FBI produces and provides to White House the final investigation report—not available to the nominee
- The nominee may not publicly disclose his/her nomination until the president makes an announcement
- Nomination signed by the president (sometimes preceded by a White House announcement of an intent to nominate)

Confirmation Process:

- Nomination delivered to Senate, which must be in session to receive nomination
    - Nomination received by Office of the Executive Clerk and assigned a Presidential Nomination Number (PN)
    - Nomination referred to committee of jurisdiction
- FBI final investigation report must be made available to SASC chair and ranking member
- OGE Form 278e plus a letter from the nominee to the SASC chairman regarding conflicts of interest
- Letter from OGE documenting its review of the nominee's Form 278e
- Letter from the DAEO of the department or agency in which the nominee will serve assessing the nominee's compliance with laws, regulations, and policies to prevent conflicts of interest

- o SASC ethics policy compliance:
    - o Divest holdings over $15,000 in companies appearing in the "Top 10" slots of the GSA Top 100 DOD Contractors listing over the last five fiscal years
- o SASC Questionnaire Part A and Part B
- o Copies of last three federal tax returns
- o List of all published writings (print and online)
- o Copies of formal speeches made in the previous five years on matters relevant to the nominee's prospective position
- o Potential interviews with Committee staff (upon request)
- o Courtesy calls with SASC chairman, ranking member, and any other senators on committee
- o Advanced Policy Questions (APQs)
- o Confirmation hearing
- o Questions For the Record (QFRs)
- o Favorable vote out of Committee
- o Favorable vote on the Senate floor

Appointment Process:

- o Secretary of the Senate transmits a resolution of confirmation to White House
- o President signs warrant of appointment
- o Nominee takes oath of office and assumes new duties and responsibilities of confirmed position

Post-government Restrictions:

- o Title 18 restrictions:
    - o 1-year cooling-off period restricts former officials from representing anyone other than the government back to their former agency or component
    - o 2-year ban on post-government involvement in "particular matters" pending under a former

government employee's official responsibility in the 1 year before leaving government
- o Permanent ban on taking a private role in a program in which the official "personally and substantially participated" (e.g., a major decision-maker) during their government service
- o McCain provision:
  - o Prohibits any DOD former PASs, senior civilian executives, and senior military officers from engaging in lobbying contacts and lobbying activities with certain Executive Branch officials inside and outside of DOD. In some cases, even 'behind-the-scenes' advice to a new private sector employer is prohibited under the same one or two-year restrictions
- o Additional restrictions based on an administration's ethics pledge

D: Template Letter from an Officer Nominee to the Chairman of the SASC

Dear Mr. Chairman:

This letter provides information on my financial and other interests for your consideration in connection with my nomination for the position of _____. It supplements U.S. Office of Government Ethics Form 278e (OGE Form 278e), Executive Branch Public Personnel Financial Disclosure Report, which has already been provided to the Committee and summarizes my financial interests.

To the best of my knowledge, none of the financial interests listed on my OGE Form 278e will create any conflict of interest in the execution of my new governmental responsibilities. [If the nomination is to a designated acquisition position, add: I have no holdings [other than Excepted Investment Funds and Mutual Funds, as applicable] over the OGE-recognized *de minimis* standard in, or liabilities to, any organization on the list of "Top 10" DOD contractors during the preceding five years, as published by the Department of Defense Standards of Conduct Office.]

During my term of office, neither I nor any member of my immediate family will invest in any entity that would create a conflict of interest with my governmental duties. I do not have any present employment arrangements with any entity other than the DOD and have no formal or informal understandings concerning any further employment with any entity.

I have never been arrested or charged with criminal offenses other than minor traffic violations. I have never been party to any civil litigation. To the best of my knowledge, there have never been any lawsuits filed against any agency of the federal government or corporate entity with which I have been associated, reflecting adversely on the work I have done at such agency or corporation. I know of no incidents or matters reflecting adversely on my suitability to serve in the position to which I have been nominated.

To my knowledge, I am not presently the subject of any governmental inquiry or investigation.

I am a member of certain organizations and professional societies, as indicated in my responses to the Senate Armed Services Committee Questionnaire. None of these should pose any conflict of interest with my governmental responsibilities.

I trust that the preceding information will be satisfactory to the Committee.

Sincerely,

Officer's signature and signature block

E: PRACTICAL TIPS TO IMPROVE VETTING

A few practical tips to inform White House vetting, with a view to avoiding common issues that tend to delay the confirmation process:

If a statute creating a position for which Senate confirmation is required indicates that a nominee must have certain demonstrated abilities and qualifications, the White House should pay close attention and ensure it can articulate how its nominee meets these requirements. Lip service in this regard will not suffice.

Almost every recent president has emphasized that his nominees will meet extremely high ethical standards and that his administration will be "the most ethical" in memory. Inevitably, these same presidents nominate one or two individuals who patently fail to meet far more basic standards—failing to pay income taxes, for example. This "do as I say, not as I do" dichotomy fosters Senate and SASC distrust, not only of the nominee at issue but of all nominees to come. A president should follow this example only if he or she wants to subject the raft of his or her nominees to enhanced scrutiny of their financial disclosure forms, divestiture proposals, and tax returns... all of which adds days, if not weeks, to the Committee vetting process.

The White House can expedite the confirmation process writ large by investing additional time during the initial vetting stage in a comprehensive examination of a potential nominee's social media—all of it. A social media audit can validate a candidate's background or raise hitherto unknown and serious concerns about a candidate's qualifications, ideologies, judgment, temperament, and maturity. Politicians and those who wish to engage in the political milieu garner attention, approval from like-minded

persons, and sometimes financial contributions by loudly opposing certain ideologies, parties, and people via social media. One
would be amazed by the depth of political vitriol that a single post
(comprising no more than 280 characters) can convey. Individual
senators or the members of the political party on the receiving end
of that vitriol will not hesitate to use past political grandstanding
on social media against a nominee during confirmation. This concern applies to both parties. Watchdog groups, activists, reporters,
and Senate staffers will inevitably dig into a nominee's social media, seeking even one ill-advised post that can be used to derail a
nomination. To avoid such embarrassment, the president and the
White House Presidential Personnel Office must ensure that *they*
turn up any potentially damaging information first and that anything they do find is subject to unflinching consideration of the
likely consequences before any decision is made to put a candidate
forward. The doubters among you need only review the nominations of Ms. Sue Fulton and Ms. Neera Tanden.

BIBLIOGRAPHY

9/11 Commission Recommendations: The Senate Confirmation Process for Presidential Nominees. Library of Congress. Congressional Research Service. Nov. 22, 2004.

Adams, Bruce, and Mark, Friedman. *The Senate Rubberstamp Machine: A Common Cause Study of the U.S. Senate's Confirmation Process.* Washington: CC, 1977.

Bell, Lauren Cohen. *Warring factions: Interest groups, money, and the new politics of Senate confirmation.* Ohio State University Press. 2002.

Carey, Maeve P. *Presidential Appointments, the Senate's Confirmation Process, and Changes Made in the 112th Congress.* DIANE Publishing Company. 2011.

Congressional Research Service. *Floor Time to Process all Pending Military Nominations on the Executive Calendar.* Memorandum to Senator Jack Reed, August 23, 2023.

Council for Excellence in Government's Presidential Appointee Initiative. *A Survivor's Guide for Presidential Nominees.* Brookings Institution Press. 2000.

Department of Defense Nominee Gouge Book (ed. 2019-2020).

Examining the Senate Confirmation Process and Federal Vacancies. Hearing before the Committee on Homeland Security and Governmental Affairs, United States Senate, One Hundred Seventeenth Congress, Second Session, March 3, 2022. U.S. Government Publishing Office.

Fisher, Louis. *Constitutional Conflicts Between Congress and the President*. Sixth edition, revised. Lawrence, Kansas: University Press of Kansas, 2014.

Galina, Carlos, Paul Hitlin, and Mary-Courtney Murphy. *Slow Nominations and Confirmations Pose a Threat to National Security*. Partnership for Public Service's Center for Presidential Transition. May 24, 2022.

Gerhardt, Michael J, Neal Devins, and Mark A Graber. *The Federal Appointments Process: A Constitutional and Historical Analysis*. Durham: Duke University Press. 2001.

Green, Joseph Michael. *Your Past and the Press! Controversial Presidential Appointments: A Study Focusing on the Impact of Interest Groups and Media Activity on the Appointment Process*. Dallas: University Press of America. 2004.

Hammond, Thomas H., and Jeffrey S. Hill. *Deference or preference? Explaining Senate confirmation of presidential nominees to administrative agencies*. Journal of Theoretical Politics 5.1 (1993): 23-59.

Lewis, David E. *The Politics of Presidential Appointments: Political Control and Bureaucratic Performance*. Princeton University Press, 2008.

Light, Paul Charles. A Government Ill-Executed: *The Decline of the Federal Service and How to Reverse It*. Harvard University Press. 2008.

Mackenzie, G. Calvin, editor. *Innocent Until Nominated: The Breakdown of the Presidential Appointments Process*. Brookings Institution Press, 2001.

Mackenzie, G. Calvin. *The Politics of Presidential Appointments*. London: Collier Macmillan. 1981.

Marcum, Cheryl Y., Lauren R. Sager Weinstein, Susan D. Hosek, and Harry J. Thie. *Department of Defense Political Appointments: Positions and Process*. Santa Monica, CA: RAND Corporation. 2001.

Olson, Theodore B. *The Senate Confirmation Process: Advise and Consent, Or Search and Destroy?* National Legal Center for the Public Interest. 2006.

Ornstein, Norman, and Thomas Donilon. *The Confirmation Clog*. Foreign Affairs, vol. 79, no. 6, 2000, pp. 87–99.

Partnership for Public Service and Center for Presidential Transition. *Unconfirmed: Why Reducing the Number of Senate-confirmed Positions Can Make Government More Effective*. August 2021.

Punaro, Major General Arnold L. *The Ever-Shrinking Fighting Force*. McLean, VA: The Punaro Press. 2021.

Punaro, Arnold L. with David Poyer. *On War and Politics: The Battlefield Inside Washington's Beltway*. Annapolis, MD: The Naval Institute Press. 2016.

Sollenberger, Mitchel A. *The President Shall Nominate: How Congress Trumps Executive Power*. Lawrence, Kan: University Press of Kansas. 2008.

Strauss, David A., and Cass R. Sunstein. *The Senate, the Constitution, and the Confirmation Process*. The Yale Law Journal 101.7 (1992): 1491-1524.

INDEX

ENDNOTES

1. O'Neill Jr, James, "Promotion for James? Senate Group Should Up Colonel Stewart's Air Force Rank" Washington Daily News, p. 4, April 4, 1957.
2. Air Force Nominations for Reserve General Officers: Hearings Before the United States Senate Committee on Armed Services, 85th Congress, First Session, May 2, 1957.
3. In the same hearing, just after Senator Smith's questioning regarding Stewart, Senator Stuart Symington asked, "Even though he may not have observed all the rules... his interest in the reserve would mean that young people would be more interested in the Air Force?"
4. Associated Press, "Former Arizona Governor Accused of Having AF General Reassigned" February 14, 1967.
5. Richard B. Russell Library for Political Research and Studies (University of Georgia Libraries), Richard B. Russell Collection, Series I, Box 11 (File 21), Athens, May 2022.
6. U.S. House, Committee on Oversight and Government Reform, United States Government Policy and Supporting Positions (Plum Book), 2020.
7. Council for Excellence in Government & The Presidential Appointee Initiative, "A Survivor's Guide for Presidential Nominees," Brookings Institution Press, 2000.
8. Interestingly enough, the Trump Administration complied with this principle very strictly, even in the absence of specific SASC guidance on this point.
9. Kaczynski, Andrew, Em Steck, and Nathan McDermott, "Democrats on Key Senate Committee Oppose Top Pentagon Pick as More Inflammatory Tweets," CNN, June 15, 2020.
10. Five other Principal Staff Assistants (PSAs) are a mix of career and political senior executives appointed by the Secretary of Defense. None of these five is subject to Senate confirmation.

11. The Army has a total of five assistant secretaries, the fifth being the Assistant Secretary for Civil Works, who exercises supervision of the unique civil works functions of the U.S. Army Corps of Engineers. The Air Force also has five assistant secretaries, the fifth of whom is responsible for unique Space Force Acquisition and Integration functions.

12. U.S. Senate Committee on Armed Services. "History," https://www.armed-services.senate.gov/about/history.

13. The Legislative Reorganization Act of 1946, Pub. L. 79-701, section 102, 60 Stat. 815, August 2, 1946.

14. Punaro, Arnold, The Ever-Shrinking Fighting Force, 2021, Punaro Press.

15. U.S. Senate Historical Office, "Monrad Charles Wallgren," Biographical Directory of the United States Congress.

16. Richard B. Russell Papers, Series 1, Richard B. Russell Library for Political Research and Studies, The University of Georgia.

17. Department of Defense, "David Packard," Historical Office, Office of the Secretary of Defense. https://history.defense.gov/DOD-History/Deputy-Secretaries-of-Defense/Article-View/Article/585238/david-packard/.

18. "Roll-Call in the Senate On Warnke Selection." The New York Times, March 10, 1977.

19. U.S. Senate Committee on Armed Services, "Nominations," https://armed-services.senate.gov/nominations.

20. Committee on Foreign Relations, "Background Information on the Committee on Foreign Relations of the United States Senate", U.S. Government Printing Office, 2000; Judiciary.senate.gov/nominations

21. O'Brien, Connor, "Senate confirms Pentagon nominee after battle over tweets, Mideast views," Politico, April 27, 2021, https://www.politico.com/news/2021/04/27/senate-approves-colin-kahl-pentagon-484826.

22. U.S. Senate Committee on Armed Services, "Advance Policy Questions for Dr. Mark T. Esper Nominee for Appointment to Be Secretary

of Defense," 2019, https://www.armed-services.senate.gov/imo/media/doc/Esper_APQs_07-16-19.pdf.

23. U.S. Senate Committee on Armed Services, "Advance Policy Questions for Dr. Mark T. Esper Nominee for Secretary of the Army," 2017, https://www.armed-services.senate.gov/imo/media/doc/Esper_APQs_11-02-17.pdf.

24. U.S. Senate Committee on Armed Services, "Advance Policy Questions for Mr. Dana Deasy Nominee for Appointment to be Department of Defense Chief Information Officer," 2019, https://www.armed-services.senate.gov/imo/media/doc/Deasy_APQs_10-29-19.pdf.

25. U.S. Senate Committee on Armed Services, "Advance Policy Questions for Mr. Shon Manasco Nominee for Appointment to be Under Secretary of the Air Force," 2020, https://www.armed-services.senate.gov/imo/media/doc/Manasco_APQs.pdf.

26. The reprogramming process is initiated when DOD proposes to use funds appropriated by Congress for one purpose for another preferred purpose. The longstanding agreement between DOD and the Congress requires DOD to submit its reprogramming proposals—usually at quarterly intervals—to all four congressional defense committees (the Senate and House Armed Services Committees and the Senate and House Appropriations Committees), all of which must concur before the reprogramming can occur.

27. Senate, Congress. "United States Government Policy and Supporting Positions (Plum Book), 2020". Government. U.S. Government Publishing Office, November 30, 2020. https://www.govinfo.gov/app/details/GPO-PLUMBOOK-2020

28. Partnership for Public Service Center for Presidential Transition, "Presidential Transition Guide," 2020, https://presidentialtransition.org/wp-content/uploads/sites/6/2018/01/Presidential-Transition-Guide-2020.pdf.

29. Congressional Research Service, Presidential Transition: Issues Involving Outgoing and Incoming Administrations, L. Elaine Halchin, May 17, 2017.

30. Public Law 108-458, Subtitle F, section 7601, Presidential Transition, 118 Stat. 3856-3858.

31. I worked with dozens of DASDs and Senate Directors over the years, and they don't get much better than Jane Mathias in the Clinton administration and Captain Mike Vitali (USN) in the Obama and Trump administrations. In the beginning of the Trump Administration, Pete Giambastiani took on the role of Principal Deputy Assistant Secretary of Defense for Legislative Affairs. Laura McAleer and James Thomas were the Senate DASDs. Together, the four of us handled most of the Trump DOD nominations.

32. Ohio State University Libraries, The Lantern, "Metzenbaum urges Bush to reject Stello," November 14, 1989, pp. 1-2.

33. "Panel Hears Plea on Energy Nominee, Matthew L. Wald," The New York Times, November 16, 1989, Section B, page 11.

34. Three Mile Island Alert Newsletters, February 13, 1990, in the Archives & Special Collections of the Waidner-Spahr Library, Dickinson College, Carlisle, PA.

35. "Bush Withdrawing Nominee to Nuclear Weapons Post," Associated Press, April 25, 1990.

36. Stello's duties in this role included overseeing efforts to restart idled reactors at the Savannah River nuclear weapons plant in South Carolina. Ultimately, he was promoted to the level of principal deputy assistant secretary at the Department of Energy, focusing on safety and quality in defense programs. Near the end of his career, the Defense Nuclear Facility Safety Board named an annual award for Stello, in recognition of his work as a proponent of nuclear safety.

37. Each calendar year, the General Services Administration (GSA) publishes a list of the Top 100 Contractors for each federal department and agency. The DOD Standards of Conduct Office (SOCO) maintains the list of entities appearing in the "Top 10" DOD slots over the last five fiscal years and usually updates that list within 30-45 days after GSA issues an updated Top 100 list, often in mid-calendar year. The calendar year 2022-2023 DOD "Top 10" list (which includes all companies in the "Top 10" over the period of fiscal years 2017-2022)

comprises 14 companies: Analytic Services Inc.; BAE Systems PLC; Bechtel Group Inc.; The Boeing Company; General Dynamics Corporation; Humana Inc.; Huntington Ingalls Industries, Inc.; L3Harris Technologies, Inc.; Lockheed Martin Corporation; Modernatx Inc.; Northrop Grumman Corporation; and United Technologies Corporation. The "Five Year DOD Top 10 Contractor List" is published on the publicly accessible website of the DOD Standards of Conduct Office at https://dodsoco.ogc.osd.mil/Portals/102/Documents/Conflicts/CY2022%2023%20Five%20Year%20Top%2010%20List%20FY17%2021.pdf.

38. National Defense Authorization Act for Fiscal Year 2020, Pub. L. 116–92, § 921(a), Dec. 20, 2019, 133 Stat. 1560.

39. Office of Government Ethics regulations at title 5, Code of Federal Regulations, section 2640.202, currently permit such stocks to be retained unless they exceed $15,000 in value.

40. DOD SOCO defines a "sector fund" as a "fund that concentrates its investments in an industry, business, single country other than the United States, or bonds of a single state within the United States." In contrast, a diversified fund includes a mutual "fund that does not have a stated policy of concentrating its investments in one industry, business, or single country other than the United States." See https://dodsoco.ogc.osd.mil/Portals/102/OGE%20Form%20450%20Nov%202019_accessible.pdf (last accessed on January 29, 2023).

41. SASC had a long-standing requirement that any nominee who had a pension based on a defense company's performance needed to insure that pension so as to remove any incentive to favor that company in any decisions. The nominee was already required to divest any of that company's stock.

42. Recusal from such decisions would be required by 18 U.S.C. § 208, a law that carries criminal penalties if violated. A waiver of the recusal requirement may be granted only when a DAEO determines in writing that the interest of the Government in the PAS official's participation in a decision involving a former employer through which the

346

official is entitled to defined benefit retirement plan payments outweighs any appearance of impropriety.

43. A Certificate of Divestiture is not an employee benefit. Rather, it is designed to reduce the financial burden of complying with ethics laws. 6 U.S.C. § 1043; 5 Code of Federal Regulations § 2634.1001-1008.

44. Eckstein, Megan, "Financier Philip Bilden Withdraws from SECNAV Nomination." USNI News. February 27, 2017. https://news.usni.org/2017/02/26/philip-bilden-withdraws-secnav.

45. Given that Senate confirmations—particularly those of civilian nominees—can take some time, and the possibility that through no fault of his or her own, a nominee may never be confirmed, the 90-day divestiture period is not triggered until confirmation. 5 Code of Federal Regulations § 2634.802.

46. For this purpose, "diversified" means the fund does not have a stated policy of concentrating in any industry, business, single country other than the United States, or the bonds of a single state within the United States.

47. When the PAS files his or her income taxes, he or she should complete part IV of IRS Form 8824 to defer payment of capital gains on the sale of the asset based on the Certificate of Divestiture.

48. E.O. 12834, "Ethics Commitments by Executive Branch Appointees," 58 Federal Register 5911, January 22, 1993; E.O. 13490, "Ethics Commitments by Executive Branch Personnel," 74 Federal Register 4673, January 21, 2009; E.O. 13770, "Ethics Commitments by Executive Branch Appointees," 82 Federal Register 9333, January 28, 2017; and E.O. 13989, "Ethics Committees by Executive Branch Personnel," 86 Federal Register 7029, January 20, 2021.

49. Wilson, George C., "Consultant Paisley's Method Big Risks for Big Gains," The Washington Post, June 28, 1988.

50. Howe, Robert F., "Paisley Guilty in Fraud Case," The Washington Post, June 15, 1991.

51. United States Court of Appeals for the Armed Forces website, https://www.armfor.uscourts.gov/ (last accessed on February 17, 2023).

52. Code of Conduct for Federal Judges, effective March 12, 2019; Canon 1, Commentary; Canon 3(A)(6) (a judge should not make public comment on the merits of a matter pending or impending in any court.)

53. Once confirmed, a CAAF judge is required to conduct a personal review of cases for conflicts, develop a list identifying financial conflicts for use in conflict screening, review and update the list at regular intervals, and employ the list in automated conflict screening.

54. Senate Rule XXXI, paragraph 6, of the Standing Rules of the Senate. Nominations not acted upon at the time of a recess of more than 30 days or at the end of a session of Congress will be returned to the White House.

55. A "session day" is any calendar day on which the Senate meets, including days that the Senate meets in pro forma session. The day on which the Committee chairman notifies the executive clerk that "requested information [has been] received" from the nominee is considered day one of the 10-session-day count.

56. Greene, Michael, "Consideration of Privileged Nominations in the Senate," Congressional Research Service, R46273, January 23, 2023, p.5.

57. Per Senate Order of March 10, 2005.

58. When the nomination is received in the Senate it is referred to the Select Committee on Intelligence; when reported by the Select Committee on Intelligence, it is sequentially referred to the Committee on Armed Services for 30 calendar days pursuant to S. Res. 470 of the 113th Congress.

59. Per Senate order of January 7, 2009.

60. S. Res. 470 of the 113th Congress provides for the nomination to be referred first to the Senate Select Committee on Intelligence, then to be sequentially referred to the Committee on Armed Services for 30 calendar days, and when reported by the Committee on Armed Services, to be sequentially referred to the Committee on Homeland

Security and Governmental Affairs for 20 calendar days under the authority of the order of January 7, 2009.

61. S. Res. 28 of the 112th Congress

62. U.S. Constitution, Article II, section 2.

63. The National Security Act of 1947, Pub. Law 80-253, § 202, 61 Stat. 495, July 26, 1947. Later codified at 10 U.S.C. § 113.

64. McInnis, Kathleen, "The Position of Secretary of Defense: Statutory Restrictions and Civilian-Military Relations," Congressional Research Service, R44725, January 6, 2021.

65. That Congress was not universally in favor of an exception is reflected in the final votes on the measure. The measure passed the House by a vote of 220-105, with 101 representatives not voting and three representatives answering "present" to the roll call. In the Senate, the measure passed by a vote of 47-21, with 28 senators not voting.

66. Office of Congressman Walter Jones, "Defense Bill Passes Committee, Jones Authors Several Provisions for Military," press release, May 10, 2007, https://jones.house.gov/press-release/defense-bill-passes-committee-jone-athors-several-provisions-military-1.

67. National Defense Authorization Act for Fiscal Year 2008, Pub. L. 110-181, Div. A, title IX, § 903. The law changed 10 USC § 113(a) to read as follows: "There is a Secretary of Defense, who is the head of the Department of Defense, appointed from civilian life by the President, by and with the advice and consent of the Senate. A person may not be appointed as Secretary of Defense within seven years after relief from active duty as a commissioned officer of a regular component of an armed force."

68. U.S. Congress, Senate Committee on Armed Services, Civilian Control of the Armed Forces, 115th Cong., 1st sess. January 10, 2017.

69. Sen. Tammy Duckworth (D-IL).

70. It became Public Law 115-2, 131 Stat.6, January 20, 2017.

71. Sen. Gillibrand, long a member of the SASC, was also one of the 17 Democrats who had voted against a waiver for Mattis.

72. It became Pub. L. 117-1, 135 Stat. 3, January 22, 2021.

73. Pub. L. 117–81, Div. A, title IX, § 901(a), 135 Stat. 1867, Dec. 27, 2021.

74. 10 USC § 132 (A person may not be appointed as Deputy Secretary of Defense within seven years after relief from active duty as a commissioned officer of a regular component of an armed force.)

75. 10 USC § 133a (as pertains to the Under Secretary of Defense for Research and Engineering); 10 USC § 133b (as pertains to the Under Secretary of Defense for Acquisition and Sustainment); 10 USC § 134 (as pertains to the Under Secretary of Defense for Policy); 10 USC § 135 (as pertains to the Under Secretary of Defense for Comptroller); 10 USC § 136 (as pertains to the Under Secretary of Defense for Personnel and Readiness); and 10 USC § 137 (as pertains to the Under Secretary of Defense for Intelligence and Security).

76. 10 USC § 7013 (as pertains to the Secretary of the Army); 10 USC § 8013 (as pertains to the Secretary of the Navy); 10 USC § 9013 (as pertains to the Secretary of the Air Force).

77. 10 USC § 138b(2). It is presumed that Congress established a cooling off period for this Assistant Secretary of Defense because of the Service secretary-like duties and responsibilities associated with the position.

78. 10 USC § 139. Pub. L. 116–283, Div. A, title IX, § 913(c), 134 Stat. 3804, Jan. 1, 2021. The Chief Diversity Officer is appointed by the Secretary of Defense.

79. Pub. L. 116–283, Div. A, title IX, § 913(b), Jan. 1, 2021, 134 Stat. 3803. The Senior Advisor is appointed by the secretary of the Military Department concerned or the Commandant of the Coast Guard, as appropriate.

80. Department of Defense, "George C. Marshall," Historical Office, Office of the Secretary of Defense, https://history.defense.gov/Multimedia/Biographies/Article-View/Article/571266/george-c-marshall/.

81. 10 USC § 101-18506.

82. Lipton, Eric, and Julie Turkewitz, "Pentagon Pushes for Weaker Standards on Chemicals Contaminating Drinking Water," The New York Times, March 14, 2019,

https://www.nytimes.com/2019/03/14/us/politics/chemical-stand-ards-water-epa-pentagon.html.

83. Senate Armed Services Committee, 116th Cong., 2d sess., Hearing to consider the nominations of the Honorable Kenneth J. Braithwaite to be Secretary of the Navy, the Honorable James H. Anderson to be the Under Secretary of Defense for Policy, and General Charles Q. Brown, Jr., for reappointment to the grade of General and to be the Chief of Staff of the United States Air Force, May 7, 2020.

84. Senate Armed Services Committee, 115th Cong., 1st sess., Hearing to consider the nominations of Mr. Robert F. Behler to be Director of Operational Test and Evaluation, Dr. Dean L. Winslow to be Assistant Secretary of Defense for Health Affairs, Mr. Thomas B. Modly to be Under Secretary of the Navy, and Mr. James F. Geurts to be Assistant Secretary of the Navy for Research, Development, and Acquisition, November 7, 2017.

85. Johnston, David, "Clinton's Choice for Justice Dept. Hired Illegal Aliens for Household," The New York Times, January 14, 1993.

86. Johnston, David, "Clinton Not Fazed by Nominee's Hires," The New York Times, January 15, 1993.

87. "The Lesson of Zoë Baird," New York Times, Opinion, January 23, 1993, Section 1, page 20.

88. "Charles Stimson," The Heritage Foundation, https://www.heritage.org/staff/charles-stimson.

89. Stimson, Cully, "Sen. Kirsten Gillibrand's 'Military Justice Destruction Act'" The Daily Signal, June 10, 2016. https://www.dailysignal.com/2016/06/07/senator-kirsten-gillibrands-military-justice-destruction-act/.

90. Brown, David, Connor O'Brien, and Daniel Lippman, "Nominee for Top Pentagon Personnel Job Withdraws after Op-Ed Surfaces," Politico, February 4, 2020, https://www.politico.com/news/2020/02/04/pentagon-op-ed-david-patterson-110761.

91. Richard Cohen, "Holbrooked," The Washington Post, July 13, 1999.

92. Ferrechio, Susan, "The chopping block: Trump's list of fired IGs," Washington Examiner, May 18, 2020, https://www.washingtonexaminer.com/news/congress/the-chopping-block-trumps-list-of-fired-igs.

93. Note: the Biden Administration totals only includes data through January 2023.

94. Note: the Obama Administration data excludes a handful of holdovers from the Bush administration.

95. Alderete, Jaqlyn, and Christina Condreay, "Most Nominations Withdrawn From Consideration by the Senate Happen Prior To Receiving a Committee Hearing," Center for Presidential Transition, March 18, 2021, https://presidentialtransition.org/blog/most-nominations-withdrawn-happen-prior-to-receiving-a-committee-hearing/.

96. "Biden Administration political appointees: Who is filling key roles," The Washington Post, retrieved March 31, 2023, https://www.washingtonpost.com/politics/interactive/2020/biden-appointee-tracker/.

97. DMDC Data, "Active Duty Military Personnel by Rank/Grade and Service," July 31, 2023.

98. DMDC Data, "Selected Reserves by Rank/Grade," July 31, 2023.

99. A "promotion" is an appointment of an officer to a higher pay grade. Pay grades are administrative classifications used primarily to standardize compensation across the military services. States promote National Guard officers, but these promotions must be federally recognized for officers to wear the insignia or to receive the pay of their new grade when under federal orders. The federal recognition process is designed to ensure that National Guard officers meet federal promotion requirements.

100. Dellinger, Walter, "The Constitutional Separation of Powers Between the President and Congress," United States Department of Justice Office of Legal Counsel, May 7, 1996, p. 144, n. 54 ("even the lowest ranking military or naval officer is a potential commander of United States armed forces in combat—and, indeed, is in theory a commander of large military or naval units by presidential direction or in the event of catastrophic casualties among his or her superiors");

Bradbury, Steven G., "Offices of the United States Within the Meaning of the Appointments Clause," United States Department of Justice Office of Legal Counsel, April 16, 2007, p. 91 (Explaining that a military officer's authority to command the forces of the United States draws its legitimacy from the president himself as "Commander in Chief" of the armed forces of the United States; the president cannot reasonably be expected to command every soldier, or any soldier, in the field and so delegates his authority to command to officers he commissions.)

101. Appointments that result from Military Department accession programs, including commissions awarded through a Military Service Academy, the Reserve Officers' Training Corps, or via direct commission.

102. See, e.g., 10 U.S.C. § 531(a)(2) ("Original appointments in the grades of major, lieutenant colonel, and colonel in the Regular Army, Regular Air Force, and Regular Marine Corps in the grades of lieutenant commander, commander, and captain in the Regular Navy, and in the equivalent grades in the Regular Space Force shall be made by the President, by and with the advice and consent of the Senate"); 10 U.S.C. § 12203(a) ("Appointments of reserve officers in commissioned grades of lieutenant colonel and commander or below... shall be made by the President alone. Appointments of reserve officers in commissioned grades above lieutenant colonel and commander shall be made by the President, by and with the advice and consent of the Senate...").

103. Exec. Order No. 13358, 69 Fed. Reg. 58, 797 (Sept. 28, 2004); Exec. Order No. 13384, 70 Fed. Reg. 43, 739 (July 27, 2005). There are two types of officers in DOD: warrant officers (pay grades W-1 to W-5) and commissioned officers (pay grades O-1 to O-10). Per Executive Order, the Secretary of Defense has the authority to approve appointments and promotions for officers in the active component pay grades of W-1 to W-5 and O-1 to O-3 and appointments and federal recognition and appointments in the reserve component pay grades of W-1 to W-5 and O-1 to O-5. The President and Senate approve

appointments and promotions for officers in the active component pay grades of O-4 to O-10 and the appointment and federal recognition of National Guard officers in pay grades of O-6 and above.

104. The promotions and appointments of commissioned Coast Guard Officers are processed by the Senate Committee on Commerce, Science, and Transportation—not by the SASC.

105. In 2011, Congress changed the law to specify that the Chief of the National Guard Bureau was a member of the Joint Chiefs of Staff. Pub. L. 112-81, § 512.

106. Presidential Executive Order 12344, Naval Nuclear Propulsion Program, dated February 1, 1982.

107. 10 U.S.C. § 601.

108. On November 2, 2023, the Senate confirmed two service chiefs, along with Lt. Gen. Christopher Mahoney to be the Assistant Commandant of the Marine Corps. The Senate took this unusual step because the Commandant, Gen. Eric Smith, suffered a medical emergency several days earlier on October 29. With no Assistant Commandant confirmed at the time because of Tuberville's hold, the 3-star deputy commandant for combat development and integration had to fleet up to Performing the Duties of the Commandant. This episode highlighted the dangers of Tuberville's strategy and the need to ensure the smooth and steady confirmation of our military leaders.

109. The Senate's actions to "confirm" the retirements of 3- and 4-star general and flag officers in these high grades were such high-profile events that they became a magnet for all manner of complaints against the retiring officer. Some of these complaints had long been known to the Senate, while others seemed to come out of the woodwork once it became known that the officer intended to leave service. Investigating, reviewing, and adjudicating these complaints became such a drain on SASC time and effort that the Committee decided to delegate the grade determination function to the Secretary of Defense. The Senate modified 10 U.S.C. § 1370(c), in section 502 of the National Defense Authorization Act for Fiscal Year 1996, Pub.

L. 104-106, Feb. 10, 1996, eliminating the requirement for Senate advice and consent on the retirement in grade of 3- and 4-star officers. Section 502 substituted a requirement that the Secretary of Defense certify to the President and Congress that a 3- or 4-star officer had served on active duty satisfactorily in that grade before approving the officer's retirement in grade. Today, the White House, the President of the Senate, the Speaker of the House of Representatives and the chairman and ranking member of the Senate and House Armed Services Committees regularly receive 3- and 4-star retirement certification letters from the Secretary of Defense. The SASC takes no action on these notifications, but Committee professional staff uses them to inform SASC members of the retirement of senior general and flag officers in which they may have an interest.

110. McMichael, William H., The Mother of All Hooks: The Story of the U. S. Navy's Tailhook Scandal, New Brunswick, New Jersey: Transaction Publishers, 1997.
111. Hearings before the Committee on Armed Services of the United States Senate, 108th Congress, S. Hrng 108-652, Allegations of Sexual Assault at the U.S. Air Force Academy, March 31, 2003, p. 4.
112. S. Hrg 108-856, Nominations Before the Senate Armed Services Committee, Second Session, 108th Congress, Nominations of Dr. Francis J. Harvey to be Secretary of the Army; Richard Greco, Jr., to be Assistant Secretary of the Navy for Financial Management; and Gen. Gregory S. Martin, USAF, for reappointment to the grade of General and to be Commander, United States Pacific Command, October 6, 2004, p. 342.
113. S. Hrg. 108-856, p. 357.
114. Gerstel, Steve, "Senate Panel Denies Two Generals Promotions," UPI, July 24, 1987.
115. By July of 1987, the NDAA for FYs 1988 and 1989 had already been passed in the House and received in the Senate. The Senate did not enact a separate version of the NDAA that year, but in October, passed the House version of the NDAA with an amendment—an amendment with which the House disagreed. Conference on the bill

began later that month, with both houses of Congress agreeing to the final bill in mid-November. The NDAA for FYs 1988 and 1989 was presented to the President shortly after Thanksgiving that year and signed into law on December 4, 1987.

116. The National Defense Authorization Act for Fiscal Year 1989, Public Law 100-456, title V, section 501(a), September 29, 1988, 102 Stat. 1965, codifying the addition of a new subsection (c) to 10 U.S.C. § 615.

117. Public Law 102-190, National Defense Authorization Acts for Fiscal Years 1992 and 1993, 105 Stat. 1355-1358 section 504(a), adding new subsection (a) to existing 10 U.S.C. § 615, December 5, 1991, and 504(b), adding new subsection (f) to 10 U.S.C. § 616.

118. 10 U.S.C. § 616(e).

119. 10 U.S.C. § 611(c). The primary set of Secretary of Defense regulations on officer promotions is promulgated in Department of Defense Instruction 1320.40, DOD Commissioned Officer Promotion Program Procedures, last updated on December 16, 2020.

120. 10 U.S.C. § 611(a).

121. Boards for promotion to each grade at or above O-4 are generally convened annually, by can be convened more or less frequently, "whenever the needs of the service require." See 10 U.S.C 611(b).

122. 10 U.S.C. § 616(c).

123. 10 U.S.C. § 615(a)(2).

124. Department of Defense Instruction 1320.04, "Military Officer Actions Requiring Presidential, Secretary of Defense, or Under Secretary of Defense for Personnel & Readiness Approval or Senate Confirmation," Incorporating Change 1, dated June 30, 2022.

125. National Defense Authorization Act for Fiscal Year 2020, Pub. L. 116–92, § 502(a), (b), Dec. 20, 2019; William M. (Mac) Thornberry National Defense Authorization Act for Fiscal Year 2021, Pub. L. 116–283, § 505(c)(1), (2), Jan. 1, 2021.

126. DODI 1320.14, para 3.4c(4).

127. DAA for FY 2023, § 519.

128. If the secretary of the Military Department determines that the promotion selection board has acted contrary to law, regulation, or the secretary's guidance to the board, the secretary must return the report to the board for corrective action. Once the board conducts such proceedings as may be necessary to revise the report to be consistent with law, regulation, and the secretary's guidance, it resubmits the revised report to the secretary. See 10 U.S.C. § 618(a)(2).

129. The chairman must review any selection board report that considered officers serving on, or who have served on, the Joint Staff or are joint qualified officers (See 10 U.S.C. § 618(b)). The chairman also reviews and provides advice and comment on all nominations for promotion to a general or flag officer grades (See DODI 1320.04, Enclosure 2, paras 3c and 3g).

130. Title 10, U.S. Code, sections 7233 (as to officers of the Army), 8167 (as to officers of the Navy and Marine Corps), or 9233 (as to officers of the Air Force and Space Force). Although presented in slightly different formats, the requirements imposed by each section of the Code are essentially the same. They provide that all commanding officers and others in authority in the Service are required: (1) to show in themselves a good example of virtue, honor, patriotism, and subordination; (2) to be vigilant in inspecting the conduct of all persons who are placed under their command; (3) to guard against and suppress all dissolute and immoral practices, and to correct, according to the laws and regulations of the Service, all persons who are guilty of them; and (4) to take all necessary and proper measures, under the laws, regulations, and customs of the Service, to promote and safeguard the morale, the physical well-being, and the general welfare of the officers and enlisted persons under their command or charge.

131. DODI 1320.04, Encl 3, para 1b(3)(b).

132. DODI 1320.14, para 3.5f. The Secretary of Defense will invariably follow the recommendation of the secretary of a Military Department to withhold the name of the officer from the scroll.

133. DODI 1320.04, Encl 5, para 6b(7).

134. DODI 1320.04, Enclosure 3, para 1b(2)(b).

135. DODI 1320.04, Encl 5, para 8.

136. 10 U.S.C. § 618(d). "The secretary of the Military Department may make a recommendation that an officer's name be removed from a board report."

137. 10 U.S.C. § 164 establishes the duties of combatant commanders and 10 U.S.C. § 604 refers to the "commander of a combatant command" positions as "Joint 4-star officer positions."

138. 10 USC § 601. In accordance with the Glossary of DODI 1320.04, a position of "importance and responsibility" is one designated by the President to carry the grade of lieutenant general or vice admiral or general or admiral. The President may assign to any such position an officer of the Army, Navy, Air Force, Marine Corps, or Space Force who is serving on active duty in any grade above O-6. An officer assigned to any such position has the grade specified for that position if he is appointed to that grade by the President and confirmed by the Senate.

139. Pub. L. 102–190, § 502(a), December 5, 1991, 105 Stat. 1354.

140. DODI 1320.04, Encl 3, para 2f.

141. DODI 1320,04, Encl 3, para 2f.

142. DODI 1320.04, Encl 6, para 1g.

143. DODI 1320.04, Enclosure 6, para 2.

144. DOD Instruction 1320.02, "Frocking of Commissioned Officers," dated May 10, 2022, defines "frocking" as "Authorizing an officer who has been selected for promotion and, if required, confirmed by the U.S. Senate, to wear the insignia and uniform of and assume the title of the next higher grade before being promoted to that grade." A frocked officer is not paid at the higher rate of pay and may not assume any legal authority associated with the grade to which frocked. Further the officer does not accrue seniority or time in grade in the higher grade. Each Military Service is authorized a specific number of frocking allocations that may be used when an officer meets certain requirements. Secretaries of the Military Departments are authorized to frock an officer to the grades of O-4 through O-6. The Under

Secretary of Defense for Personnel & Readiness is authorized to frock an officer to a general or flag officer grade, subject to notifying Congress in writing of the intent to do so.

145. S. Res. 28 of the 112th Congress.

146. Senate Rule XXXI, paragraph 6, of the Standing Rules of the Senate. Nominations not acted upon at the time of a recess of more than 30 days or at the end of a session of Congress will be returned. In these situations, nominations are returned to OSD through the White House. The Office of the Under Secretary of Defense for Personnel & Readiness notifies the Military Departments that a nomination has been returned. If the secretary of the Military Department wishes further consideration of a nomination, it must be resubmitted as a new nomination. See also DODI 1320.04, Encl. 3, para 2h.

147. DODI 1320.04, Encl 3, para 3.

148. Each calendar year, the General Services Administration (GSA) publishes a list of the Top 100 Contractors for each federal department and agency. The DOD Standards of Conduct Office (SOCO) maintains the list of the "Top 10" DOD contractors over the last five fiscal years and refreshes that list within 30-45 days after GSA issues its updated Top 100 list annually, usually in mid-calendar year. The calendar year 2022-2023 DOD Top 10 contractor list (which includes all companies in the "Top 10" list over the period of fiscal years 2017-2022) comprises 14 companies: Analytic Services Inc.; BAE Systems PLC; Bechtel Group Inc.; The Boeing Company; General Dynamics Corporation; Humana Inc.; Huntington Ingalls Industries, Inc.; L3Harris Technologies, Inc.; Lockheed Martin Corporation; Modernatx Inc.; Northrop Grumman Corporation; and United Technologies Corporation. The "Five Year DOD Top 10 Contractor List" is published on the publicly accessible website of the DOD Standards of Conduct Office at https://dodsoco.ogc.osd.mil/Portals/102/Documents/Conflicts/CY2022%2023%20Five%20Year%20Top%2010%20List%20FY17%2021.pdf.

149. National Defense Authorization Act for Fiscal Year 2020, Pub. L. 116–92, § 921(a), Dec. 20, 2019, 133 Stat. 1560.

150. Office of Government Ethics regulations at title 5, Code of Federal Regulations, section 2640.202, currently permit such stocks to be retained unless they exceed $15,000 in value.

151. DOD SOCO defines a "sector fund" as a "fund that concentrates its investments in an industry, business, single country other than the United States, or bonds of a single state within the United States." In contrast, a diversified fund includes a mutual "fund that does not have a stated policy of concentrating its investments in one industry, business, or single country other than the United States." See https://dodsoco.ogc.osd.mil/Portals/102/OGE%20Form%20450%20Nov%202019_accessible.pdf (last accessed on January 29, 2023).

152. "Fast Rising Admiral Nominated for CNO," Daily Press, August 13, 2019, https://www.dailypress.com/news/dp-xpm-19960606-1996-06-06-9606060014-story.html.

153. Office of the Under Secretary of Defense for Personnel & Readiness Memorandum, subject: Change in Policy Regarding Officers Serving on Boards of Directors, dated November 30, 2012. This memorandum provides, "[a]fter careful study and in consultation with the Military Departments, the Department of Defense is expanding the SASC O-9 and O-10 policy to a broader class of military personnel, to avoid any suggestion of impropriety that a military leader's participation in the management of certain outside businesses suggests governmental endorsement or sanction of those businesses."

154. Shane, Leo, "Senior DOD leaders question plan to shift sexual misconduct, other serious crimes away from COMMAND," The Military Times, June 22, 2021, https://www.militarytimes.com/news/pentagon-congress/2021/06/22/senior-dod-leaders-question-plan-to-shift-sexual-misconduct-other-serious-crimes-away-from-command/.

155. Pursuant to S. Res. 400 of the 94th Congress (as amended by S. Res. 470 of the 113th Congress).

156. See 10 U.S.C. §§ 629, 14310. An officer's Promotion Eligibility Period (PEP) begins on the day the promotion board report is approved by

the appropriate authority and becomes an approved promotion list. An officer's PEP ends on the first day of the eighteenth month following the month during which the board report became an approved promotion list. Before the end of the eighteenth month, the President may extend the officer's PEP by an additional 12 months (for a total period of 30 months). The Under Secretary of Defense has the authority to approve the board reports of promotion selection boards convened to recommend officers for promotion to the grades of O-6 and below from whom confirmation by the Senate is not required. The Secretary of Defense has the authority to approve the board reports of promotion selection boards convened to recommend officers for promotion to the grades of O-6 and below for whom Senate confirmation is required. The President is the approval authority for board reports recommending officers for promotion to any general or flag officer grade.

157. DODI 1320.14, Glossary, Part II, Definitions.

158. DODI 1320.14, Glossary, Part II, Definitions.

159. The system by which complaints of unlawful discrimination or sexual harassment made by federal civilian employees are reported, adjudicated, and documented.

160. The system by which complaints of unlawful discrimination or sexual harassment made by military service members are reported, adjudicated, and documented.

161. The system in which adverse information related to individual background investigations and security clearance adjudications is maintained.

162. It is in the files of The Judge Advocate General and the Military Department General Counsel that administrative or command-directed investigations under provisions of Army Regulation 15-6, Procedures for Administrative Investigations and Boards of Officers (2016), Department of the Navy, Naval Justice School, JAGMAN Investigations Handbook (2016), and Department of the Air Force, Air Force Manual 1-101, Commander Directed Investigations (2021) are most likely to be maintained.

163. Department of Defense Instruction 1320.04, "Military Officer Actions Requiring Presidential, Secretary of Defense, or Under Secretary of Defense for Personnel & Readiness Approval or Senate Confirmation," Incorporating Change 1, dated June 30, 2022.

164. Department of Defense Instruction 1320.04, "Military Officer Actions Requiring Presidential, Secretary of Defense, or Under Secretary of Defense for Personnel & Readiness Approval or Senate Confirmation," Incorporating Change 1, dated June 30, 2022.

165. National Defense Authorization Act for Fiscal Year 2020, Pub. L. 116–92, § 502(a), (b), Dec. 20, 2019; William M. (Mac) Thornberry National Defense Authorization Act for Fiscal Year 2021, Pub. L. 116–283, § 505(c)(1), (2), Jan. 1, 2021.

166. Public Law 117-263, James M. Inhofe National Defense Authorization Act for Fiscal Year 2023, Public Law 117-263, § 521, Dec. 23, 2022.

167. DODI 1320.04, Encl 6, para 2a(2).

168. DODI 1320.04, para 3b(1).

169. DODI 1320.04, Encl 5, para 2d(2).

170. An AIS or RIS outlines the adverse or reportable information, identifies the investigative agency, discloses the findings of the investigation, describes corrective actions taken, and explains why DOD leaders continue to support the nomination.

171. Each Military Department and Service employs long-held processes that allow certain disciplinary actions (including certain noun-judicial punishment, and letters of reprimand, admonishment, or counseling) to be filed locally (so that they do not appear in the officer's permanent military record) or only temporarily (with the promise that, predicated on the officer's continued good behavior, the record of discipline will be "expunged" from the officer's file after a specified period of time). These policies are valuable tools for the professional development and rehabilitation of worthy officers. Nonetheless, there have been situations in which a record of disciplinary action related to adverse information attributable to an officer whose nomination was under consideration by the SASC was already "expunged" and no longer existed in any official military file. In many such cases,

SASC directed that the officer produce the Article 15 or reprimand from his or her personal records as a precondition to the Committee's continued processing of the officer's nomination. A word to the wise.

172. DODI 1320.04, Enclosure 5, para 1b.

173. The DOD Inspector General (DOD IG) is the primary investigative entity for all allegations involving "senior officials." Department of Defense Directive 5505.06, "Investigations of Allegations Against Senior DOD Officials," Incorporating Change 1, effective April 28, 2020, provides that allegations of misconduct against senior officials will be reported to the DOD IG within five workdays of receipt by a DOD Component. If the notification involves a military officer who has been nominated for promotion, DOD IG notifies the Under Secretary of Defense for Personnel and Readiness. The DOD IG may initiate an investigation or direct another investigative organization (e.g., a Military Department Inspector General; a command) to conduct the investigation and provide a copy of the report of investigation, including findings and recommendations to the DOD IG. It is DOD policy to vigorously investigate allegations of misconduct against senior officials. The Directive defines "senior officials" as including: any active duty, retired, reserve, or National Guard military officer in grades O-7 and above, and an officer selected for promotion to O-7 whose name is on an O-7 promotion board report forwarded to the Military Department secretary; a current or former member of the Senior Executive Service or equivalent; and a current or former presidential appointee.

174. DODI 1320.04, Enclosure 3, para 1b(3).

175. Wayne, Leslie, "Forced to Divest, Bush Aides Lose Money in a Bear Market", The New York Times, March 31, 2001.

176. More than a decade ago, in 2012, Congress enacted the bipartisan Presidential Appointment Efficiency and Streamlining Act of 2011. The Act reduced the number of positions requiring Senate confirmation by 163 and established a Working Group that provided additional recommendations on streamlining the nominee paperwork

and background check process. Although the Senate did its part by creating the Privileged Calendar, since the Act was signed into law, Congress has created even more Senate-confirmed positions. Most recommendations from the Working Group were never implemented, and a privileged nomination can languish as long as any other nomination. Since then, many new positions have been added.

177. Hamilton, Alexander. Federalist No. 76. The Federalist, April 1, 1788.

178. This new legislation could specify that those positions removed from the list of PAS officials shall be appointed by the President only, with the power of delegation to the Secretary of Defense and only to the Secretary of Defense. Applying the homespun theorem of "more choosers, less time," it's reasonable to expect that in permitting the Secretary of Defense (rather than the President) to select and appoint subordinate leaders (at least for some jobs) the full complement of DOD resources would be applied to identifying, vetting, and appointing these new leaders, decreasing dramatically the time required to complete the task at hand. To address concerns about the authority of an Acting Secretary of Defense to perform such functions, the legislation could provide that any Acting official not a PAS in his or her own right could not make such appointments and would be relegated to submitting a recommendation to the President for decision.

179. Punaro, Arnold, The Ever-Shrinking Fighting Force, 2021, Punaro Press, p. 127.

180. U.S. Senate Committee on Homeland Security and Governmental Affairs, Hearings on Examining the Senate Confirmation Process and Federal Vacancies, March 3, 2022, page 6. While confirmation times for all nominees have increased over the past decade, the time it takes to confirm privileged nominees for full-time positions has increased at a greater rate than all other nominees.

181. By the way, this is not a new recommendation—it was proposed more than a decade ago by the Working Group on Streamlining Executive Nominations.

182. Were it determined that certain information provided by the nominee should be shared only with the Executive Branch and certain information only with the Committee—this too is easily accomplished. The information provided by the nominee could automatically populate answers to comparable questions across multiple forms, each of which would be disseminated only to authorized recipients. Or users in the Executive Branch would receive coded access to only the information intended for them; likewise for users in the Senate.

183. The U.S. Electronic Signatures in Global and National Commerce Act in 2000 legislated that electronic signatures are legal in every state and U.S. territory where federal law applies.

184. The Intelligence Reform and Terrorism Prevention Act, S.2845, 108th Congress, 2003-2004 (P.L. 108-458).

185. Gold, Martin B., Senate Procedure and Practice, Third Edition, Rowman & Littlefield, 2013, p.1.

186. Nominations may be held over into the next session only by unanimous consent of all 100 senators. Not unexpectedly, as the number of nominees pending confirmation by the full Senate increases, so too does the number of nominations returned to the president between sessions. Senate Majority Leader Chuck Schumer negotiated consent for many nominations to "remain in status quo" between the first and second sessions of the 117th Congress, but 104 nominations were returned to the White House when the session adjourned on December 18, 2021. In most cases, the nomination's return had nothing to do with the qualifications of the nominee; rather the nomination had been tacitly deferred, made subject to a hold on the Senate floor, or was at stalemate over unrelated issues.

187. Darnton, John, "A U.S. Envoy Tries to Court The Court Of St. James's," The New York Times, July 14, 1996.

188. Punaro, Arnold, The Ever-Shrinking Fighting Force, 2021, Punaro Press, p. 5-8.

www.ingramcontent.com/pod-product-compliance
Lightning Source LLC
Chambersburg PA
CBHW072107270326
41931CB00010B/1478